IMAGES
of America

GREENFIELD

The Historical Society of Greenfield

I0806487

ARCADIA
PUBLISHING

ISBN 978-0-7385-8873-5

Published by Arcadia Publishing
Charleston, South Carolina

Printed in the United States of America

Library of Congress Control Number: 2011937250

For all general information, please contact Arcadia Publishing:
Telephone 843-853-2070
Fax 843-853-0044
E-mail sales@arcadiapublishing.com
For customer service and orders:
Toll-Free 1-888-313-2665

Visit us on the Internet at www.arcadiapublishing.com

To all history buffs who help preserve the rich heritage of Greenfield for the future. Your pride in the past enhances the work of the Greenfield Historical Society.

IMAGES
of America

GREENFIELD

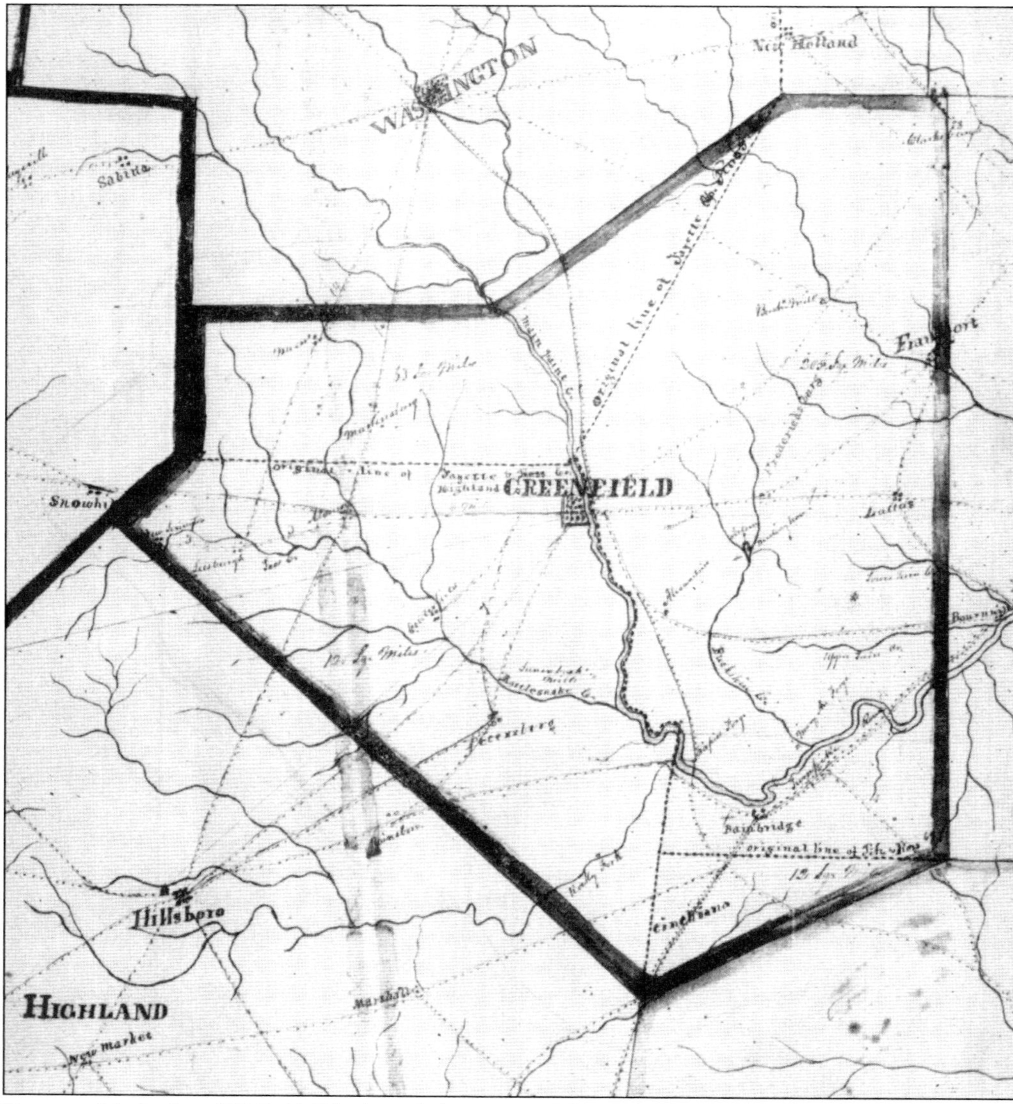

Duncan McArthur (1772–1840) platted the town of Greenfield in 1796. This 1846 map shows a potential McArthur County—a county that might have been, but never was. The original map is in the archives of the Ross County Historical Society.

On the Cover: The circus was an annual event in Greenfield as early as the 1840s. Village youth met the circus trains and paraded with them through town to watch as they set up for an afternoon performance. The picture shows a c. 1900 circus wagon filled with bears being pulled by camels. Circuses that came to town included Dan Rice, Van Amburg, John Robinson, Walter L. Moon, and Pawnee Bill. (Courtesy of the Historical Society of Greenfield, Ohio.)

Contents

ACKNOWLEDGMENTS

Since the Historical Society of Greenfield, Ohio, was founded in 1949, hundreds of volunteers have dedicated countless hours to preserving the history of Greenfield and the surrounding area. Without their hard work and love of local history, this book would not have been possible. From its early beginnings to the present time, volunteers have preserved and maintained the pictures we are using. Unless otherwise noted, all images appearing in this book were taken from the society's archives.

The book committee would like to thank the following for providing pictures: Greenfield Police Department, Greg Barr, Vicki Duff, Kenneth Eltzroth, Bill and Terry Figgins, George Foltz, Constance Ford, Ed King, Tammy McNeal, Sheri Roe, Shirley Shields, Patricia Smith, Robert Smith, Tom Smith, Lew Speakman, Susan Thompson, Janie Jinks-Weidner, Mildred Wisecup, and the Library of Congress. We also thank Arcadia Publishing editors Melissa Basilone and Sandy Shalton, who answered our many questions.

The following books were helpful in researching captions for the book: *A Greene Countrie Towne*, *Hometown Chronicles*, and *Greenfield, Ohio, Celebrating 200 Years: 1799–1999*, along with many other materials and newspapers in the society's archives.

—Jayne Honnold, chair Harold Schmidt, Judy Schmidt, Shirley Shields, and Patricia Smith

INTRODUCTION

Any book chronicling the history of Greenfield undoubtedly must include E.L. McClain and his generous gift of a school to the citizens of the town; however, Greenfield had existed for over a century when the McClain gift was made. The first recorded visit of Europeans to the area that would become Greenfield was in 1796 when Duncan McArthur surveyed the land. Impressed, he bought the land and platted the town. As early as 1799, weary settlers traveled north from the Ohio River and west from Chillicothe to form a settlement that would eventually become Greenfield, Ohio. Those early settlers—many of whom had been soldiers in the American Revolution—staked out their futures on the land along Paint Creek and the Old College Township Road between Athens and Oxford. They could not possibly imagine the change and growth their little settlement would undergo over the next two centuries.

Records exist for only a few of those early settlers. William Bell died in 1801, making him the first adult buried in Greenfield. In 1812, Noble Crawford established an inn known as the Travellers Rest in the first stone building in town. Crawford would become Greenfield's first postmaster, and his inn was the first post office. The Travellers Rest has survived the years and now, in its new location next to the Old Burying Ground on McArthur Way, serves as headquarters for the Greenfield Historical Society.

Also in 1812, Samuel Smith opened Smith's Tannery with his father, William, a Revolutionary War veteran. The tannery building remains in its original location on the northwest corner of Jefferson Street and McArthur Way.

As with all pioneer towns, essential goods and services were needed in order to prosper and grow. Families were more likely to put down roots when necessary merchandise could be easily obtained and, thus, improve the quality of life. Greenfield's early history accounts for businesses such as wool carders, hatmakers, cobblers, cabinetmakers, blacksmiths, and saddlers. The first stage coach came to Greenfield in 1818, improving access from all points on the compass.

These early settlers were eager to establish houses of worship in the vast uncharted territory. Records indicate Rev. Samuel Crothers, graduate of New York Theological Seminary, preached from 1810 to 1818 at the Hop Run Associate and Reformed Church just east of town. In 1820, the local congregation founded the First Presbyterian Church with Crothers as pastor. In 1822, the Methodist Church established a congregation here and built a church in the present-day 100 block of Mirabeau Street.

Throughout the 1830s and 1840s, Ohio towns farther south, especially those along the Ohio River, were becoming active in abolitionist activities. Greenfield, too, became quite a center for anti-slavery endeavors. The aforementioned Reverend Crothers would continue to be a community leader as he authored several widely read anti-slavery pamphlets. Congregants and other notable families including McElroy, Ghormley, Rodgers, Strain, Beatty, Wilson, Douglass, and Templeton actively supported his efforts by participating with the Underground Railroad.

By 1841, Greenfield had grown so significantly that it was designated an incorporated municipality. Around this same time, efforts were being coordinated to bring railroad service to the new city.

Residents expressed unbridled eagerness to have rail service through town as competing efforts were being made by the citizens of neighboring communities. Greenfield won the attention of officials of the Belpre-Cincinnati Railroad Company, and in 1852, local ground-breaking ceremonies featured 90-year-old Revolutionary War veteran Charles White turning the first shovel of dirt for the eagerly anticipated railroad. Two years later in 1854, the first passenger train arrived from Chillicothe. Later in the 1870s and 1880s, another railroad company, which would eventually become the Detroit, Toledo & Ironton Railroad (DT&I) came through Greenfield, further ensuring growth and prosperity.

Throughout the mid-to-late-1800s, Greenfield's entrepreneurial spirit soared. The possibilities seemed endless for enterprising, hardworking men to achieve success and even some measure of fame. In 1854, G.I. Rucker established a name for himself with Rucker's Quarry. Rucker's mansion still stands on S. Washington Street as a private home.

C.R. Patterson, a former slave, founded the C.R. Patterson & Son carriage company, and after his death, Frederick Douglass Patterson, his son, took the company into the horseless carriage era, manufacturing automobiles, buses, and truck bodies.

John M. Waddell enjoyed significant success with his Wooden Ware Works Company. Products ranging from rattraps, coffee grinders, hammocks, phonographs, store showcases and fixtures, and post office furniture were manufactured at the expansive Waddell Factory on S. Washington Street.

Other notable entrepreneurs include James A. Harps and his Never-Fail Oil Can; Thomas Browder, who invented a lifesaving net that was sold to fire departments nationwide to save victims from burning buildings; and more recently, Dr. Leslie E. Wilkin, an optometrist who became a successful hosiery salesman in the 1950s with his company Wilknit.

Then there is Edward Lee McClain, whose simple invention of a horse collar pad in 1881 led to the creation of a vast empire—the American Pad and Textile Company (TAPATCO)—which flourished for over 80 years. TAPATCO improved the design of the original horse collar and expanded its products to include life vests, hunting coats, and cotton manufacturing. In 1913, McClain and his wife, Lulu, spared no expense in leaving a legacy that is the undisputed center of pride and activity in Greenfield today. McClain High School boasts marble stairs and artwork including murals, paintings, and sculptures situated on a well-planned campus on Jefferson Street.

While innovative businessmen have been integral parts of Greenfield's history, so, too, have its military heroes. Rear Adm. Noble Irwin became head of naval aviation during World War I. The destroyer USS *Irwin* was named after him in 1943. Gen. John Edwin Hull served in World Wars I and II, and was on Gen. Dwight D. Eisenhower's staff; he retired in 1955 as the town's only four-star general.

Greenfield also lays claim to an accomplished writer and a successful musician. Frank Raymond Harris was a noted teacher, coach, principal, and superintendent of Greenfield schools in the early 1900s and even lent a hand in helping E.L. McClain plan the new high school. Harris's two histories of Greenfield, *A Greene Countrie Towne* and *Hometown Chronicles*, have been go-to resources for local historians and genealogists since their publication in 1954. Donald Eugene Lytle, known to millions of country-western music lovers as Johnny Paycheck, hails from Greenfield. Through his three-decade career, the Grammy-nominated Paycheck had six gold albums, one platinum album, and one double-platinum album.

The Greenfield Historical Society hopes that the images contained within these pages will inspire readers to collect their own histories—both with pictures and stories. The contents provided here offer just a glimpse of Greenfield's history and certainly do not tell the entire story; the histories of every resident who worked to make a better life for himself, his family, and others combine to make Greenfield what it is today.

One

Innovative Industries and Businesses

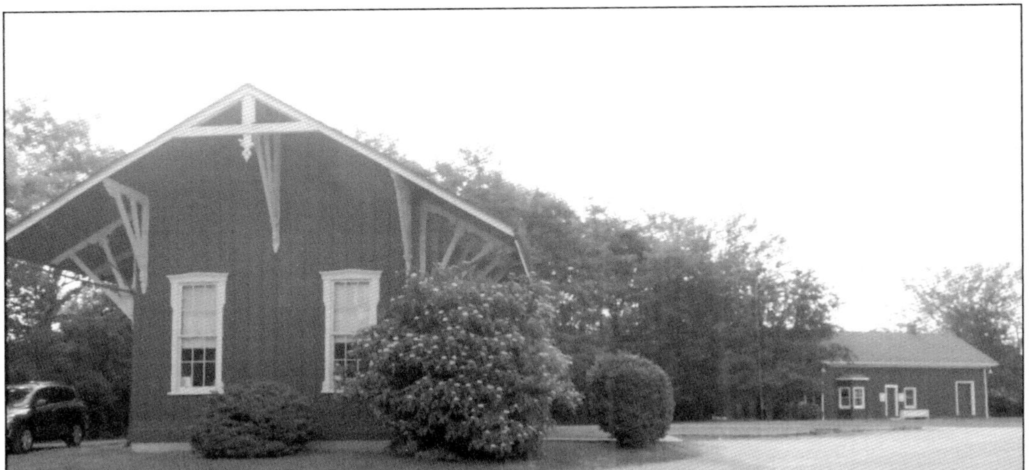

The Detroit, Toledo and Ironton Railroad (DT&I), originally the Springfield, Jackson & Pomeroy, and the Baltimore and Ohio Railroad (B&O), originally the Belpre and Cincinnati Railroad, depots are located on present-day McArthur Way. The development of these railroads was instrumental to the prosperity of Greenfield from 1854 into the 20th century.

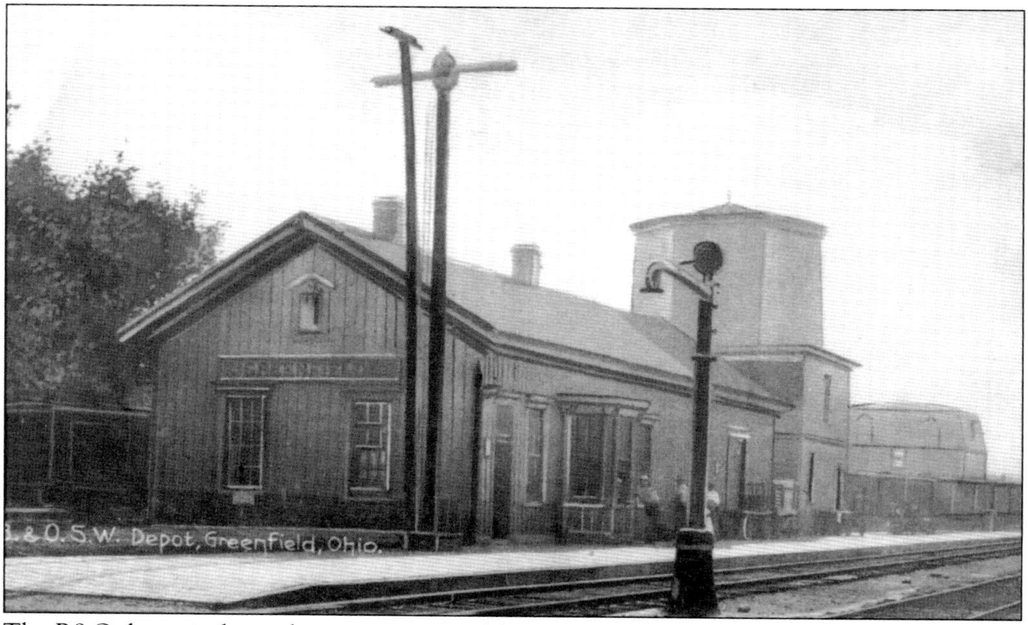

The B&O depot is shown here in its original location on S. Washington Street in about 1854. The depot was moved to McArthur Way in the 1980s. The building is currently the home of the Greenfield Historical Society's railroad and military museums.

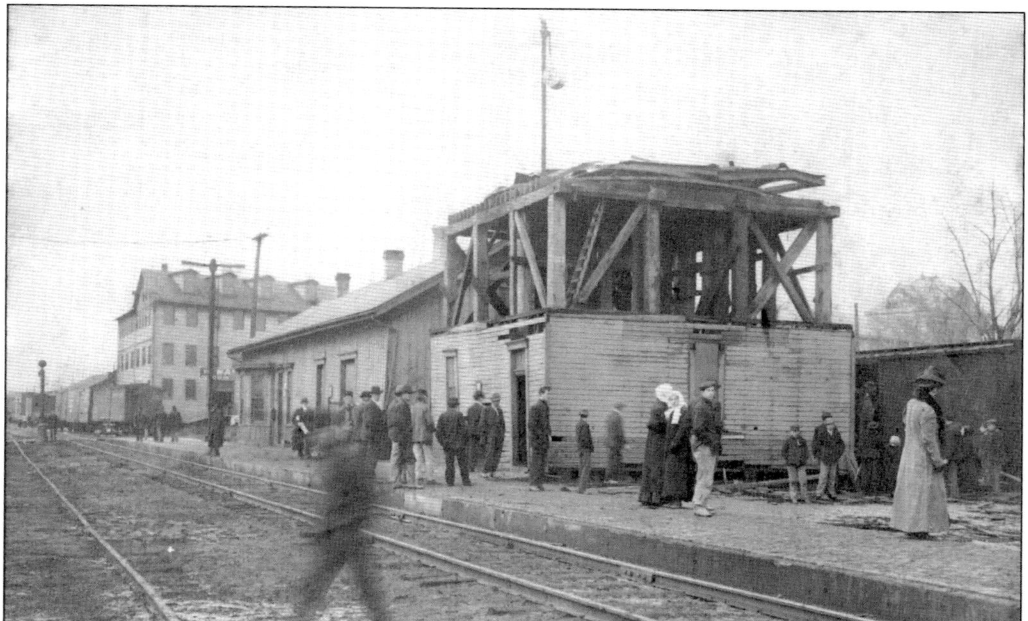

The B&O water tank disaster occurred on February 20, 1909. The water tank provided steam engines the water needed for power. The disaster took the lives of two men, Jacob Sultzberger and Boone Cable, employees of the Pad Factory who were unloading freight. The disaster was caused by the age and neglect of the tank. The tank held 58,000 gallons of water, weighing in excess of 200 tons.

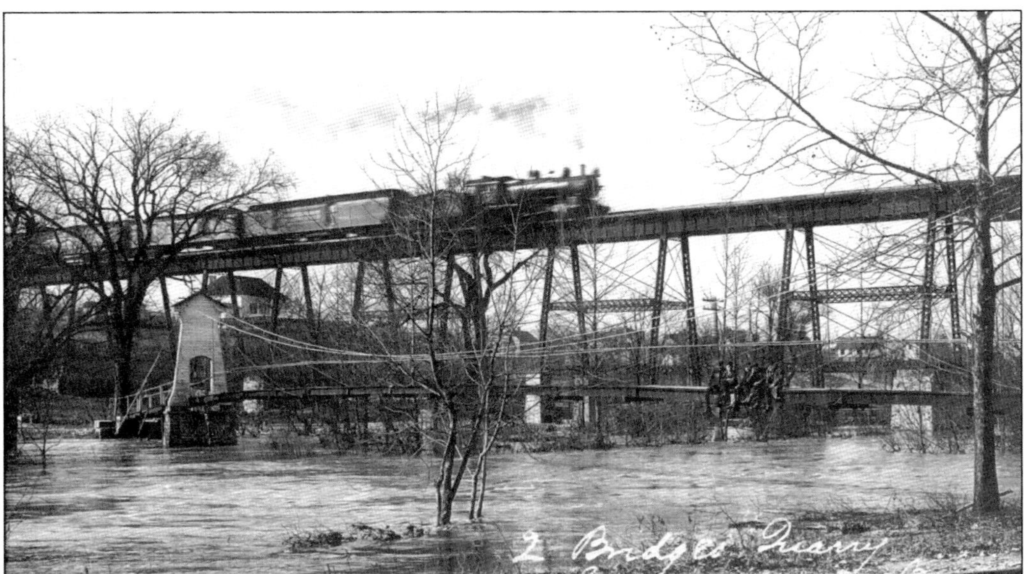

This original B&O Bridge spanned Paint Creek. Below and in front of the train trestle, the suspension footbridge also spanned Paint Creek and provided access from Greenfield to Rucker's Quarry. The trestle has been replaced by a larger concrete bridge, which can be seen on the bike path in Felson Park. The footbridge is long gone. (Courtesy of Susan Thompson.)

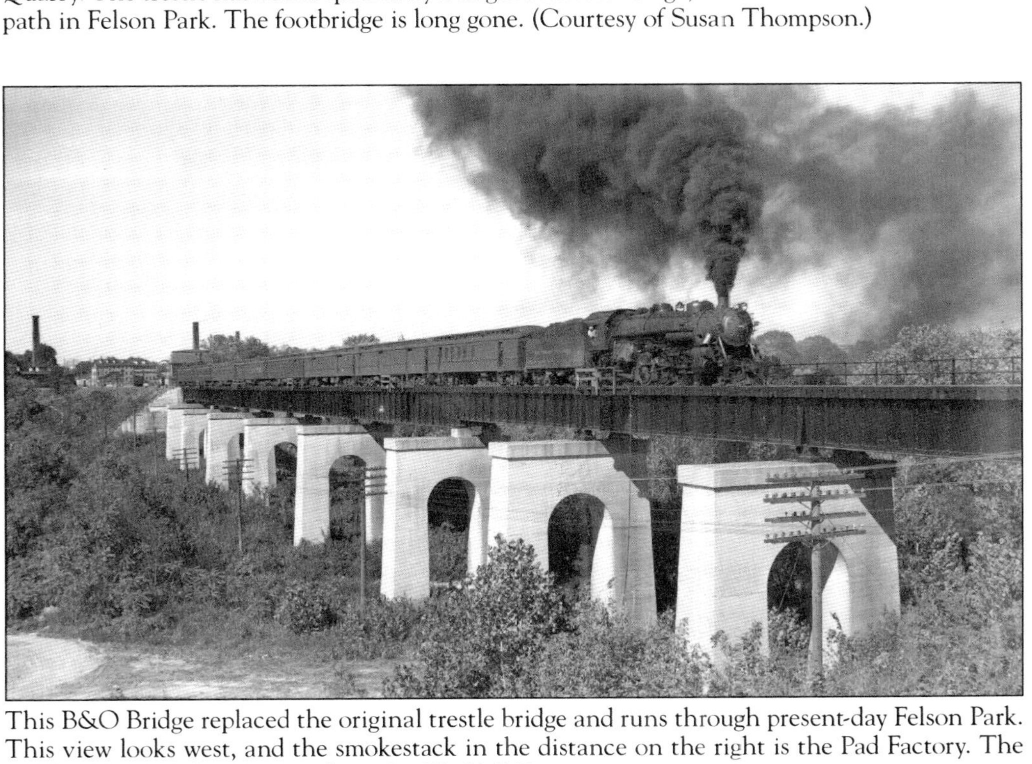

This B&O Bridge replaced the original trestle bridge and runs through present-day Felson Park. This view looks west, and the smokestack in the distance on the right is the Pad Factory. The building next to the train tracks is the Waddell Factory.

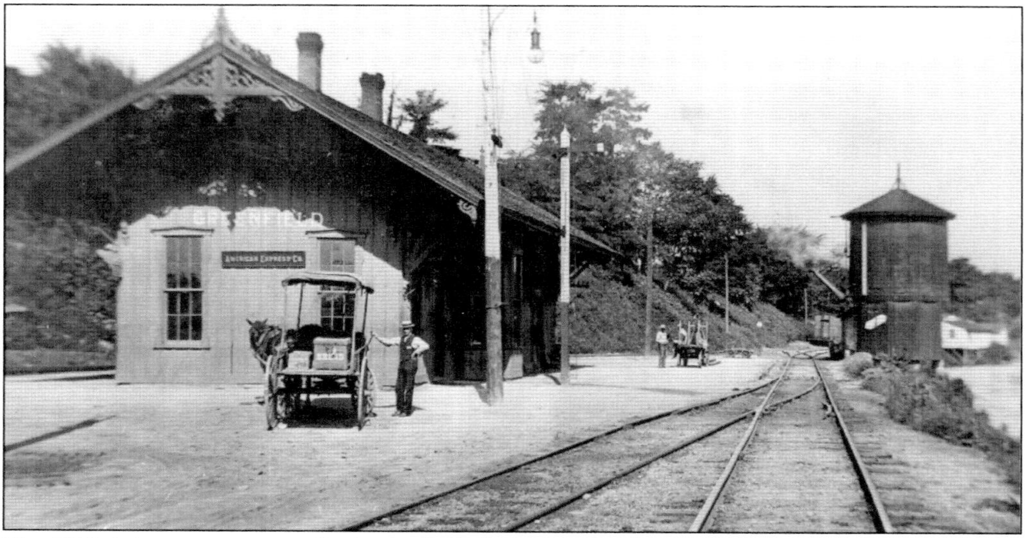

The DT&I depot was originally down the hill from McArthur Way, alongside Paint Creek. The railroad was started in the 1870s, but not finished until the 1880s because of extensive legal wrangling. The train hauled coal from southern Ohio mines to points north. It was moved to its current location on McArthur Way in the 1970s and serves as Dr. Michael Sims' Veterinary Clinic.

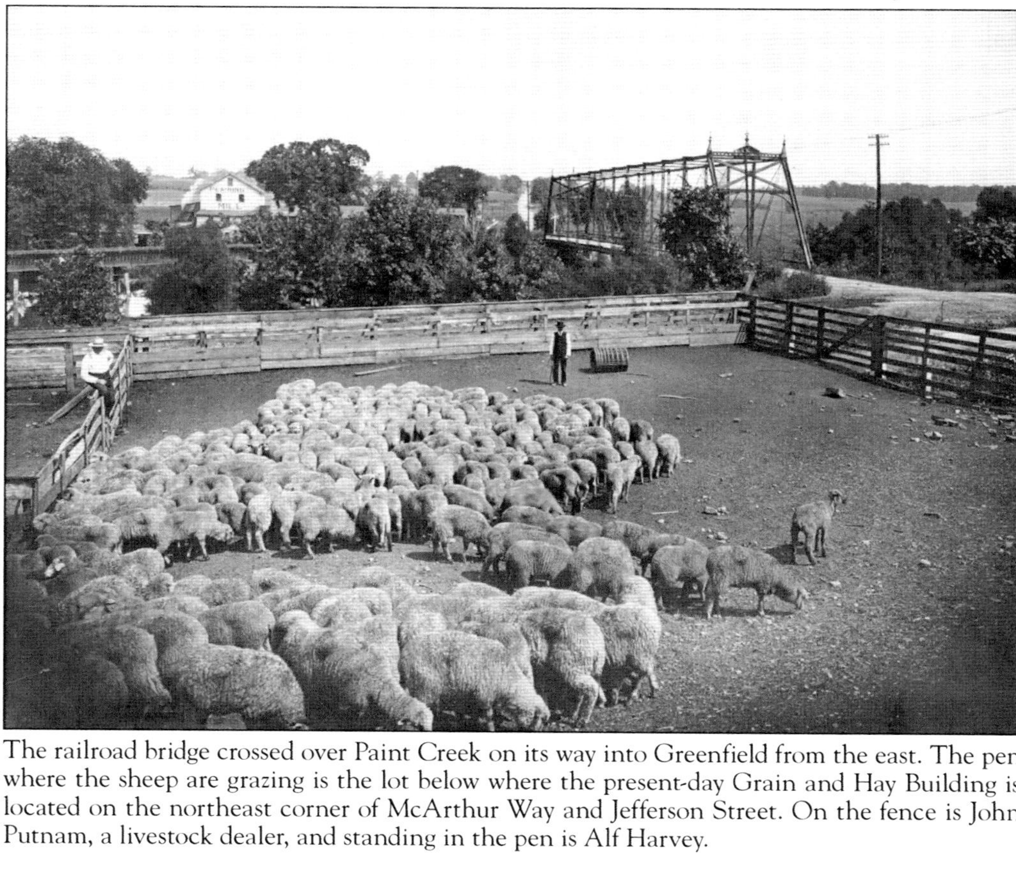

The railroad bridge crossed over Paint Creek on its way into Greenfield from the east. The pen where the sheep are grazing is the lot below where the present-day Grain and Hay Building is located on the northeast corner of McArthur Way and Jefferson Street. On the fence is John Putnam, a livestock dealer, and standing in the pen is Alf Harvey.

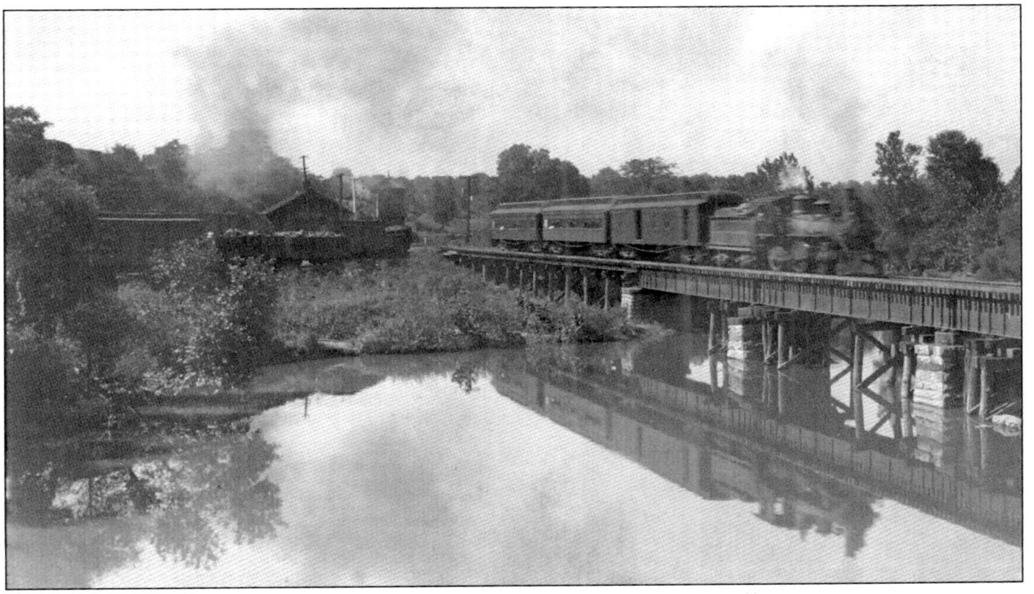

The DT&I train leaves the depot and heads south through Paint Valley. It is a passenger train with lots of windows for viewing the sights. As the train crosses Paint Creek, a reflection is created in the water.

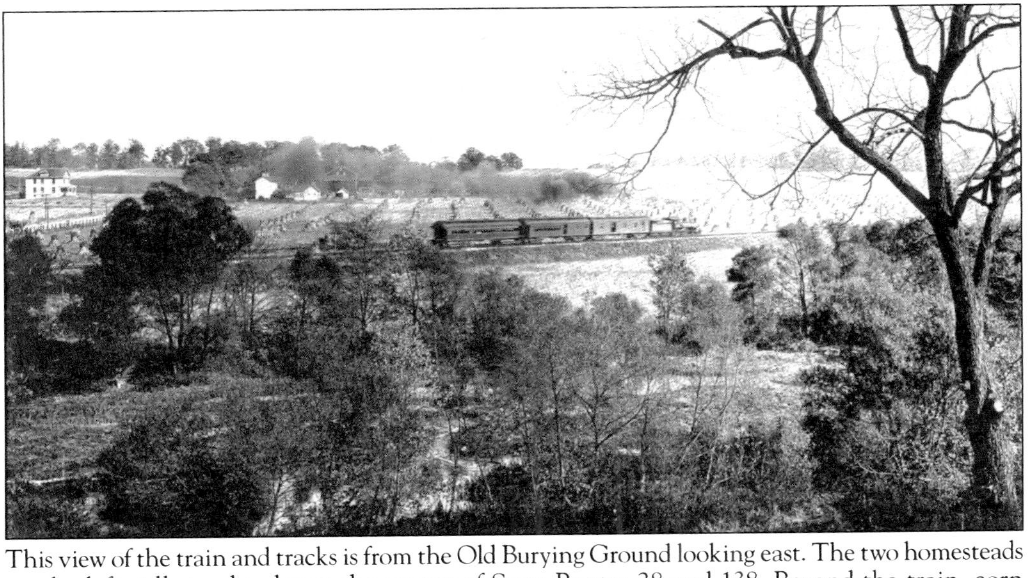

This view of the train and tracks is from the Old Burying Ground looking east. The two homesteads on the left still stand today at the corner of State Routes 28 and 138. Beyond the train, corn shocks stand in the field.

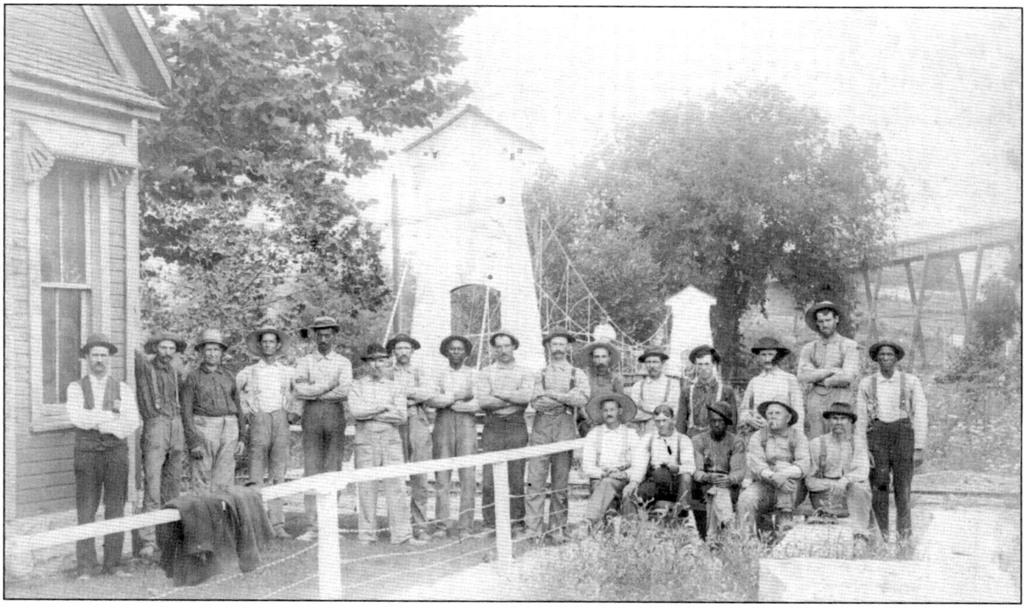

The crew of Rucker's Quarry is pictured here in front of the suspension footbridge crossing Paint Creek. Faintly showing on the right is the old train trestle. The quarry was located on 85 acres in Ross County and 13 acres in Highland County along both sides of Paint Creek.

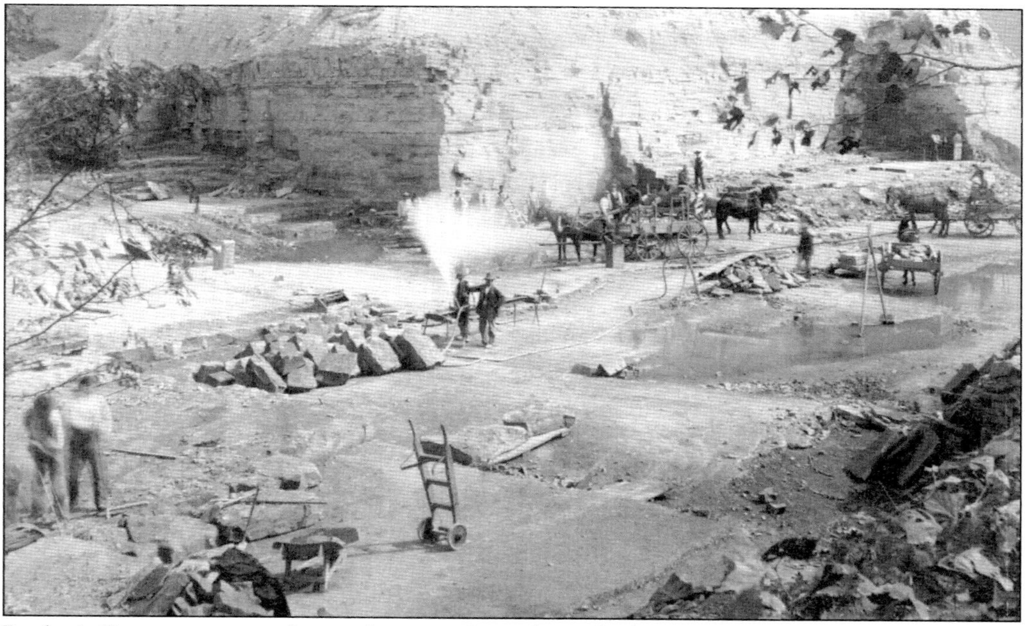

Rucker's Quarry was a productive business throughout the latter half of the 1800s and well into the 1900s. G.I. Rucker and, later, his son George W. owned and operated the quarry, which was rich with limestone. Rucker's quarried stone on a large scale for the Cincinnati market and many local markets. The limekiln operated day and night through the height of the business. (Courtesy of Tammy McNeal.)

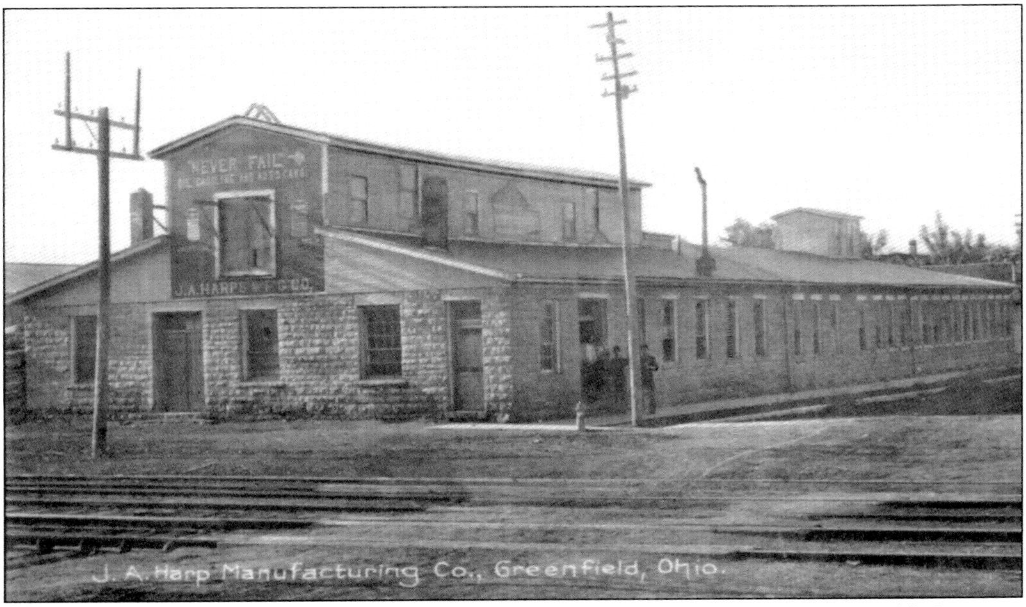

In 1902, J.A. Harps formed a manufacturing company and built this factory on S. Fifth Street in 1907. His significant product was the Never-Fail Oil Can, which "even a lady could use without soiling her gloves," according to advertisements. The can was invented by Eugene Arnott and perfected by Harps. At one point, the factory produced 1,000 oil cans per day.

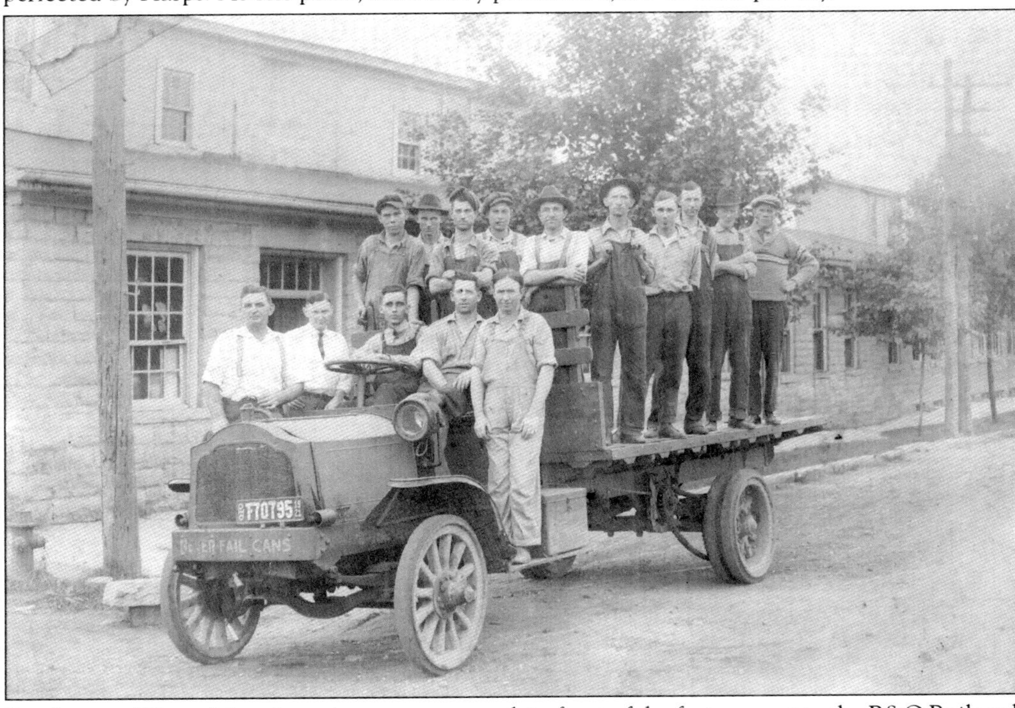

Employees of Harps Manufacturing pose on a truck in front of the factory next to the B&O Railroad. The company employed 40 workmen plus office and sales staff. Harps led an active civic life, serving on the Greenfield Board of Education and as president of the Peoples National Bank.

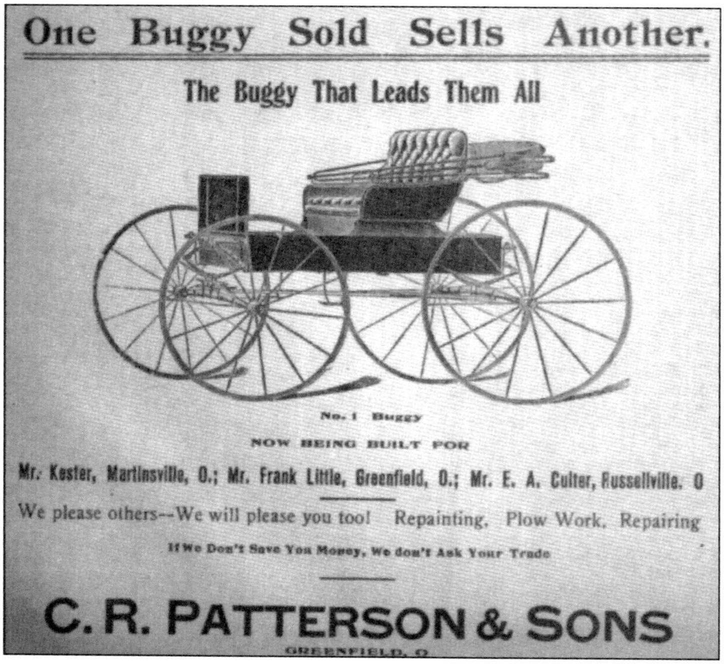

This advertisement for Patterson buggies is an example of how the company marketed its carriages nationwide. The company named buyers whose orders were currently being built, with the hope of enticing others to keep up with the Joneses.

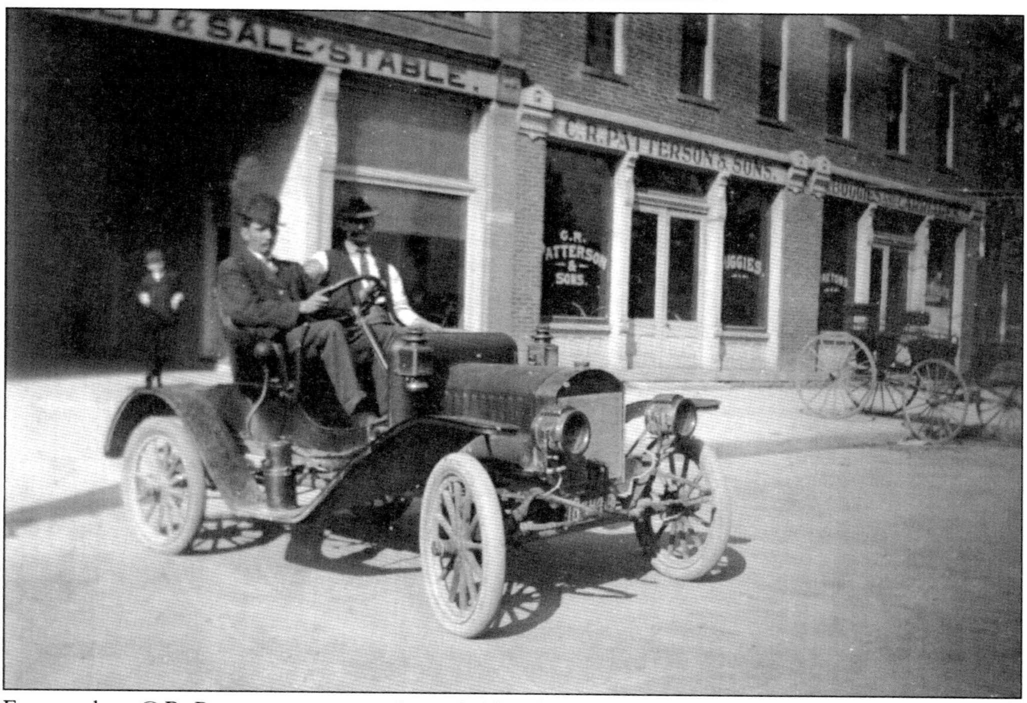

Former slave C.R. Patterson came to Greenfield and joined in the carriage-making business with a man named Lowe. Upon Lowe's death, Patterson became sole owner of the business and established his company in 1873. Here, Frederick Douglass Patterson, C.R.'s son, sits in one of the company's automobiles outside their showroom on N. Washington Street. The Patterson Company was the only African American–owned automobile manufacturing business in the United States.

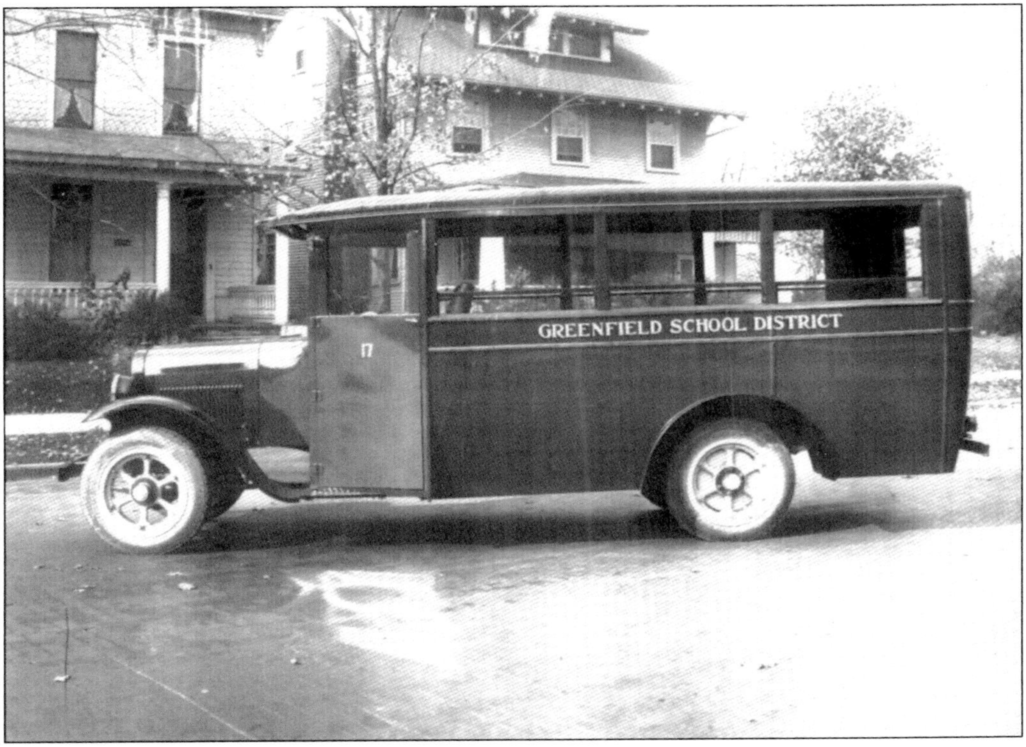

The C.R. Patterson Company provided Greenfield schools with buses for its fleet. Patterson buses were widely sold; the country of Haiti bought several buses that were driven to New York for delivery to Haitian officials.

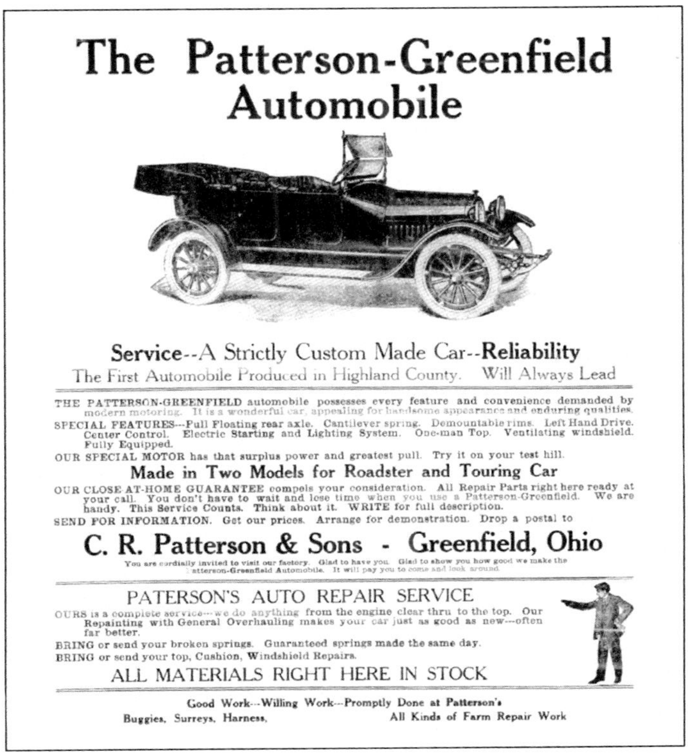

This advertisement features the Patterson-Greenfield automobile from around 1915. In addition to the auto sales, Patterson's operated an auto repair service, which enhanced their business prospects.

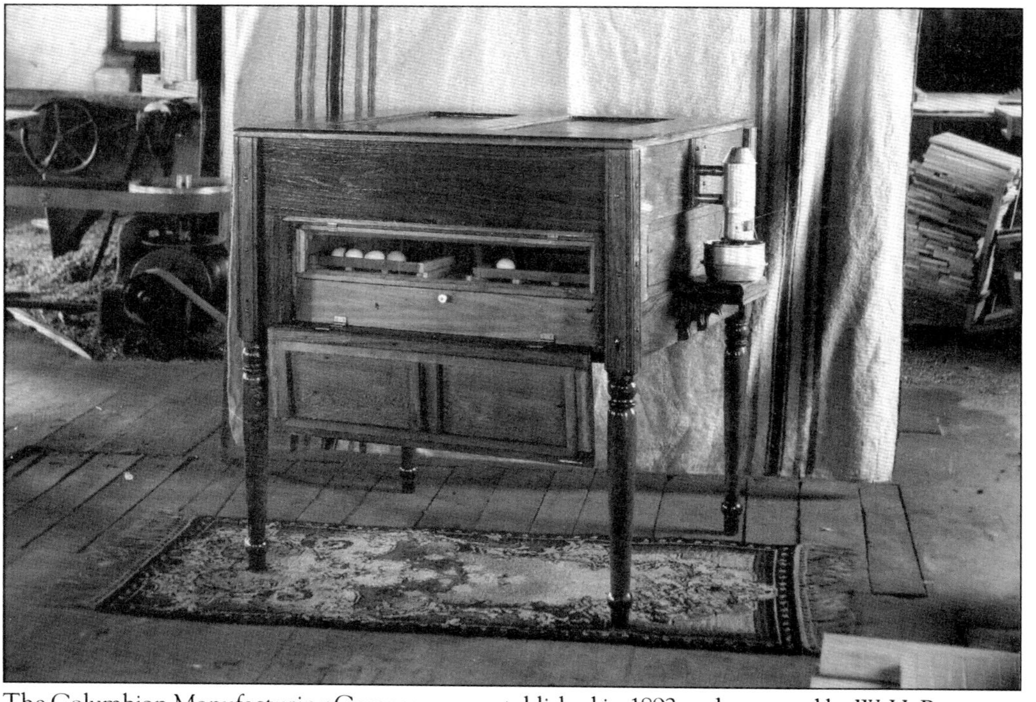

The Columbian Manufacturing Company was established in 1892 and managed by W. H. Pommert, who was known for his great business ability. Originally, the company sold products for home construction. Later, the company began patenting products such as this incubator.

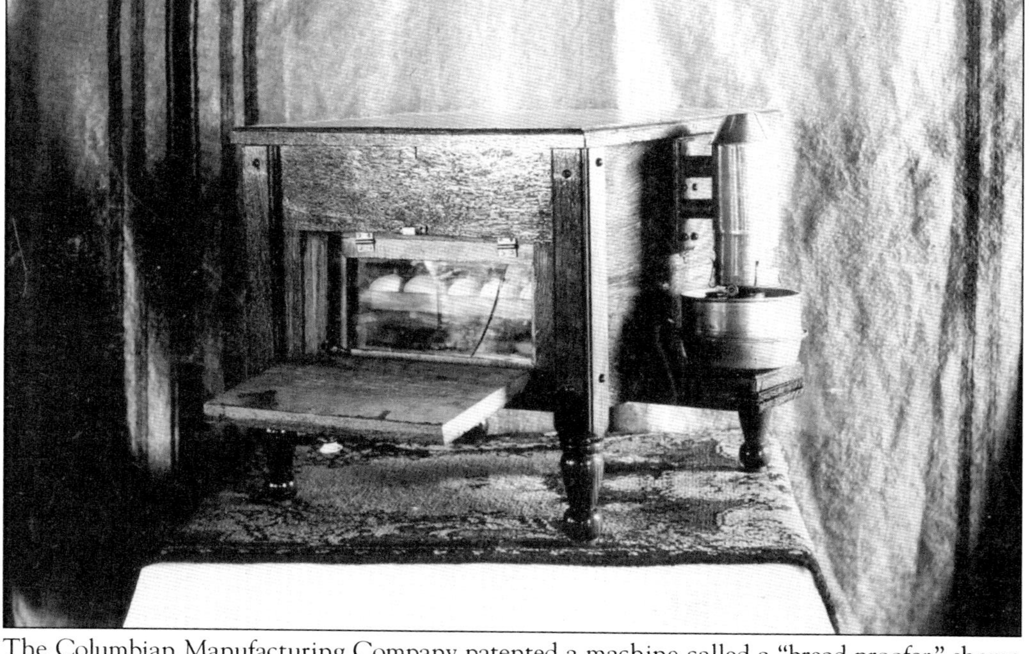

The Columbian Manufacturing Company patented a machine called a "bread proofer," shown here. Heat was applied to rising dough, decreasing the time needed to make bread.

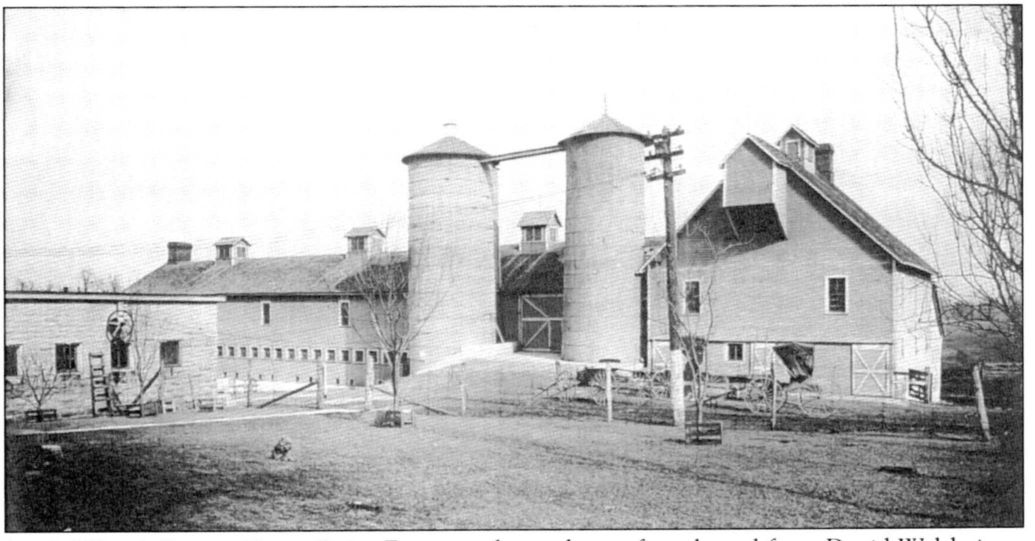

Jacob White's Spring Grove Dairy Farm was located on a farm leased from David Welsheimer and land that included the old fairgrounds. Today, this land is near Johnson Controls and the Industrial Park on Greenfield-Sabina Road. The dairy had one of the finest Jersey herds in southern Ohio at the end of the 1800s and was featured in *Country Gentleman* magazine in 1919. (Courtesy of Susan Thompson.)

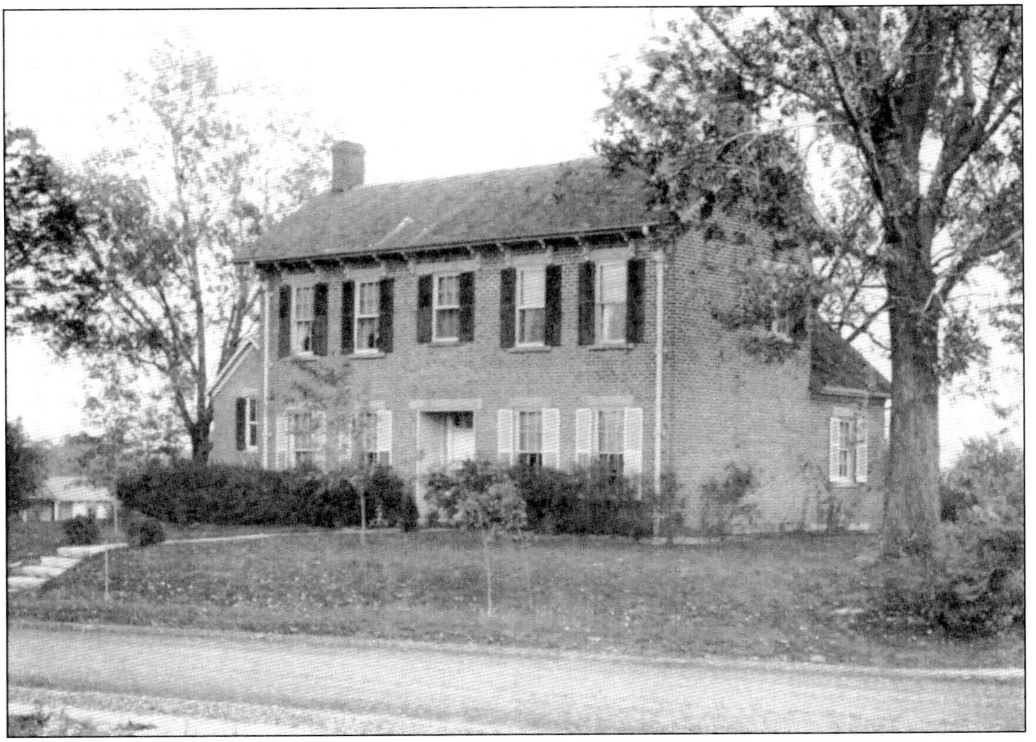

Paul Wilson, owner of Wilson Poultry in the 1920s, improved the quality of his product by importing Leghorn chickens from England to breed with his stock. Wilson sold eggs for hatching and live chicks. He lived here at the Birches, located on State Route 138 West.

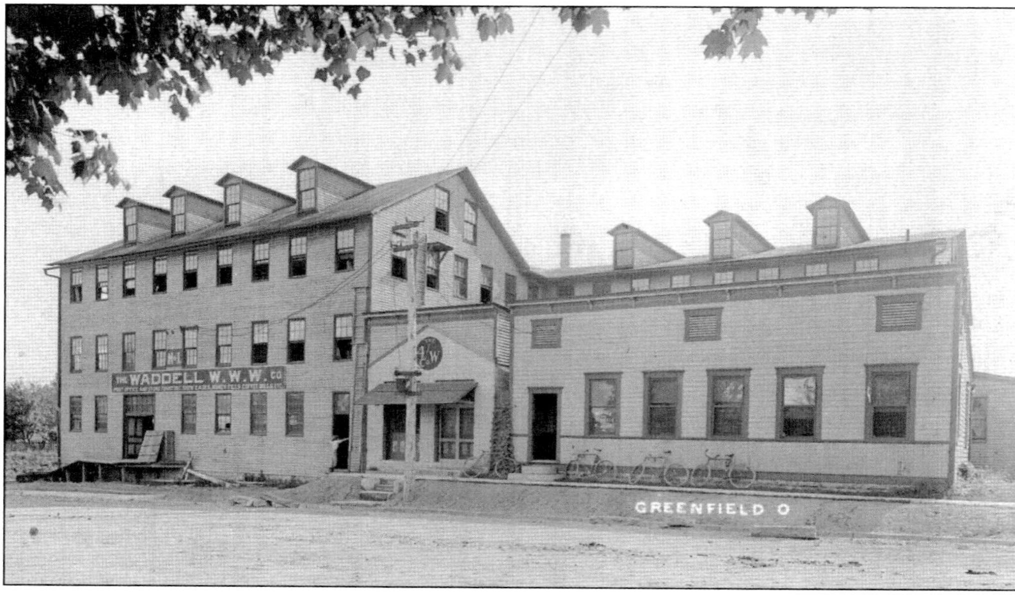

In 1889, John M. Waddell founded the Waddell Wooden Ware Works, located at 508 S. Washington Street. This structure was originally three separate buildings. The portion on the left was originally two and a half stories and was made into three and a half stories, as shown here. The company manufactured phonographs, rattraps, and coffee mills, among other things, and employed 100 people.

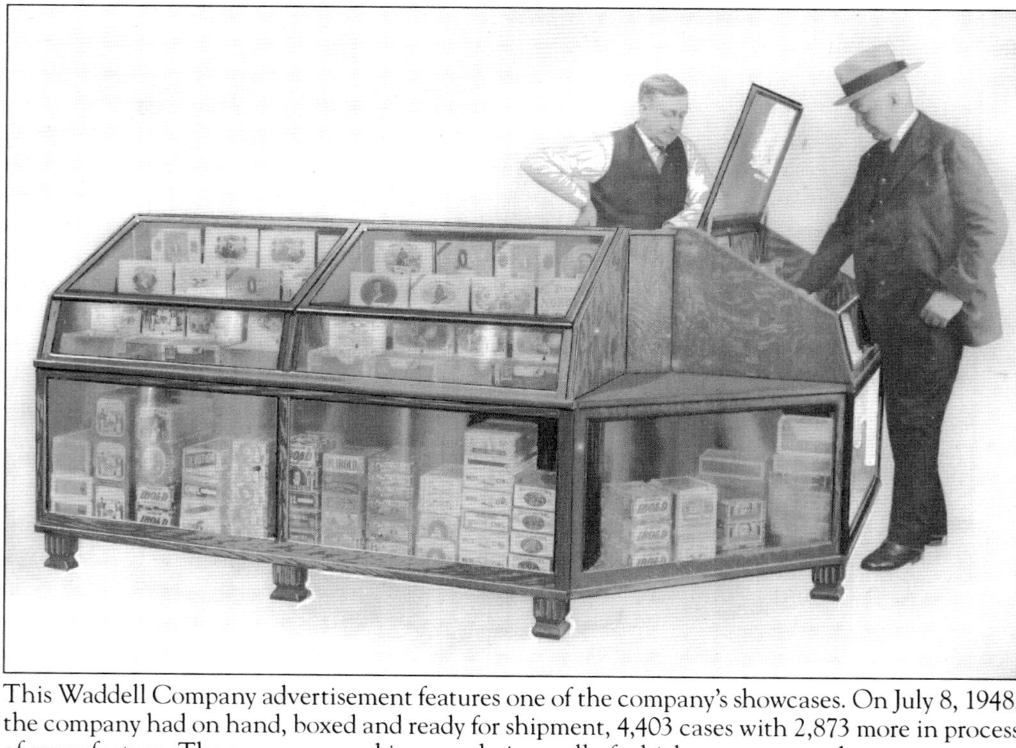

This Waddell Company advertisement features one of the company's showcases. On July 8, 1948, the company had on hand, boxed and ready for shipment, 4,403 cases with 2,873 more in process of manufacture. The company used its own designs, all of which were patented.

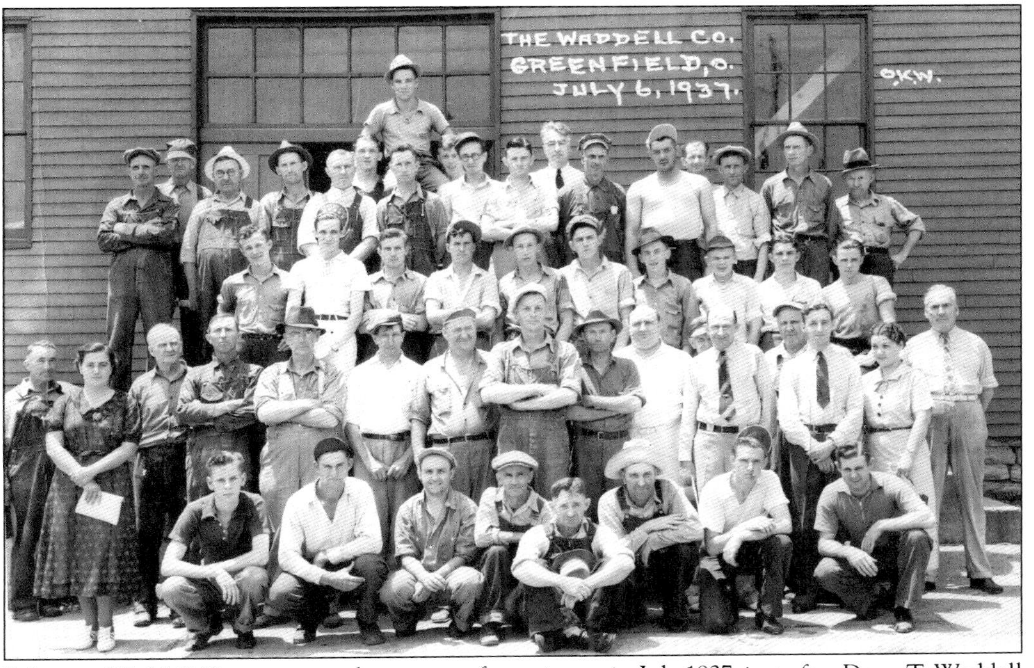

Fifty-two Waddell Company employees pose for a picture in July 1937, just after Dean T. Waddell purchased the stock held by his brothers Lew P. and Neal P. Waddell. Eventually, Dean T. Waddell was joined in business by his sons George M. and Dean M.

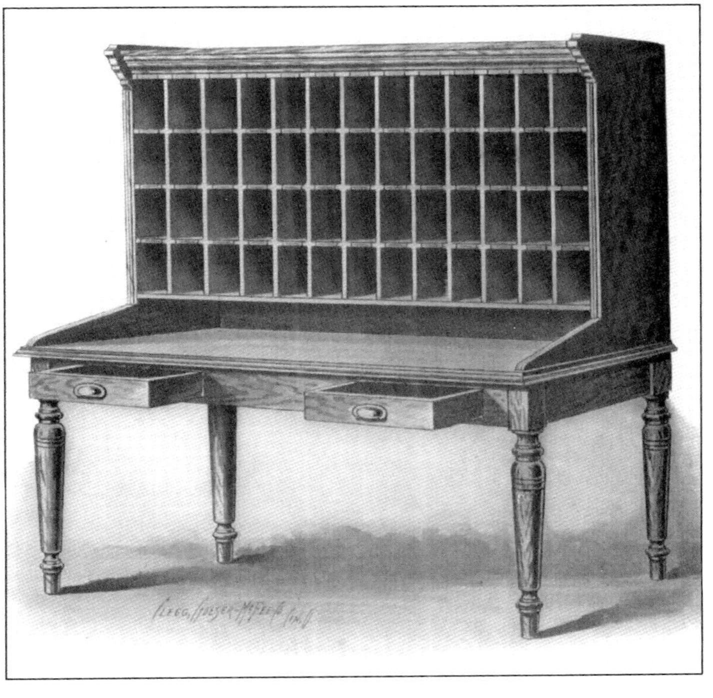

The mail-sorting table manufactured by the Waddell Company became so popular that a separate company was formed to market the postal furniture line—Waddell Postal Fixture Company. Waddell's companies sold products throughout the United States and abroad to various wholesale trades such as bakers, beauty salons, barbershops, confectioners, pharmacists, grocers, and jewelers.

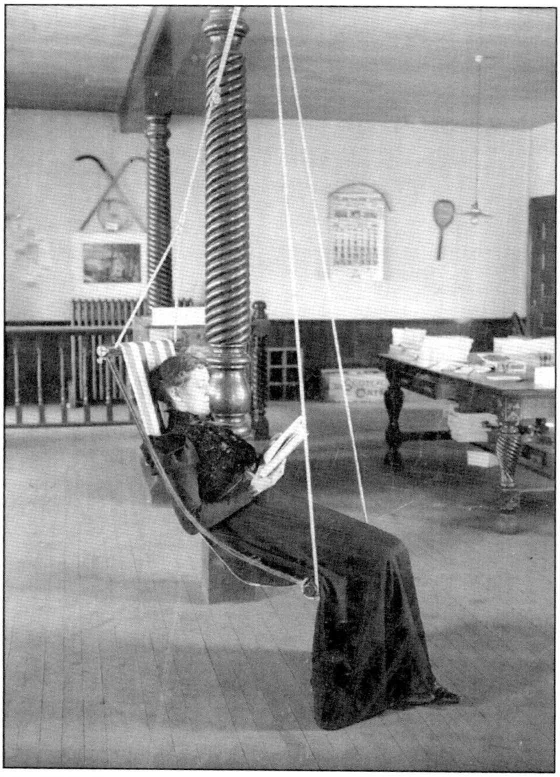

The celebrated Uwanta Hammock Chair was the most successful invention of its class ever marketed. Advertising material for the product emphasizes the innovative "deep bent side arms . . . with a wire truss buried on the underside." This construction allowed the occupant ample elbow room and was adjustable to any angle. Waddell patented the hammock on December 10, 1901.

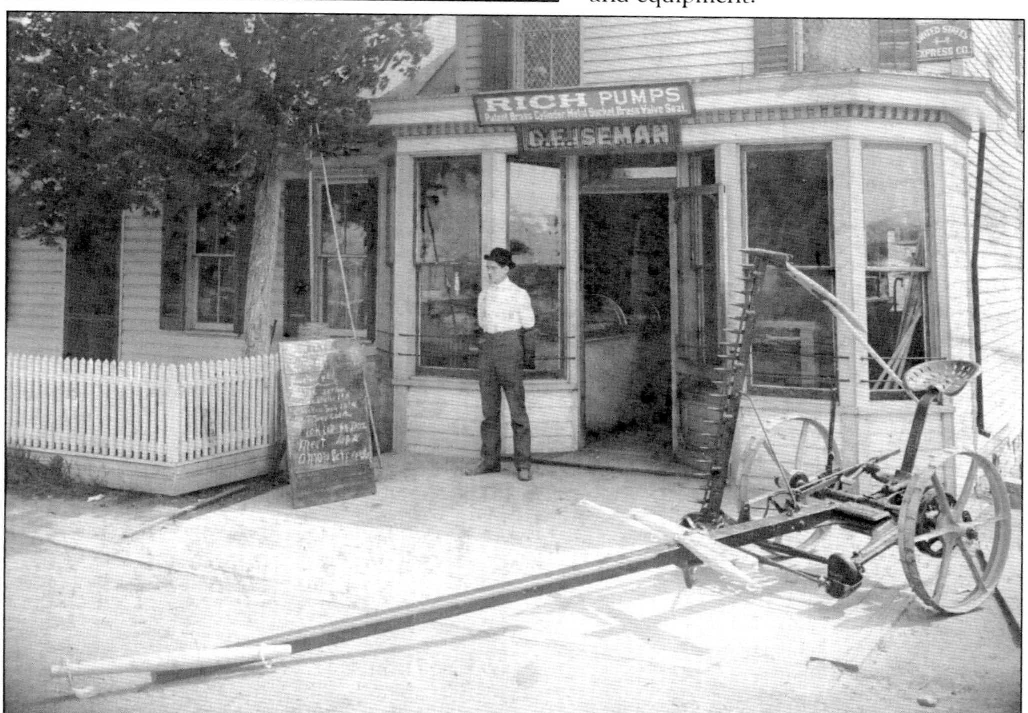

Charles Edgar Iseman owned and operated his mercantile business out of Fruitdale. The general store offered such necessities as eggs, hens, and roosters, in addition to farm implements and equipment.

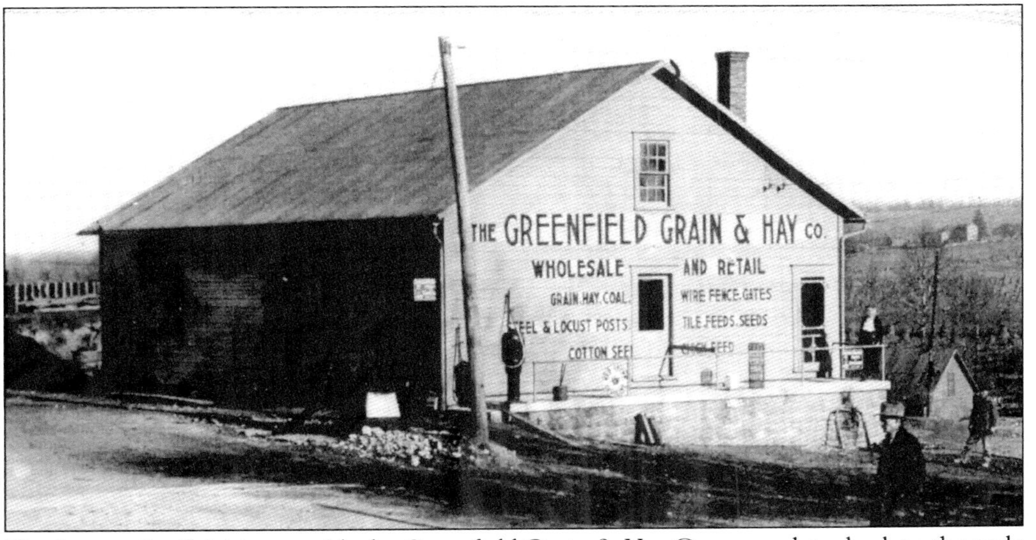

The Iseman family's history with the Greenfield Grain & Hay Company dates back to the early 1900s, when John Ellsworth Iseman and John Wood founded the business near the corner of Mirabeau and Second Streets. In 1910, Iseman bought out his partner's share and moved to Jefferson Street near Paint Creek a few years later. In 1924, John E. died, and his son Maple Dane Iseman took over the business.

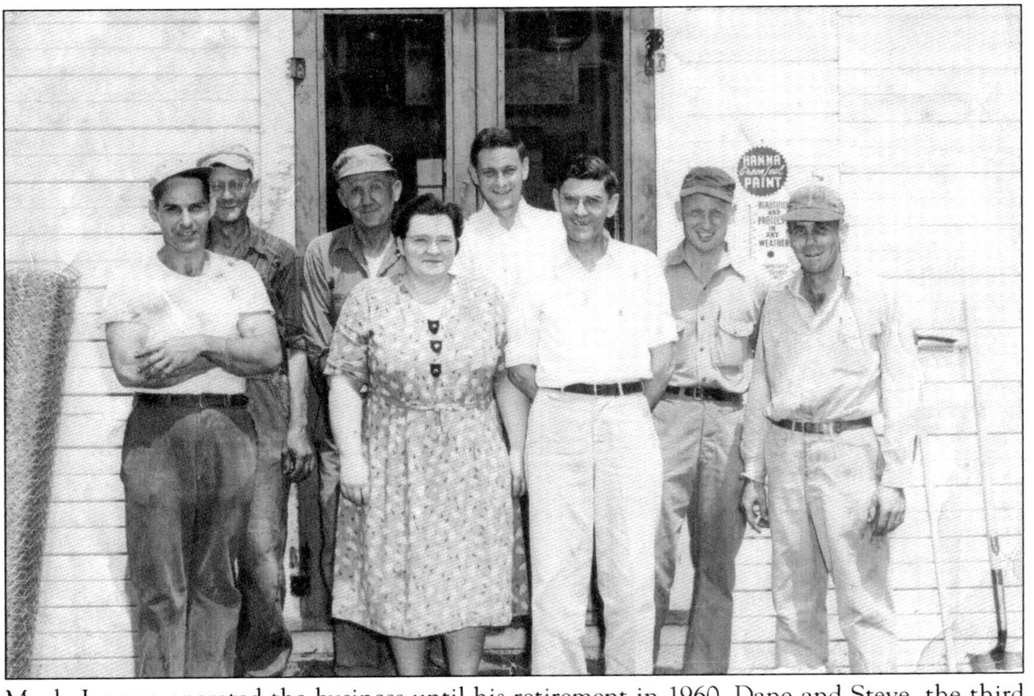

Maple Iseman operated the business until his retirement in 1960. Dane and Steve, the third and fourth generations, took over as proprietors in 1960 and 1977, respectively. Grain and Hay employees include, from left to right (first row) Orville Knisley, Stella Winegar, Maple "Mape" Iseman, and Orville "Jiggs" Everhart; (second row) Burch Taylor, Archie Lyle, Dane Iseman, and Richard Murray. The business closed in 1985.

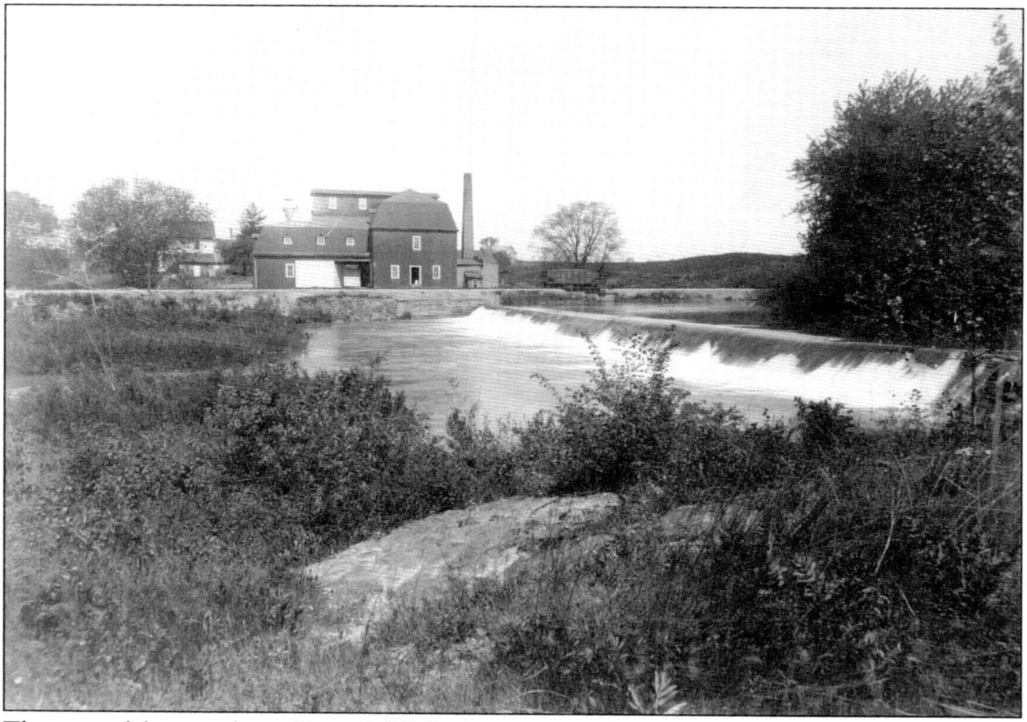

This peaceful scene shows Upper Mill, built in 1894 and known also as Island Grove Mill and Murphy's Mill. This mill and dam were located in the vicinity of present-day Island Grove Road and Wolf Road.

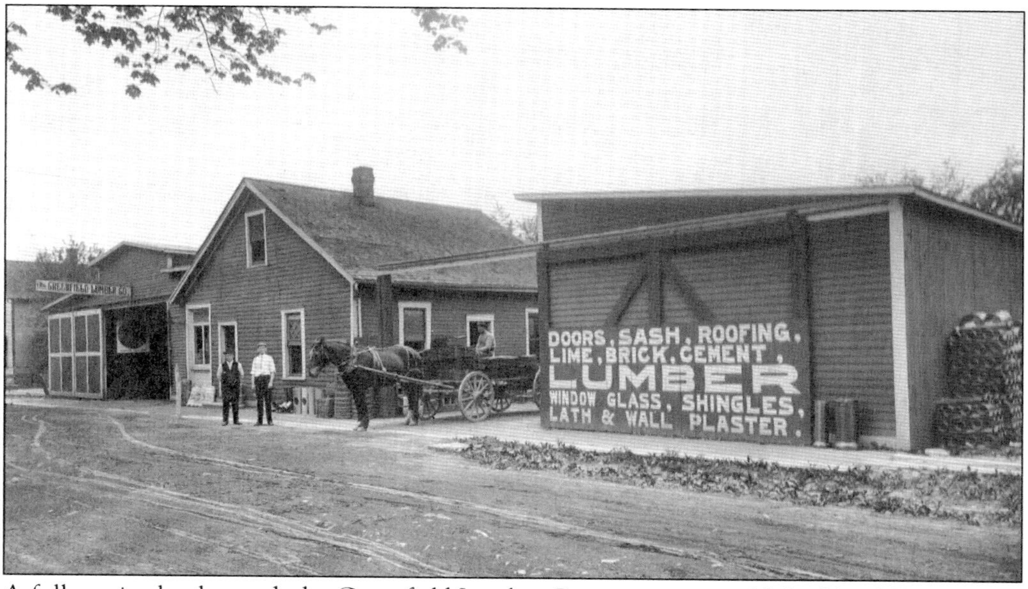

A full-service lumberyard, the Greenfield Lumber Company was established by O.E. Henry in 1895. The lumberyard was located on Summerfield Street. At some point, Henry, the president and general manager, sold the business to John J. Mertz. It later went to his son John L. Mertz.

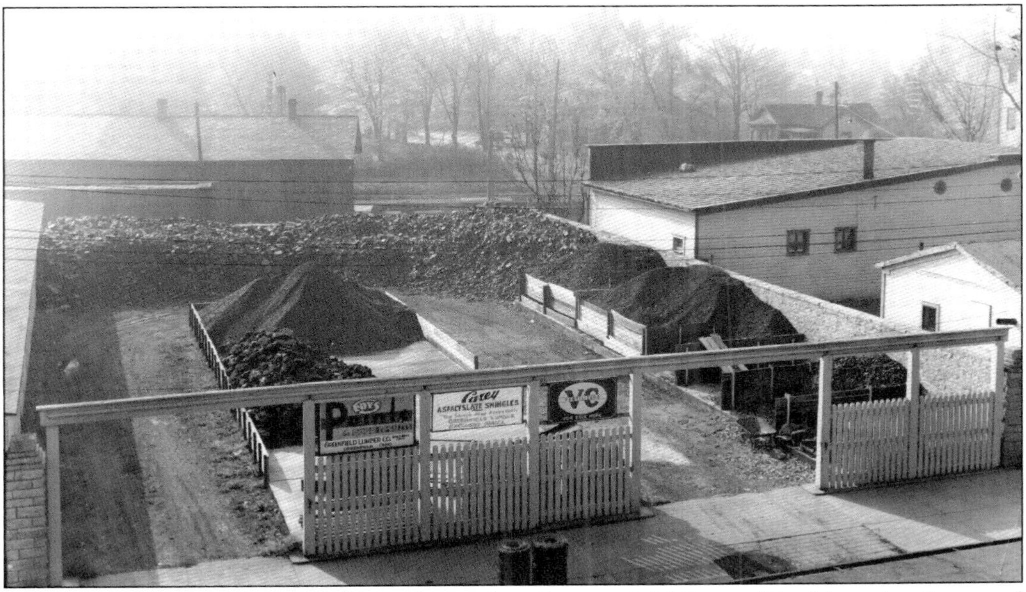

The Greenfield Lumber coal field was located on Summerfield Street. The Mertz family owned and operated the business for 33 years.

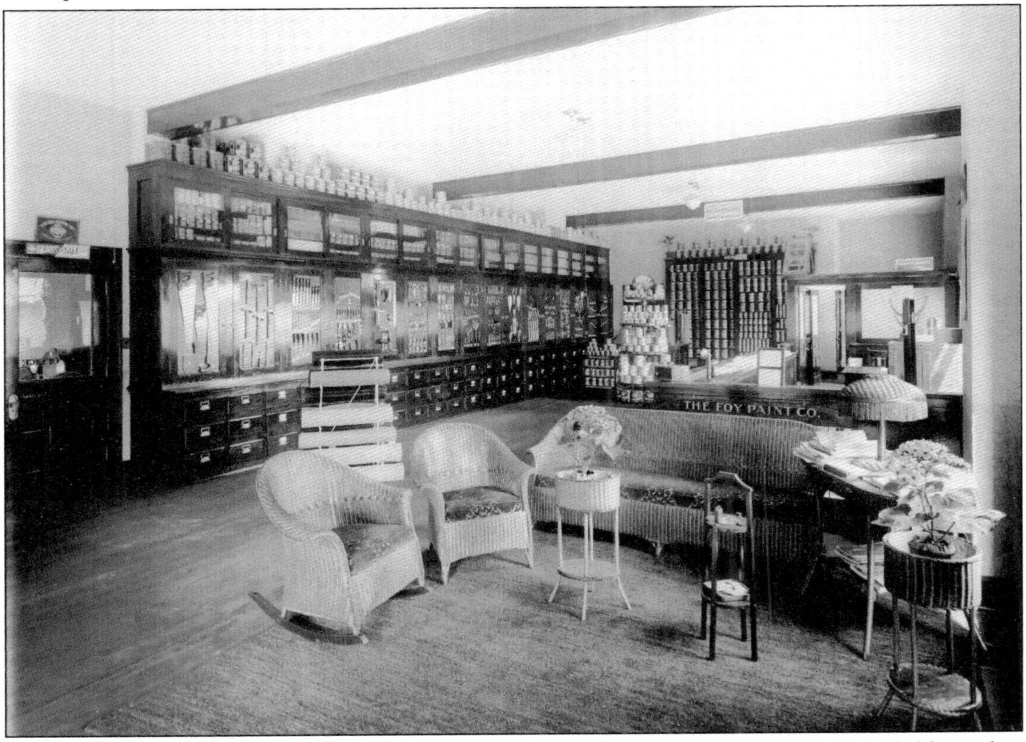

Between 1913 and 1916, a new building was constructed for the showroom of Greenfield Lumber as it expanded to include a paint store. The showroom offered shoppers a relaxed location to study options for whatever home improvements they were planning. The building is now the location of Wellers Plumbing and Heating

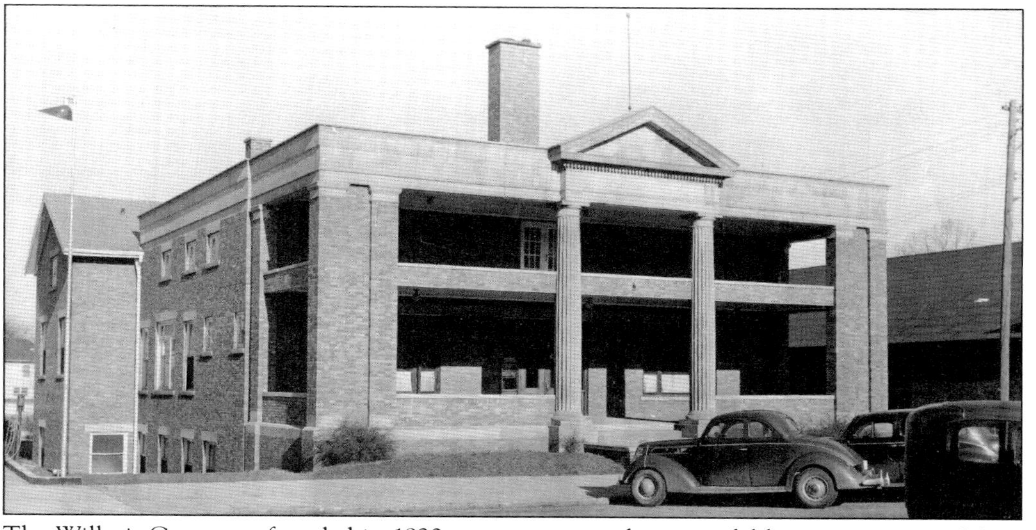

The Wilknit Company, founded in 1920, was an extremely successful hosiery company. Many people do not realize, however, that the business began when optometrist Dr. Leslie E. Wilkin began selling glasses by mail order. He changed his product to hosiery because it was so much easier to ship. This building on S. Washington Street, originally the Masonic Temple, was purchased by Wilknit in 1935.

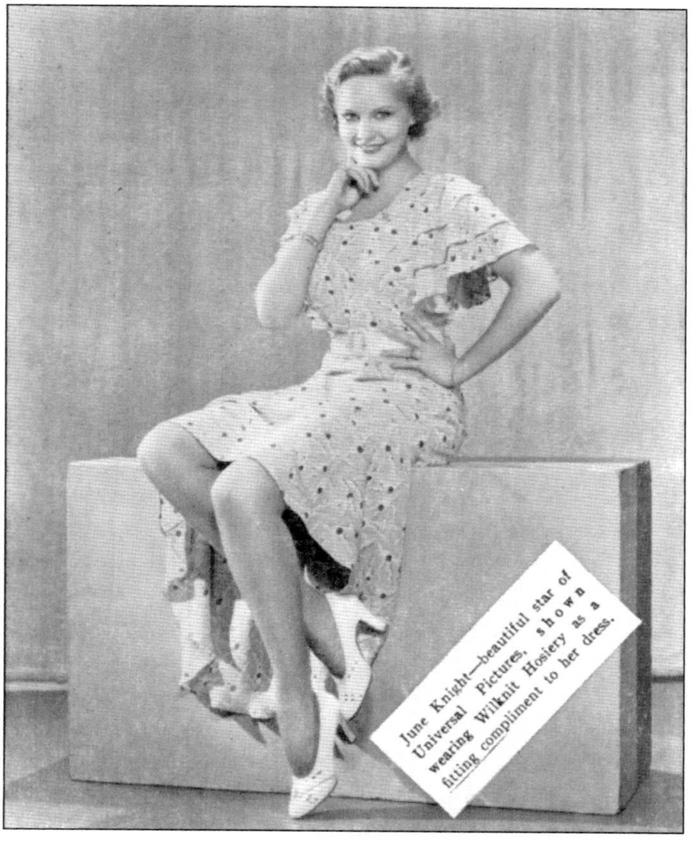

This advertisement for Wilknit Hosiery features actress June Knight. Wilknit sold and shipped nationwide a full line of men's, women's, and children's hosiery. Wilknit Company's extensive mail-order business is credited with the post offices of both Greenfield and Leesburg earning status as first-class post offices. Included among the company's customers were many Hollywood stars. First Lady Eleanor Roosevelt was also reported to have been a customer.

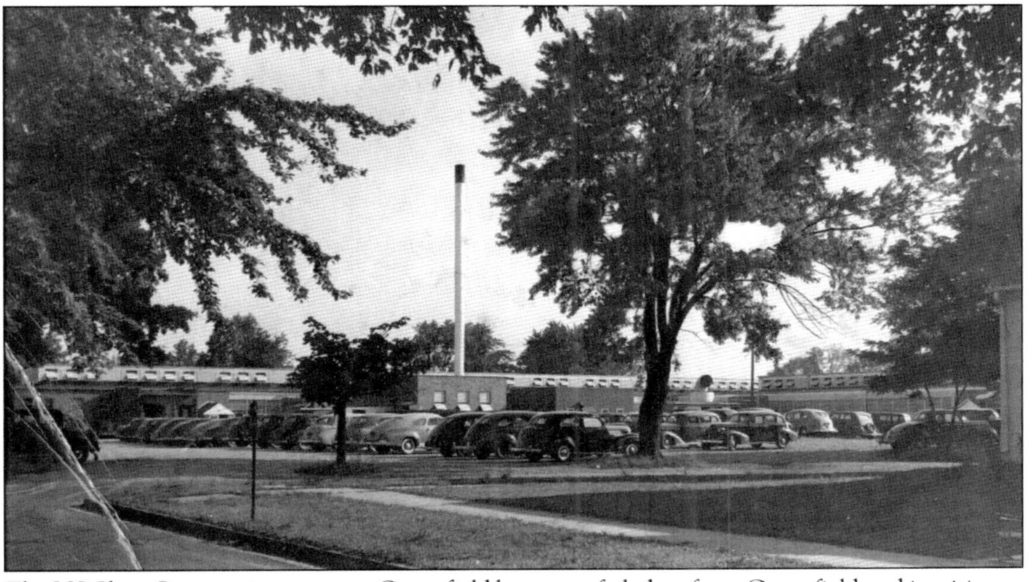

The US Shoe Corporation came to Greenfield because of pledges from Greenfield and its citizens. The Shoe Factory employed many in the Greenfield area and from as far as Chillicothe and Hillsboro. Located at Edgewood and McClain Streets, the Shoe Factory began operations in 1939 and continued into the 1980s.

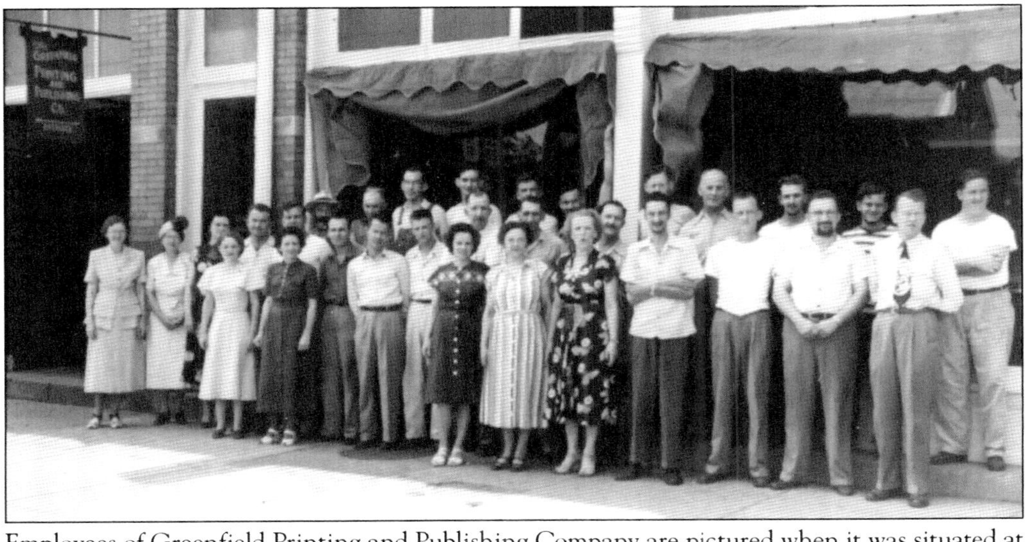

Employees of Greenfield Printing and Publishing Company are pictured when it was situated at its N. Washington Street location, which currently is the home of Southern Hills Community Bank. Greenfield Printing moved farther north on Washington Street and was later sold to Banta Publications. It is currently the site of R.R. Donnelly. (Courtesy of Lew Speakman.)

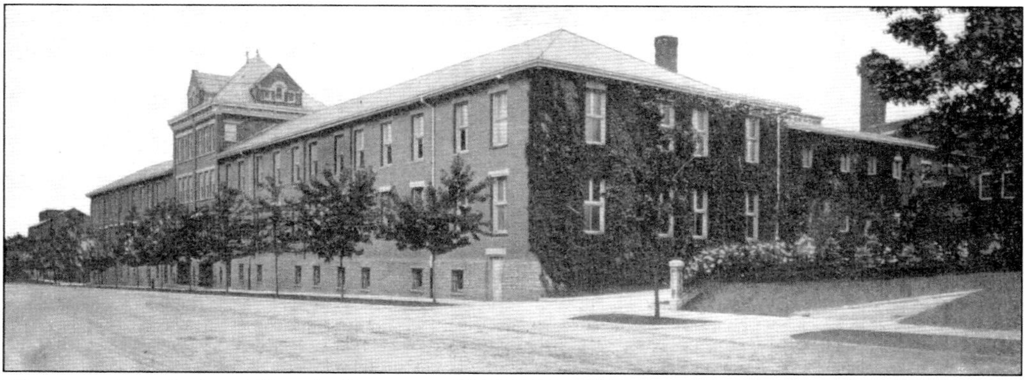

The American Pad and Textile Company (TAPATCO), known before 1903 as the E.L. McClain Manufacturing Company, was located at 410 S. Washington Street. In 1881, when he was 20, McClain designed a horse collar pad to protect the horse's neck. This became his first product, and by 1887, his company had produced over 3,600 pads. As sales increased, so did the size of the factory. (Courtesy of Susan Thompson.)

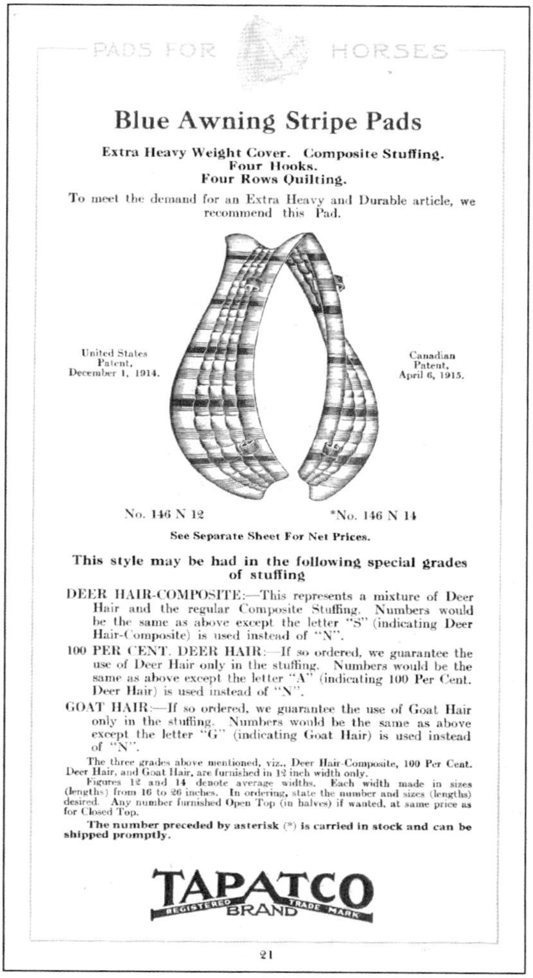

PADS FOR HORSES

Blue Awning Stripe Pads

Extra Heavy Weight Cover. Composite Stuffing.
Four Hooks.
Four Rows Quilting.

To meet the demand for an Extra Heavy and Durable article, we recommend this Pad.

United States Patent, December 1, 1914.

Canadian Patent, April 6, 1915.

No. 146 N 12 *No. 146 N 14

See Separate Sheet For Net Prices.

This style may be had in the following special grades of stuffing

DEER HAIR-COMPOSITE:—This represents a mixture of Deer Hair and the regular Composite Stuffing. Numbers would be the same as above except the letter "S" (indicating Deer Hair-Composite) is used instead of "N".

100 PER CENT. DEER HAIR:—If so ordered, we guarantee the use of Deer Hair only in the stuffing. Numbers would be the same as above except the letter "A" (indicating 100 Per Cent. Deer Hair) is used instead of "N".

GOAT HAIR:—If so ordered, we guarantee the use of Goat Hair only in the stuffing. Numbers would be the same as above except the letter "G" (indicating Goat Hair) is used instead of "N".

The three grades above mentioned, viz., Deer Hair-Composite, 100 Per Cent. Deer Hair, and Goat Hair, are furnished in 12 inch width only.

Figures 12 and 14 denote average widths. Each width made in sizes (lengths) from 16 to 26 inches. In ordering, state the number and sizes (lengths) desired. Any number furnished Open Top (in halves) if wanted, at same price as for Closed Top.

The number preceded by asterisk (*) is carried in stock and can be shipped promptly.

TAPATCO REGISTERED BRAND TRADE MARK

21

This horse collar pad from a 1919 TAPATCO catalog was one of many models made by the company. This style came in four different grades of filling and featured four clips patented by McClain to hold the pad in place. McClain owned factories in Columbus and Cincinnati, and in Ontario, Canada. He created the entire town of Atco, Georgia, when he built a mill there to manufacture cotton for his pad products.

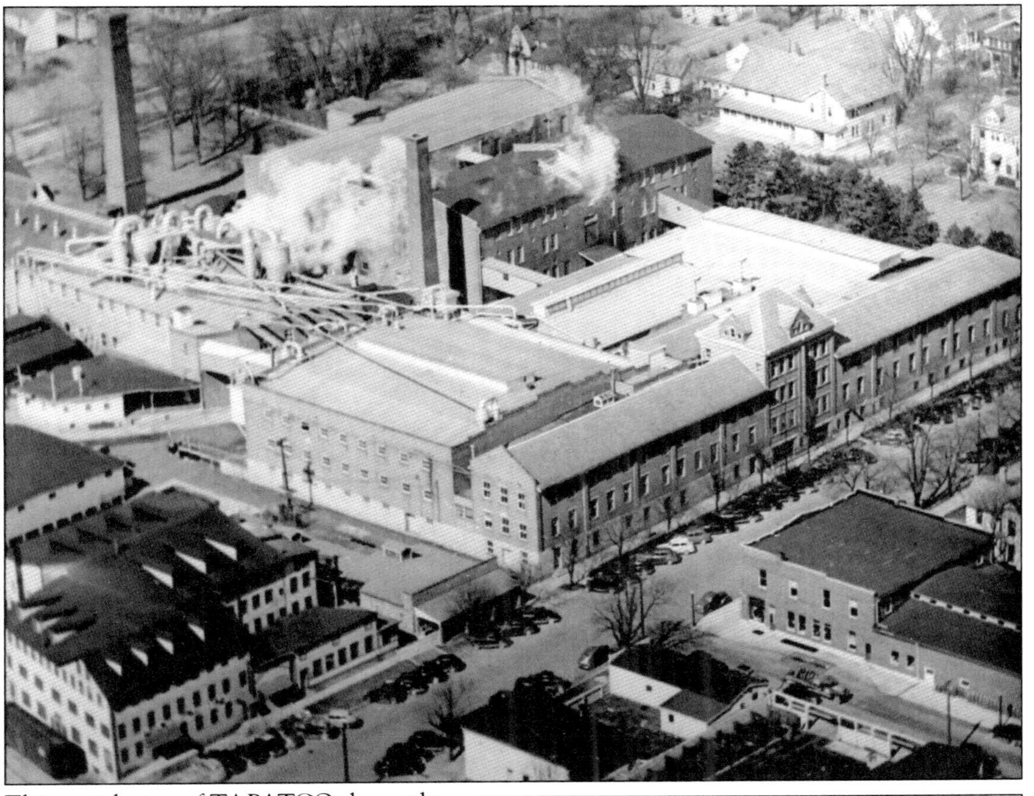

This aerial view of TAPATCO shows the sprawling factory with S. Washington Street on the east, Fourth Street on the west, and South Street on the north. South of TAPATCO in the lower left corner is the present-day Waddell Factory. Greenfield benefited from TAPATCO's success in more ways than one. McClain donated a new high school, which opened in 1915, and supported the building of a new Methodist church.

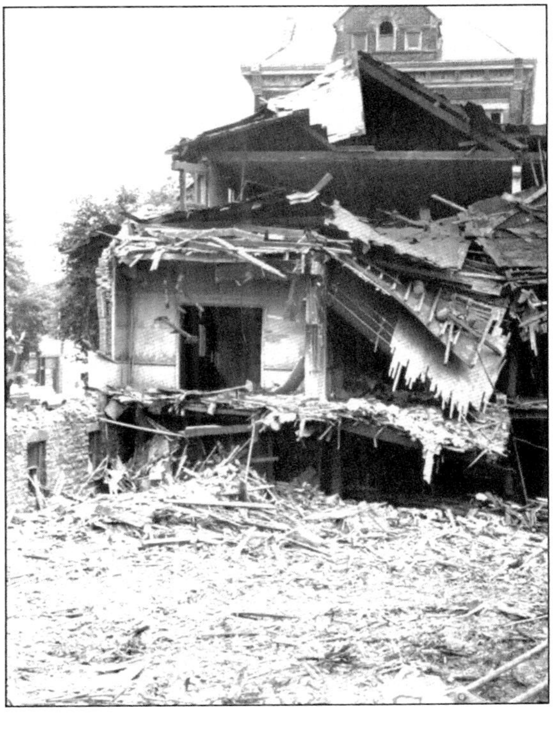

TAPATCO closed in 1962 after 81 years of business. The demolition of the factory occurred in 1981.

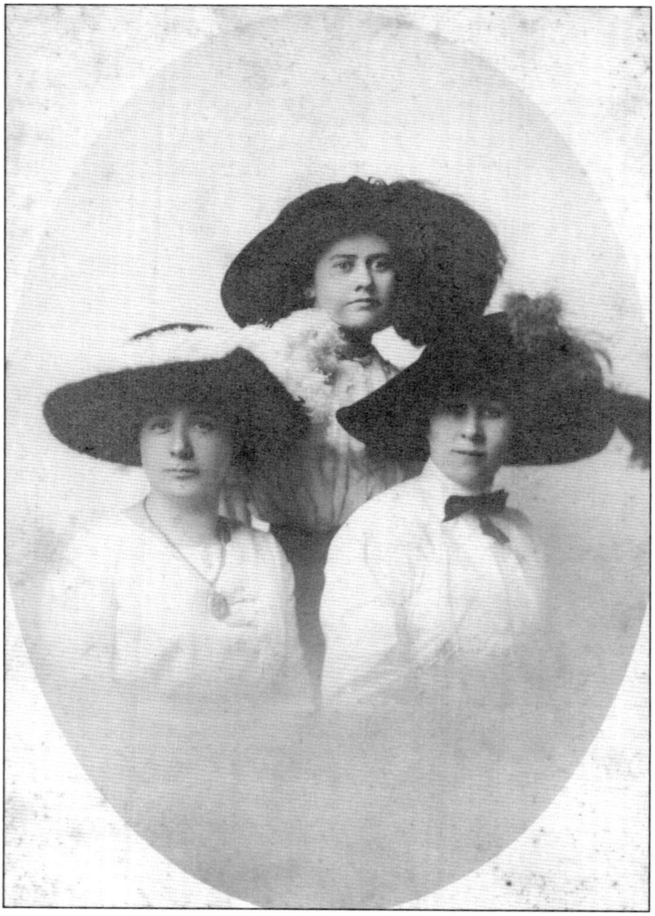

Three models display the products of the K&L Farmer Millinery shop. It is believed that these women are Lilly Free Stultz, center, with owners Kate Farmer, left, and Lucie Farmer. The building was on the site of the present-day Corner Pharmacy parking lot.

Employees pose in front of K&L Farmer Millinery in downtown Greenfield, where shoppers could buy fashionable hats and hair products. Established at 119 N. Washington Street by E. Ballard, member of an old pioneer family, the millinery was sold to Kate and Lucie Farmer around 1911.

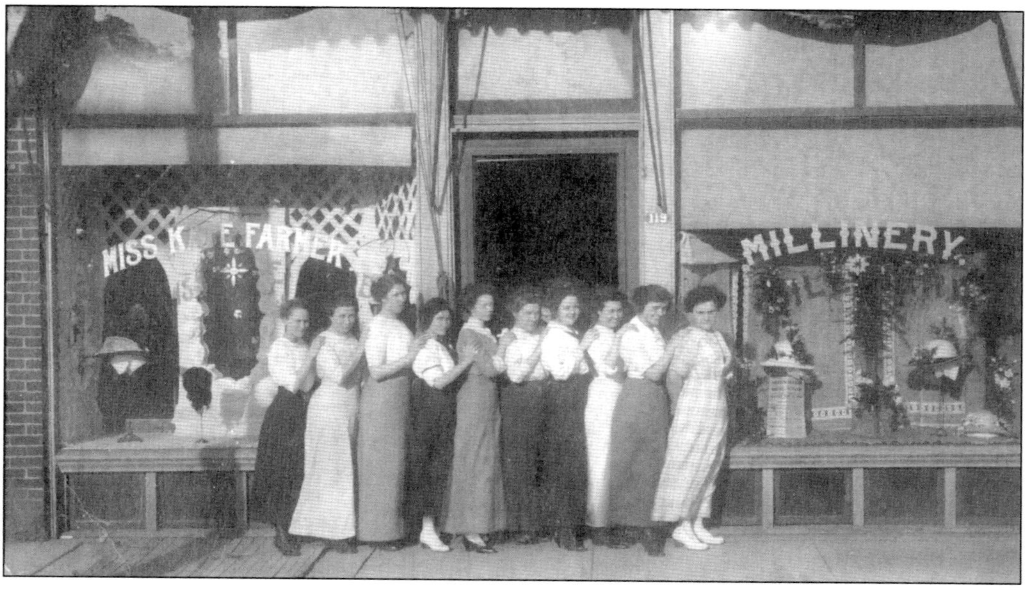

This advertisement for K&L Farmer Millinery indicates that, in addition to selling fine headwear for women, the shop also sold hair tonic for dandruff. Kate (1871–1933) and Lucie (1873–1942) Farmer were the daughters of Evan Lewis Farmer and Sarah Eunice Stewart.

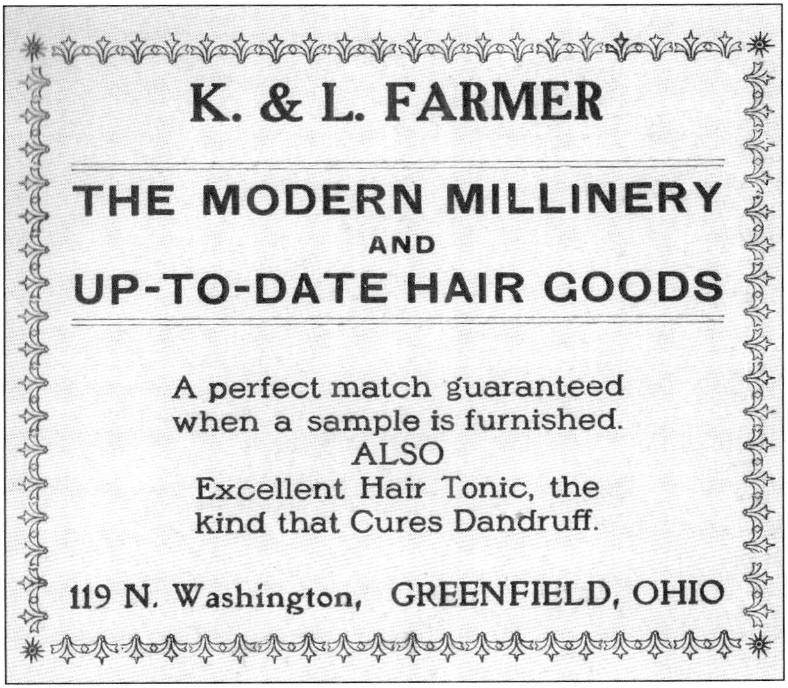

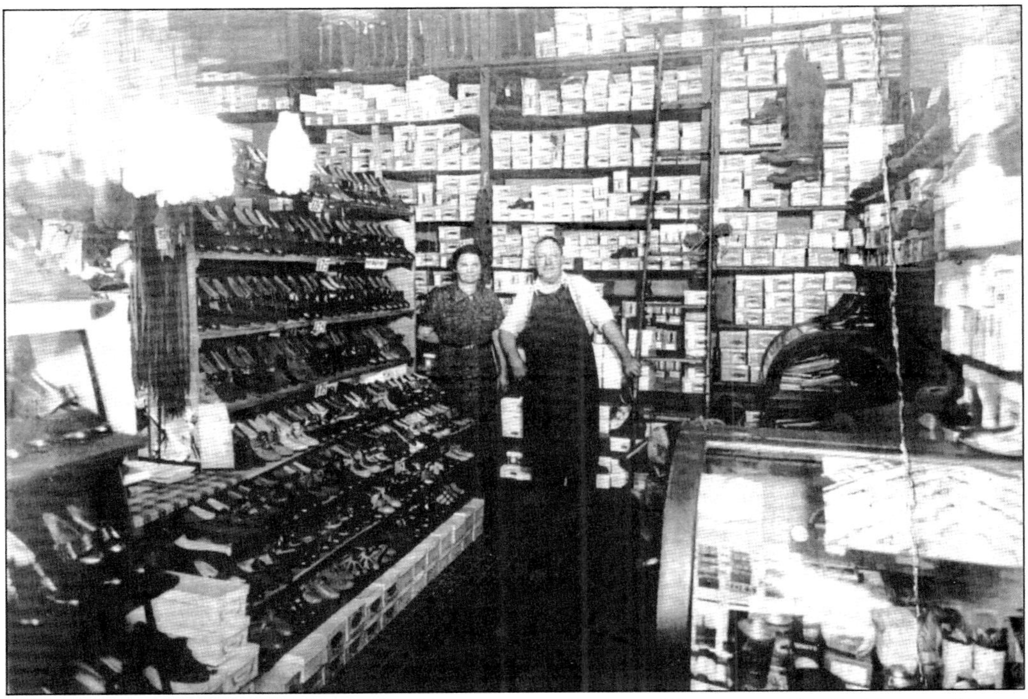

Long's Shoe Store was located in a building next to the Lyric Theater on S. Washington Street. The one-room store displayed shoes and boots in the front, with storage in the back. There is a sliding ladder on the back wall to reach stock. Signs on the shoe rack indicate that shoes cost $1.75 a pair and there were no refunds.

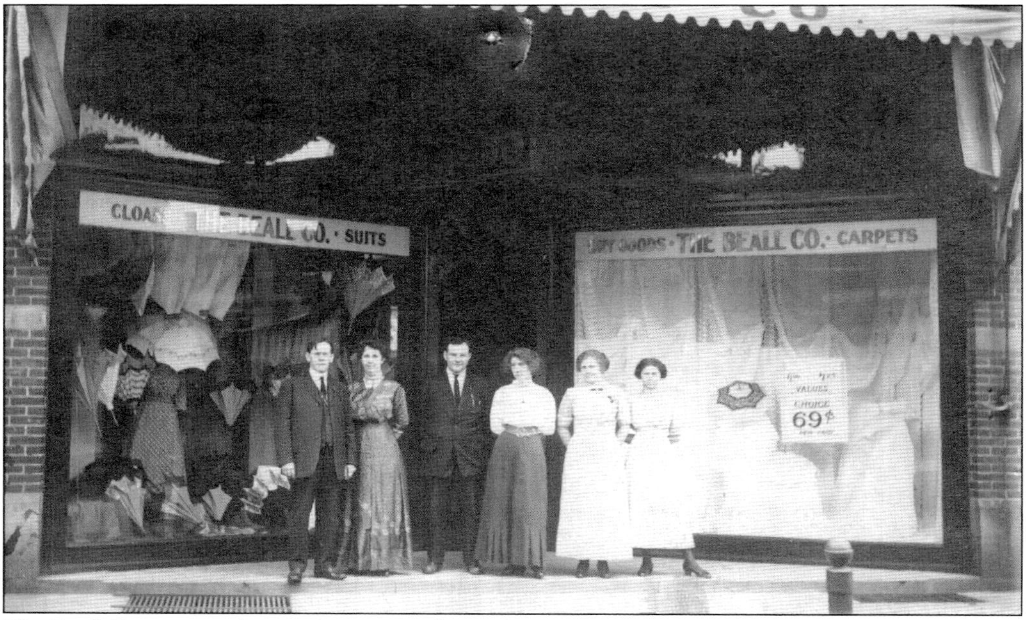

The Beall Company, a dry goods store, was located at 319 Jefferson Street. Elmer E. Beall was president and manager while his wife, Julia, served as bookkeeper and cashier. (Courtesy of Tom Smith.)

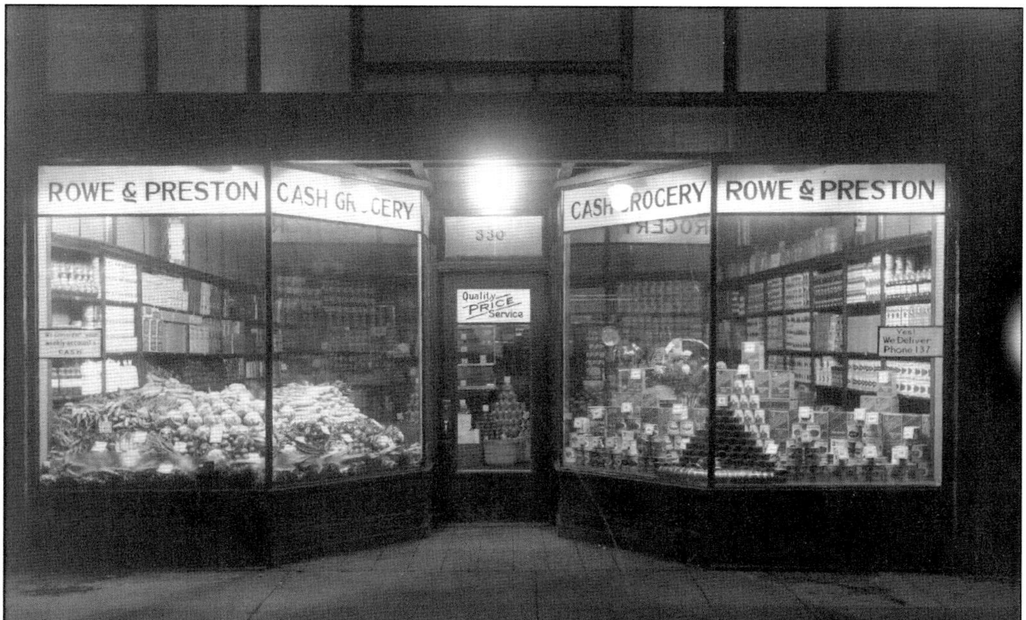

Located at 330 Jefferson Street, the Rowe & Preston Grocery carried a variety of produce and canned goods. The owners were Henry Rowe and Ed Preston, who entered into partnership in the 1930s.

Jacob Zinnecker (pictured) and his brother Henry joined a third brother, Lou, in his barbershop business in 1886. Lou had operated the barbershop since 1880 when haircuts cost 20¢ and shaves cost 10¢. At some point, Jacob acquired the business and passed it on to his sons George and Charles.

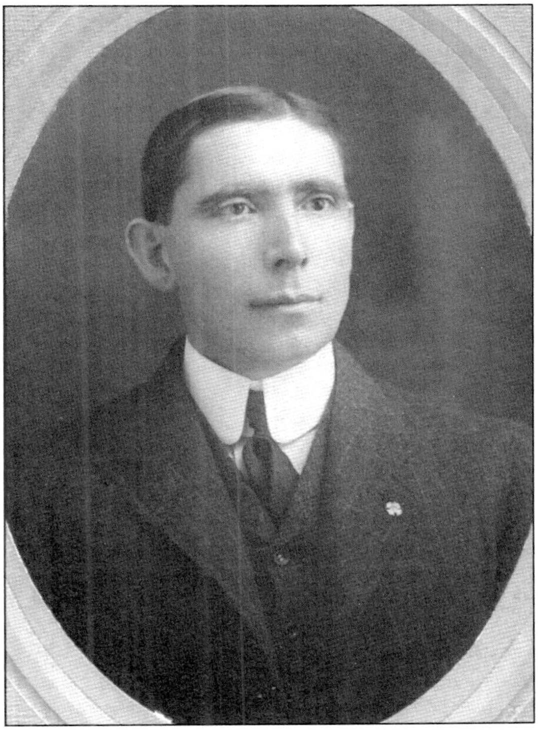

Zinnecker's Barber Shop was located on the second floor of the Smart building at the southeast corner of Jefferson and Washington Streets, the present-day site of a filling station. The barbershop later moved to 336 Jefferson Street.

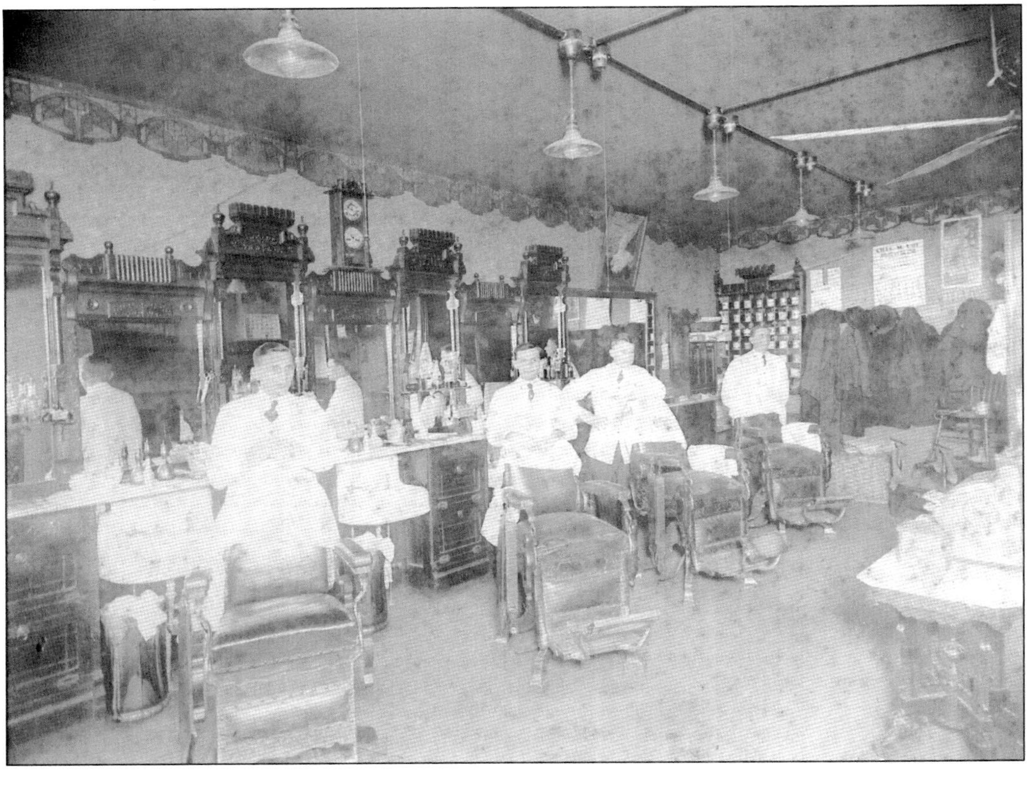

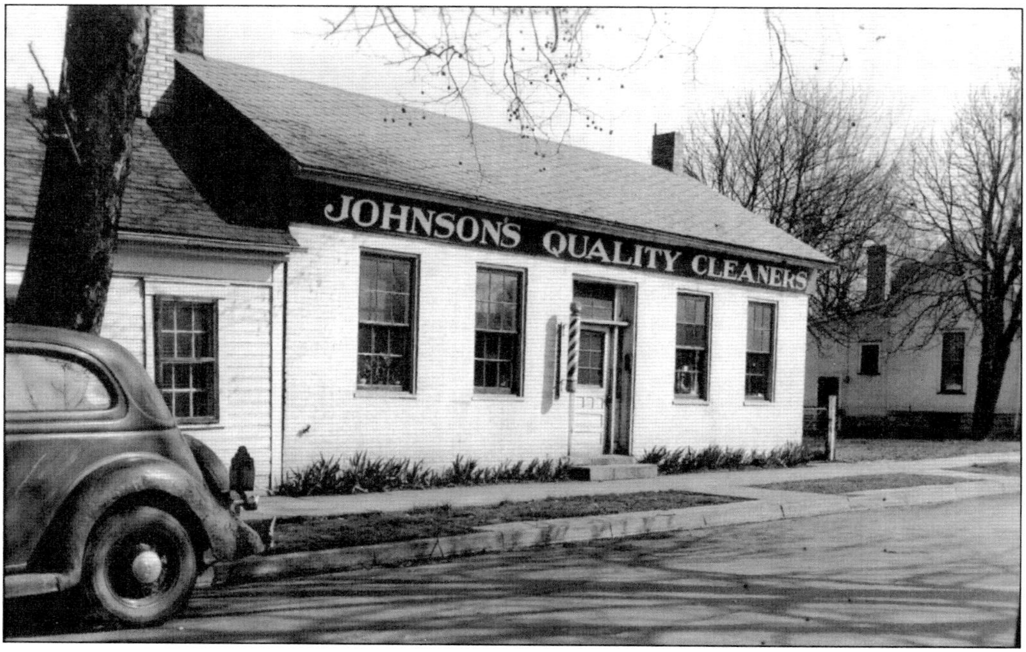

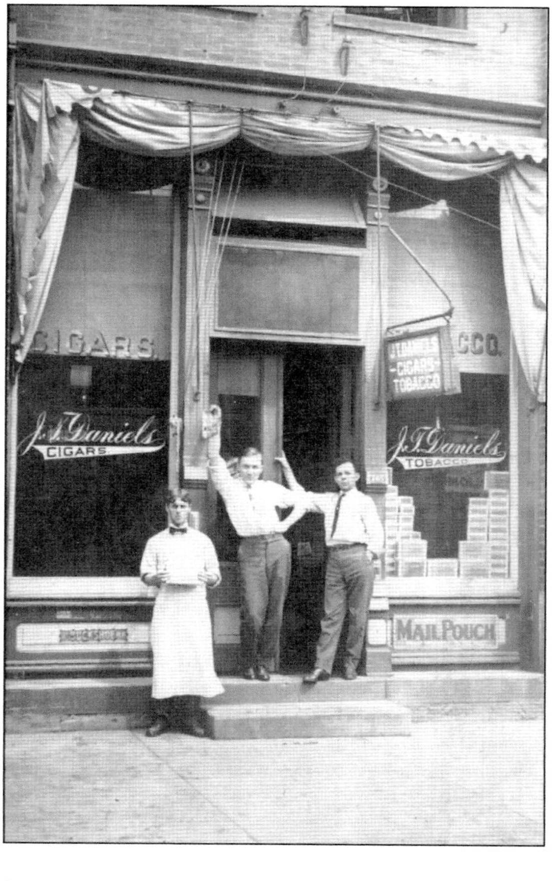

Johnson Quality Cleaners, located at 339 Lafayette Street, was owned by Allen M. Johnson.

The Daniels Cigar Store provided a complete stock of smokers' sundries for retail purchase. The cigar shop opened in 1895, and the Daniels brothers—Albert, Earnest, and John F., pictured here in front of the store—took over operations in the early 1900s. The shop included a pool hall. The manufacture of stogies ended in 1943, but the pool hall remained open until 1972. (Courtesy of Susan Thompson.)

This log cabin gas station was located on Jefferson Street just across the Paint Creek Bridge. It later became a private home.

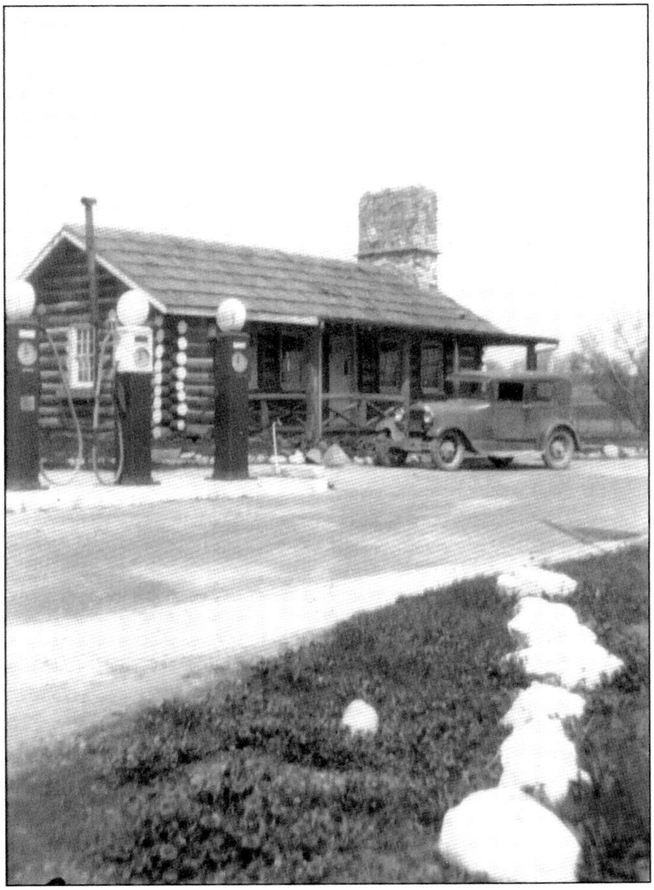

The Motor Inn, located at 233 S. Washington Street, was owned and operated by Charles R. "Unk" Davis, who purchased the land from E.L. McClain. Later, the dealership was sold to Paul Fairley and then to Gene Caplinger, who ran the business from 1968 to 1970. After his death, the business was sold to Highlander Ford. The current occupant is Visibly Green. (Courtesy of Susan Thompson.)

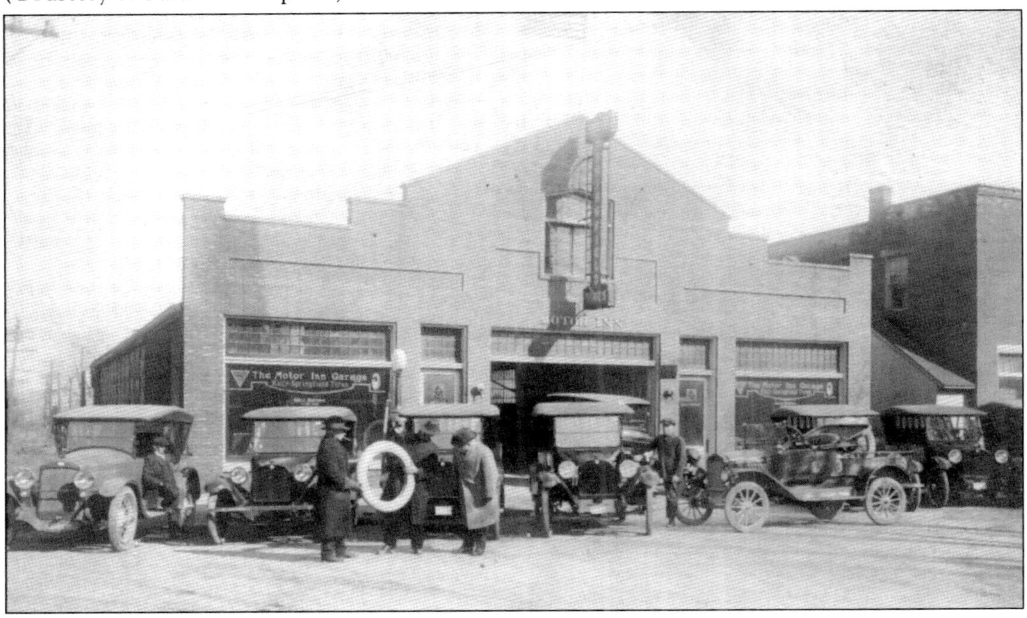

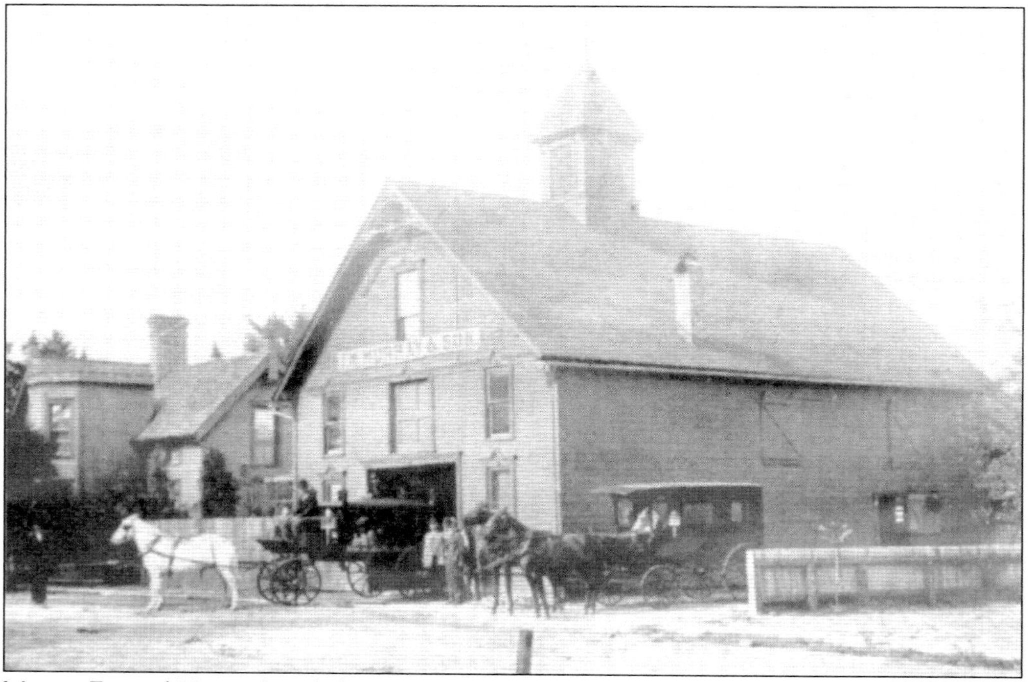

Murray Funeral Home, founded in 1851 by James M. Murray, is one of the oldest continuously running businesses in Greenfield. Prior to the automobile, sleekly groomed horses drew the funeral hearse. Funeral homes maintained stables for the horses and barns for storing carriages and hearses right on their properties.

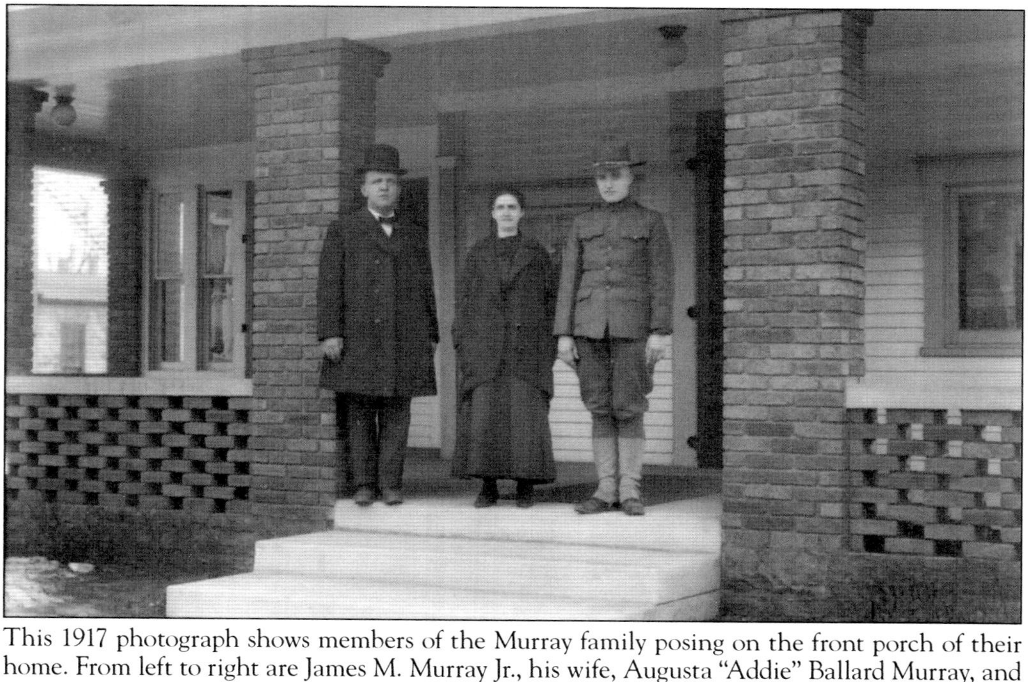

This 1917 photograph shows members of the Murray family posing on the front porch of their home. From left to right are James M. Murray Jr., his wife, Augusta "Addie" Ballard Murray, and their son Dane Ballard Murray in his World War I uniform.

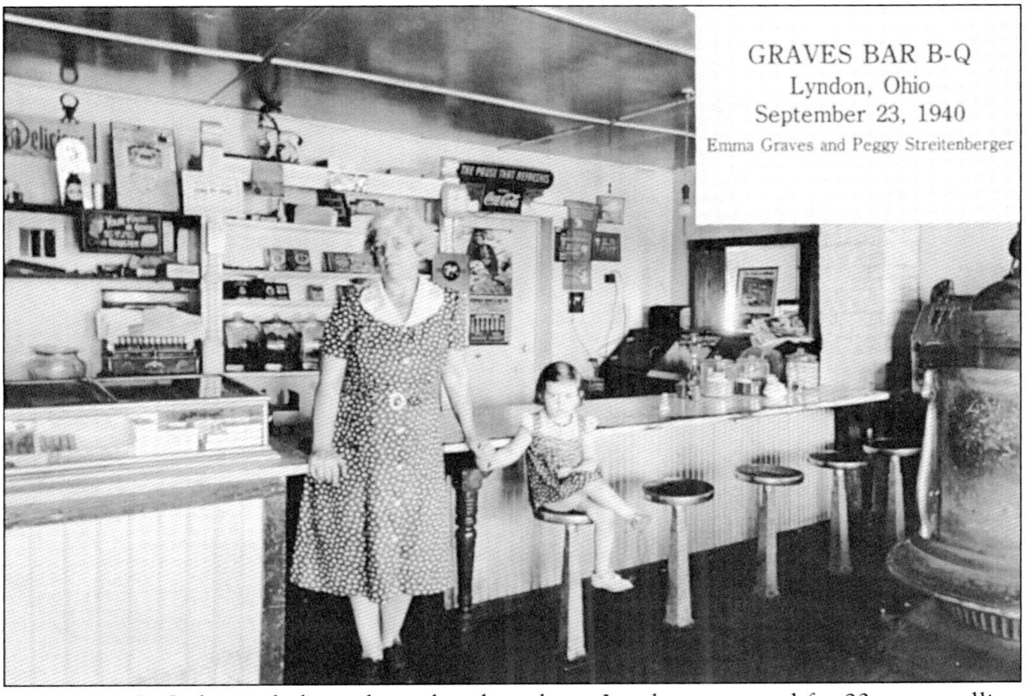

Graves Bar B-Q, located along the railroad tracks in Lyndon, operated for 23 years, selling barbecue beef and pork, coffee, and soup in addition to serving as a gasoline station. It later became a post office for Lyndon. In the picture, little Peggy Streitenberger Lucas sits with her grandmother Emma Graves, who along with her husband, Harry, owned the restaurant. (Courtesy of Lew Speakman.)

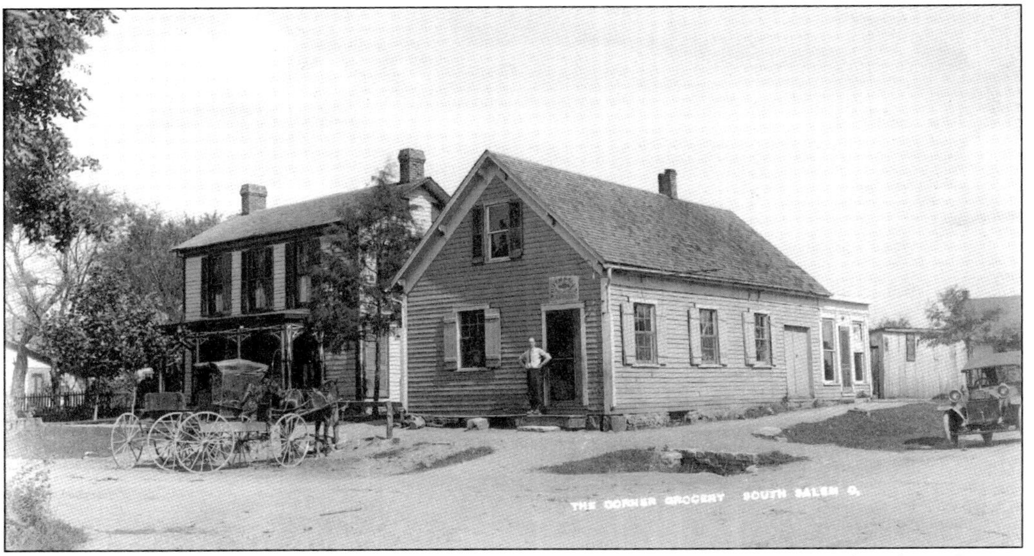

The Neely Grocery Store on the corner of Stewart and Main Streets served South Salem. Owner Emil Neely had attended Anderson College in Indiana to be a music teacher. He invented and sold a silent piano keyboard. He lived in the house attached to the grocery. The building is still standing and serves as the South Salem Post Office.

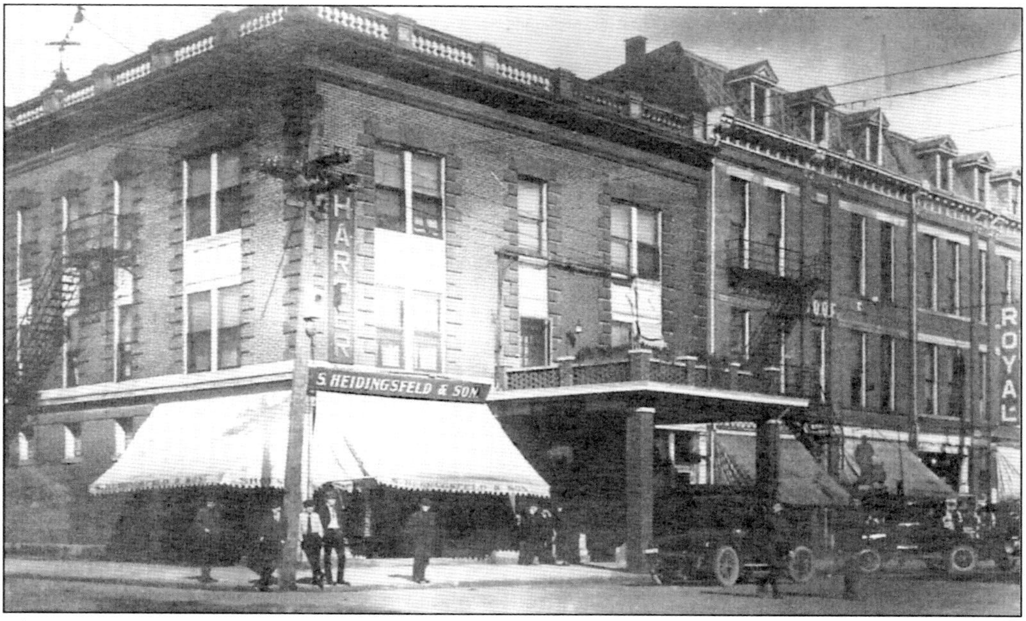

The original Harper House hotel was built in 1861 by Jesse Harper on the present-day site of the Corner Pharmacy. Harper operated a hotel until it was torn down in 1901. In 1902, Henry L. Dickey built this elegant new 51-room hotel on the same site.

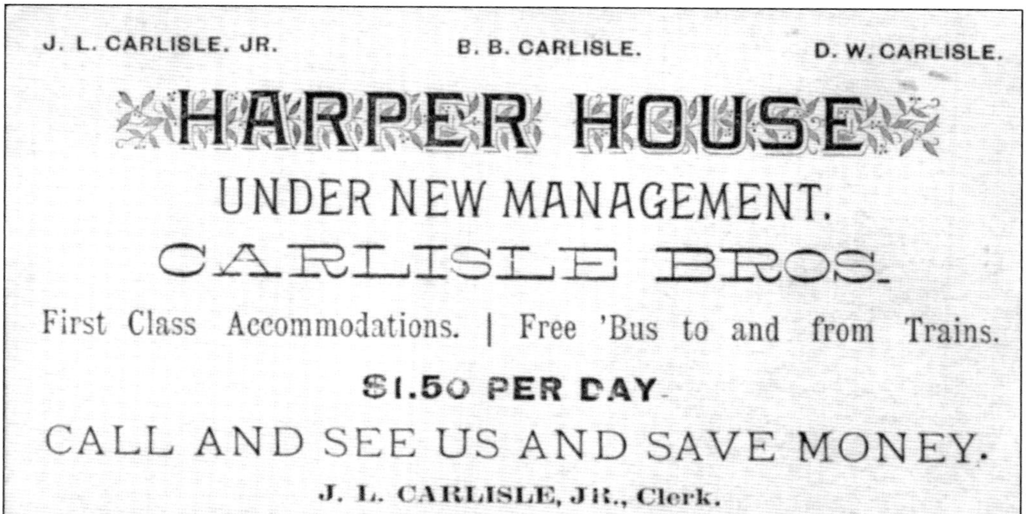

This advertisement for the Harper House, operated by the Carlisle Brothers, is from the early 1900s. Famed Greenfield educator and historian Frank Raymond Harris lived here for 36 years from 1903 through 1939 in rooms that served as his apartment. (Courtesy of Janie Jinks-Weidner.)

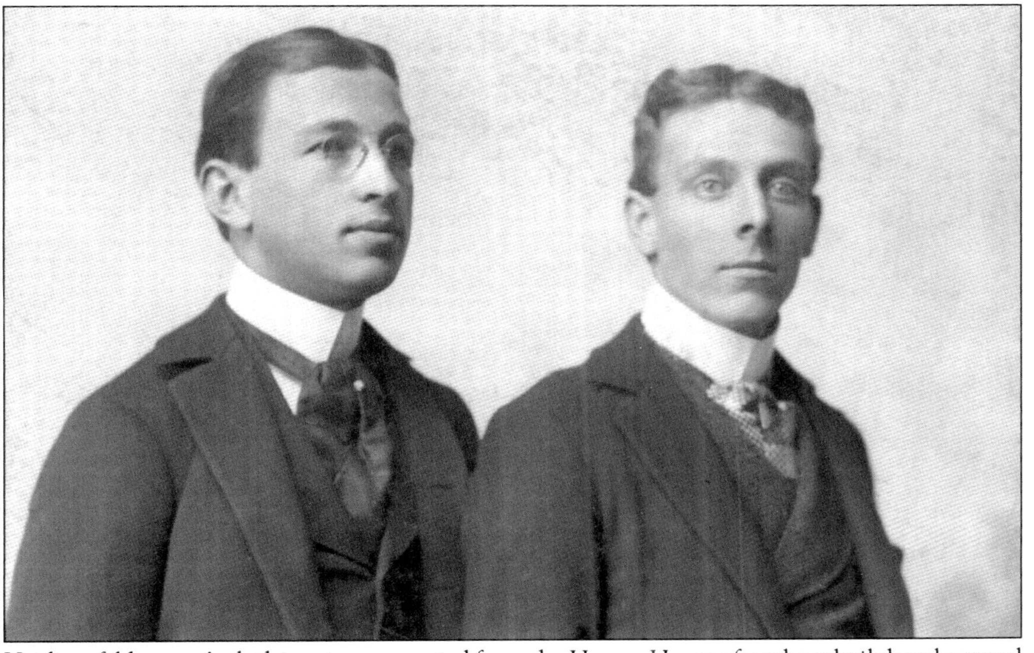

Heidingsfeld, a men's clothing store, operated from the Harper House after the rebuilt hotel opened in 1902. Pictured here are owner Oscar Heidingsfeld (left) and salesman Arnold Harvey. The original store was opened in 1860 by Oscar's father Samuel Heidingsfeld. When Oscar joined his father in business, the name became S. Heidingsfeld & Son. Their combined mercantile careers spanned nearly 75 years.

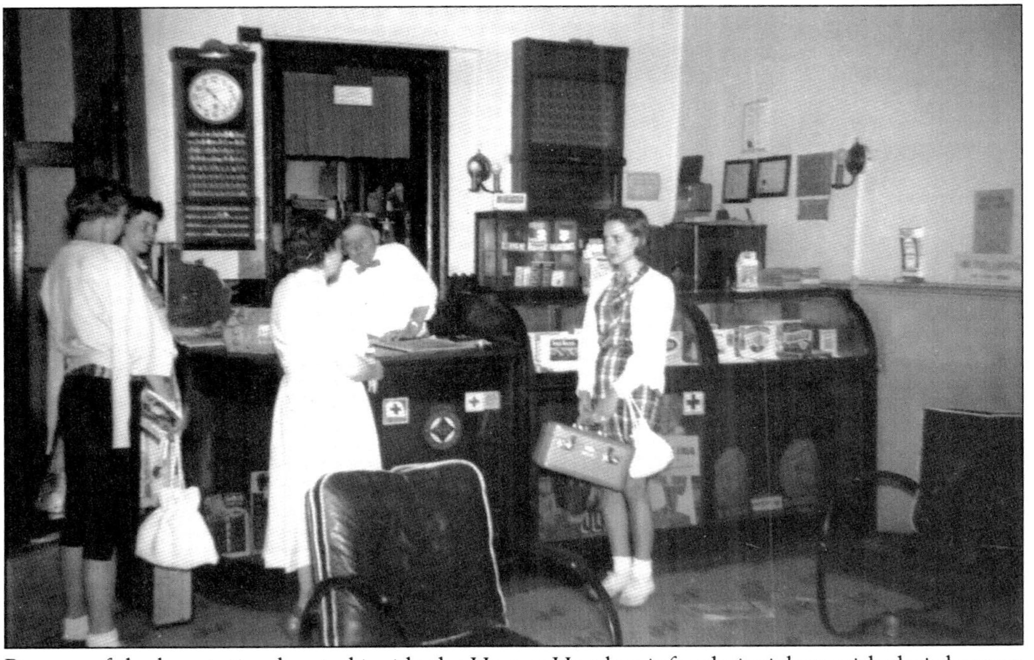

Patrons of the bus station located inside the Harper Hotel wait for their tickets with their luggage in tow.

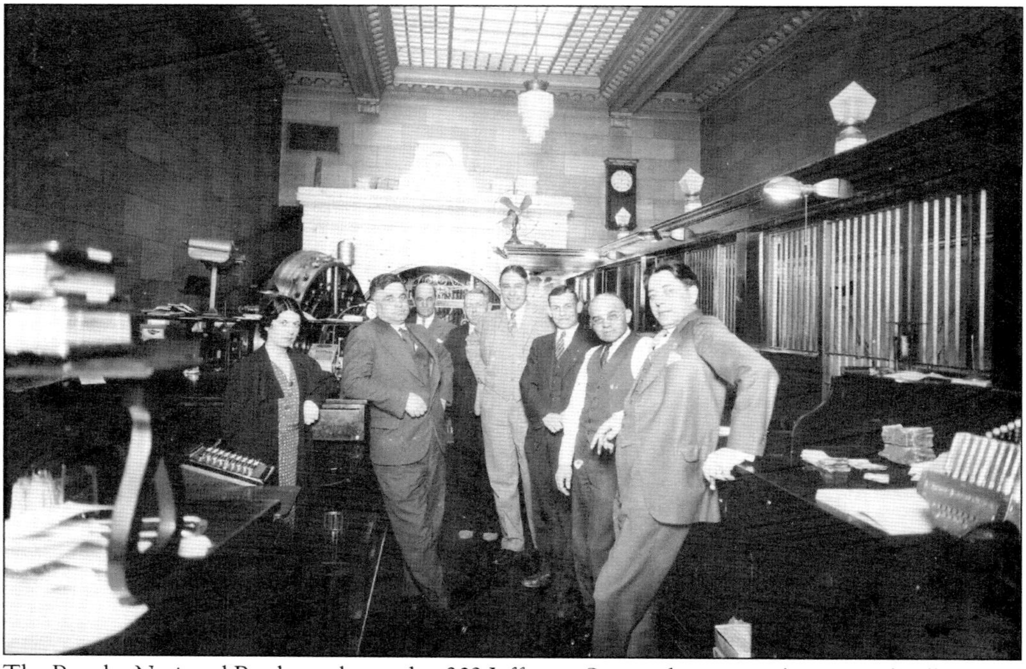

The Peoples National Bank was located at 303 Jefferson Street, the current location of Judkins and Hayes law office. Pictured from left to right are Elizabeth Smith, cashier Paul Fairley, unidentified, Clem Thoroman, Wilbur O'Dell, Wendell Shaffer, Clark Head, and Earnest Daniels.

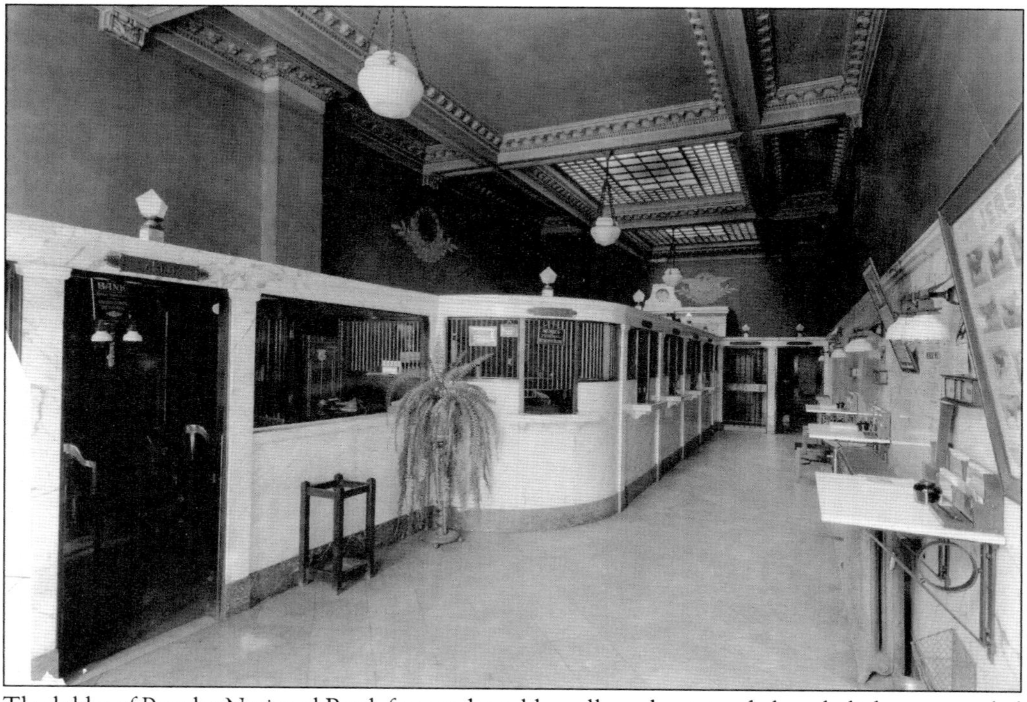

The lobby of Peoples National Bank featured marble walls and a stained glass skylight surrounded by ornate carved ceilings. The bank later moved to 117 S. Washington Street in May 1936.

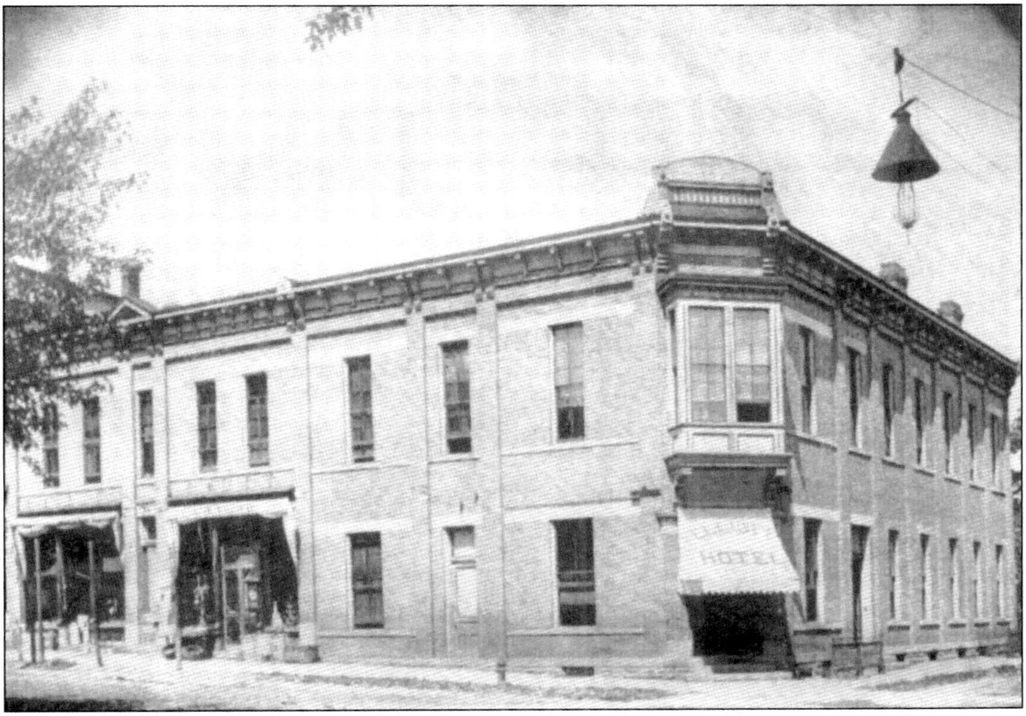

The Elliott Hotel was built by Capt. Thomas Milton Elliott on the site of the cottage of his pioneer father, Alexander. The Elliott family operated the hotel into the early 1900s. In 1911, it was owned by A.L. McWilliams and later his son, Donald. Charles Wilson and his wife operated the hotel in 1935. The building sits at the corner of S. Washington and Mirabeau Streets.

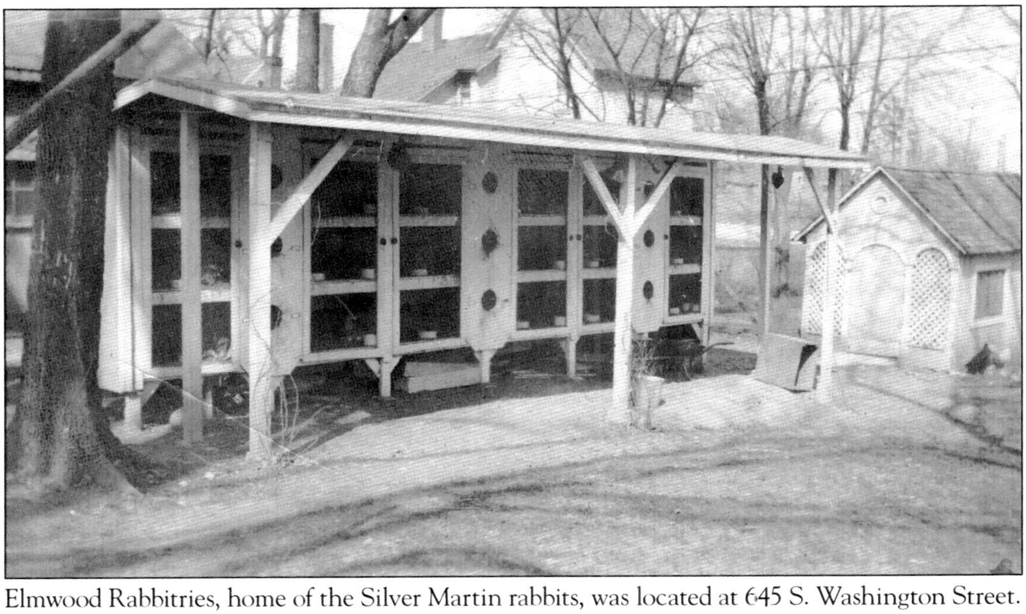

Elmwood Rabbitries, home of the Silver Martin rabbits, was located at 645 S. Washington Street.

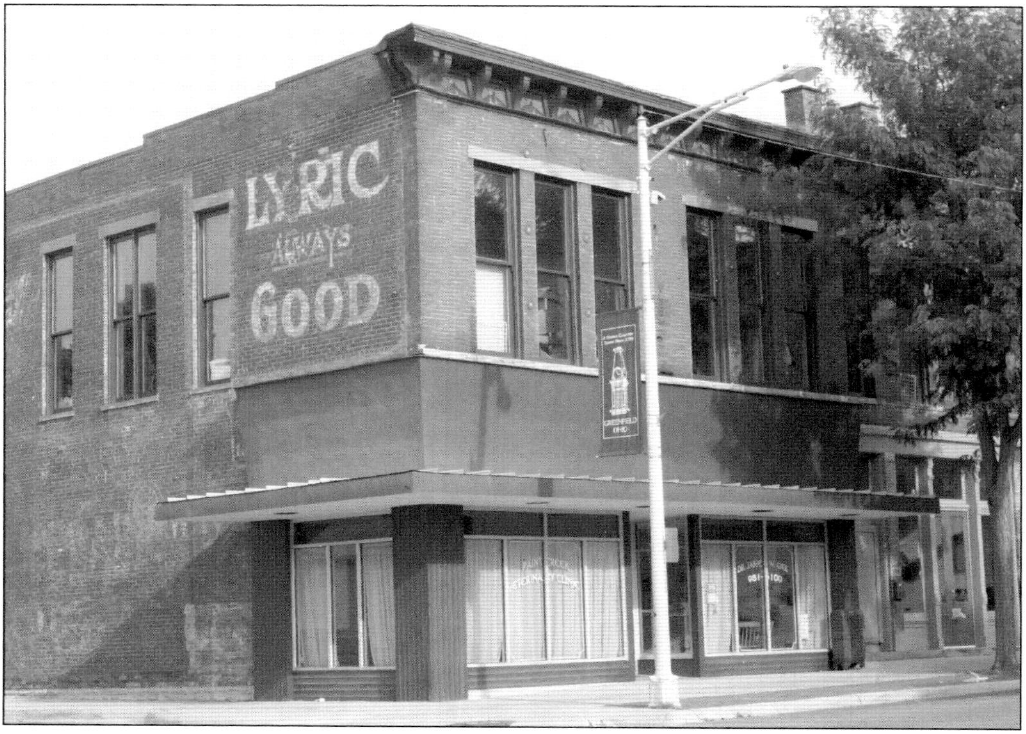

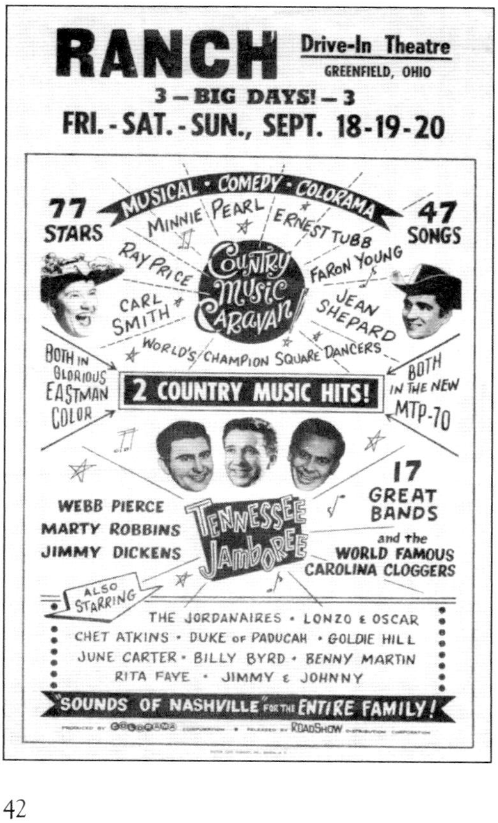

The Lyric Theater was located in this building on the northwest corner of S. Washington Street and Mirabeau Street. Records show that Harry Van Pelt owned the Lyric until 1906, when it was sold to Samuel Tilden Gray. In April 1920, Gray enlarged the Lyric and operated it through 1943. Today, this property is the location of Dr. James Orr's veterinary clinic.

This advertisement for the Ranch Drive-In Theatre announces a special three-day event featuring a number of country-western acts as well as dancers and comedians. Greenfield's first and only drive-in theater, the Ranch opened west of town under the management of K.R. Roberts in 1955. (Courtesy of Greg Barr.)

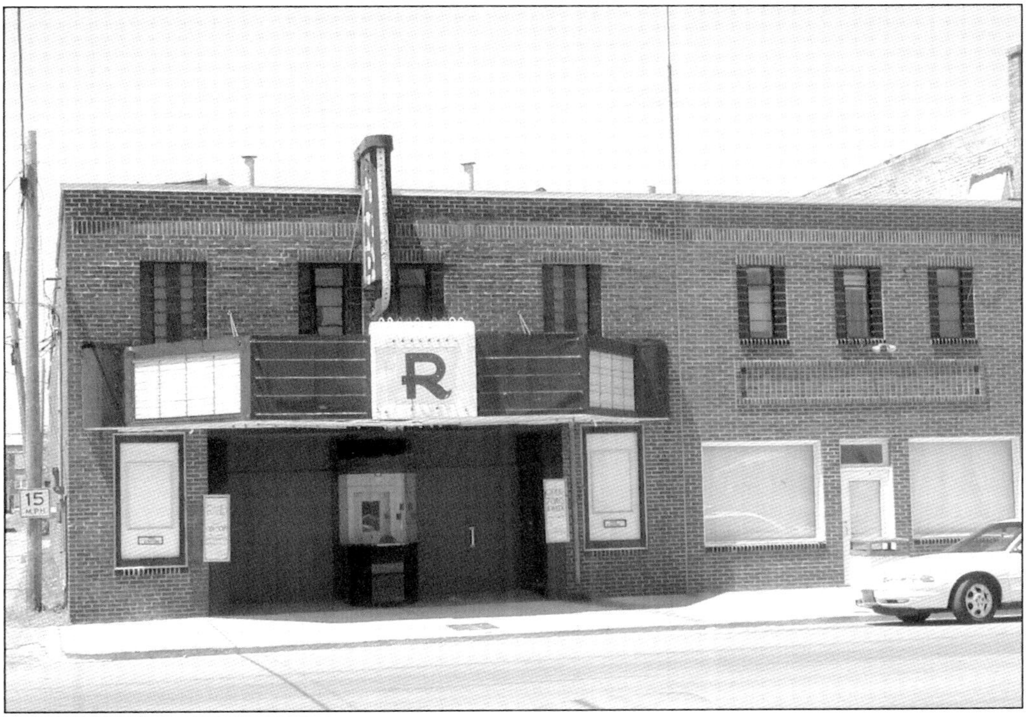

In 1937, the Rand Theater was built by Kib R. Roberts and J. Henry Davidson on Washington Street and opened under the management of Roberts with a seating capacity of 385. "Rand" stood for Roberts and Davidson. In 1946, it was rebuilt and enlarged, boasting a larger stage and 600 padded, push-back chairs. It was considered one of the finest motion picture houses in southern Ohio. (Courtesy of Greg Barr.)

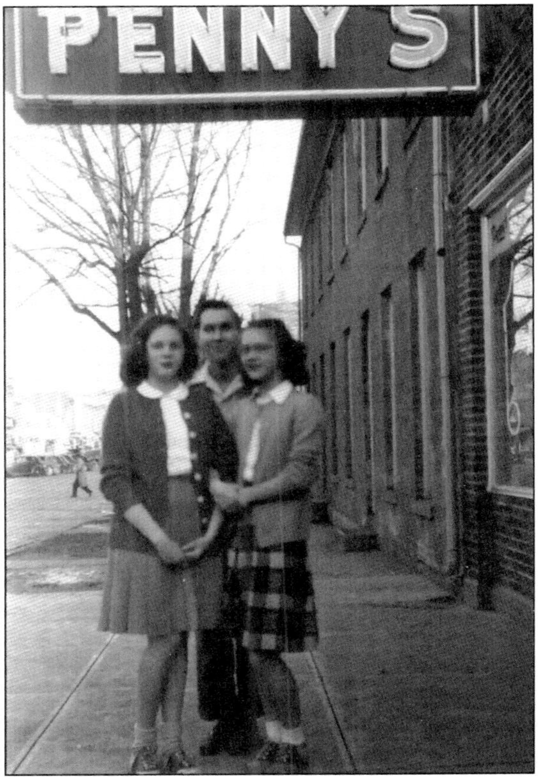

Glenn Penn owned Penny's, a popular gathering spot for teenagers in the 1940s through the early 1960s. From left to right, Pat England, David Riley, and Gloria Allen pose in front of the shop on Jefferson Street where a Subway restaurant is presently located. The shop's first locale was on N. Washington Street next to the Rand Theater. (Courtesy of Patricia Smith.)

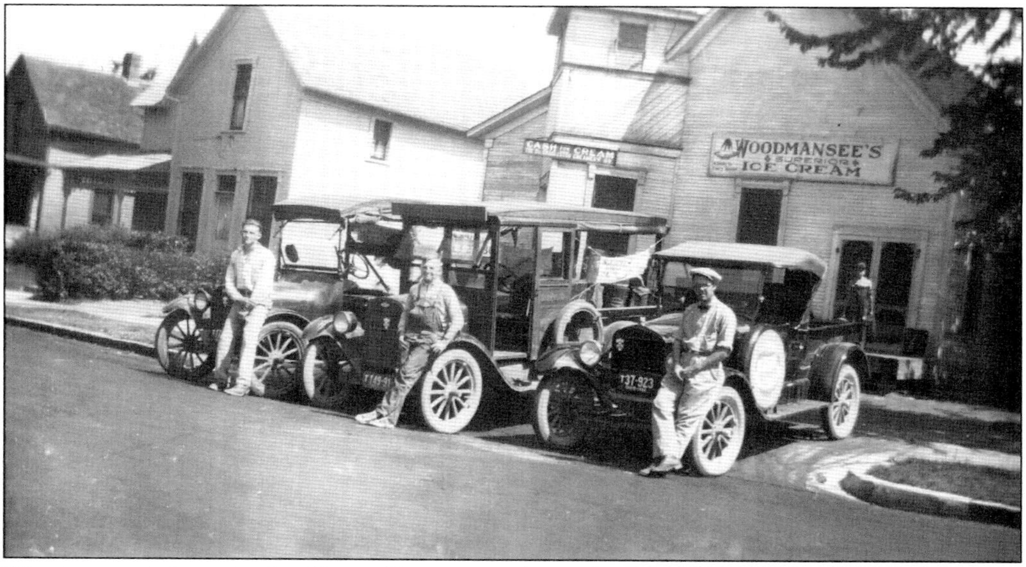

Woodmansee's Superior Ice Cream Factory was located on South Street in the building of the former Church of Christ. Forrest Woodmansee operated the Greenfield factory, having learned the business from his father. Forrest's brothers opened ice cream stores in Hillsboro and Wilmington. The family business began in 1913 when it produced three gallons for an Independence Day celebration. Forrest later served as mayor of Greenfield from 1940 to 1947.

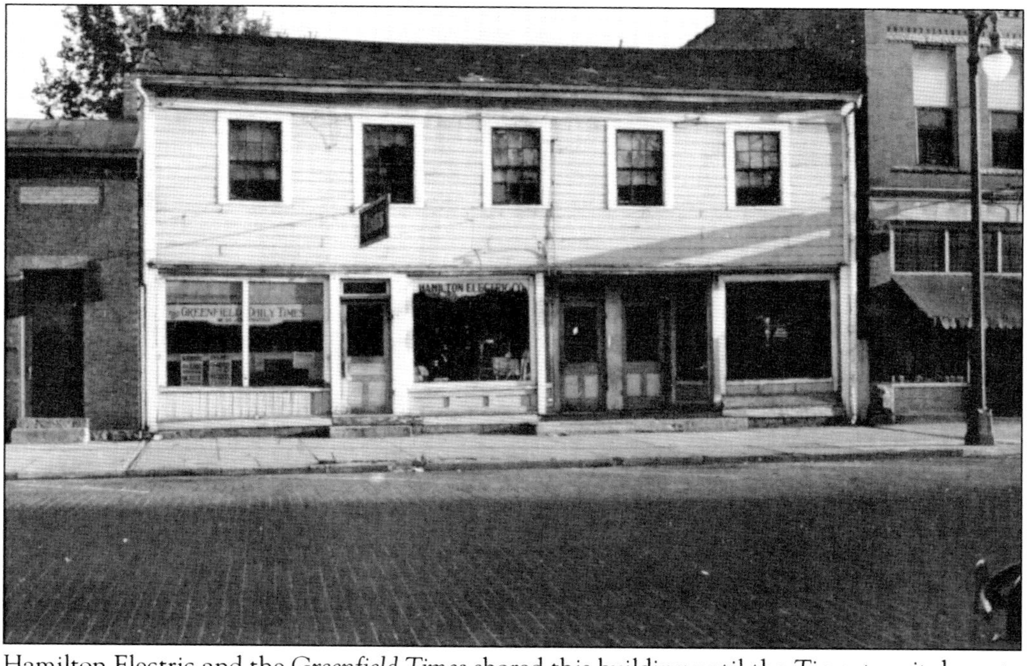

Hamilton Electric and the *Greenfield Times* shared this building until the *Times* tore it down to build the brick building on the 300 block of Jefferson Street. Hamilton's moved across the street, while the *Times* remained and expanded. It was established as a daily newspaper in 1933 with the father-son team of Emmett F. and Carlton C. Hartley as owners. Successive owners were George Fenner, Jack Schleup, and Brown Publishing Company.

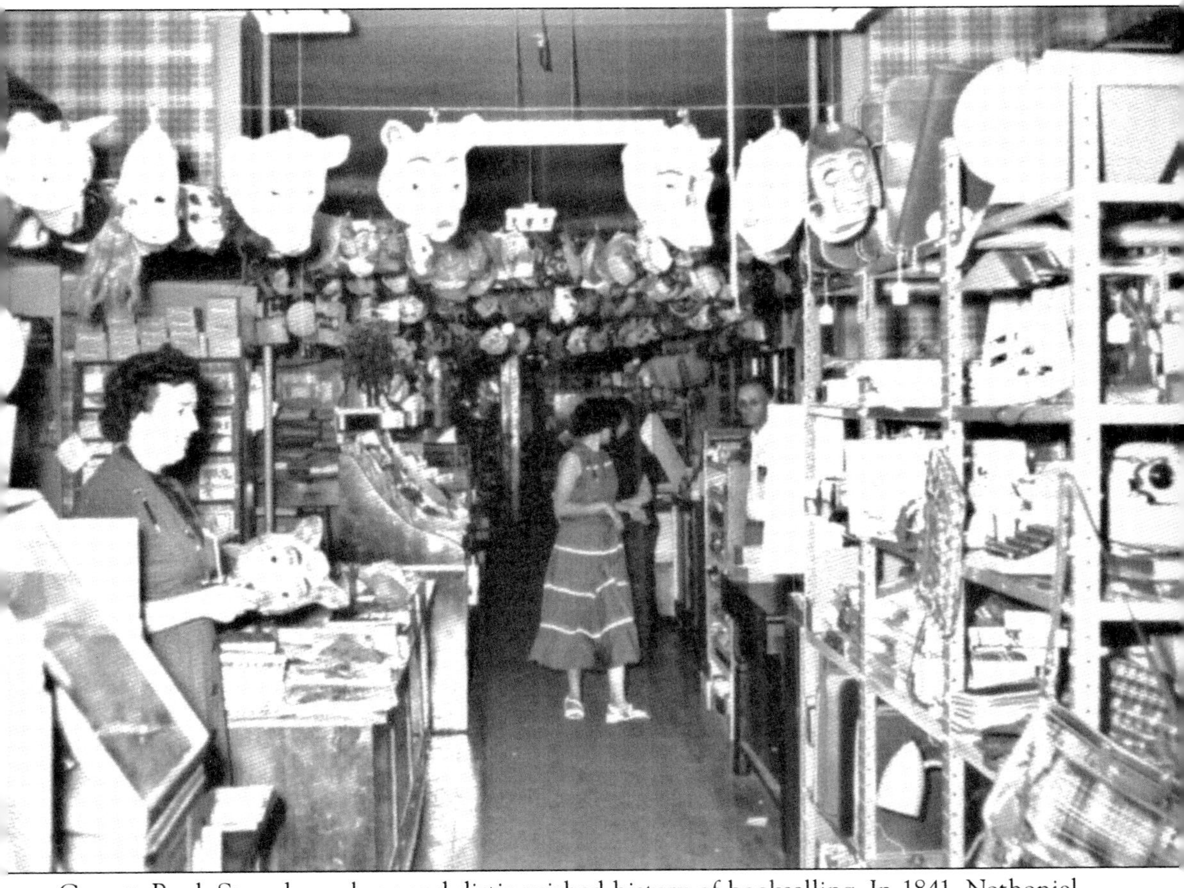

Gossett Book Store has a long and distinguished history of bookselling. In 1841, Nathaniel Pike moved from New Petersburg to Greenfield and erected a building at 207 Jefferson Street where he made and sold men's hats in the rear of the property. He rented the front portion to David Bonner, who sold books and stationery. In 1884, Pike purchased Bonner's inventory and continued the bookselling and stationery business. That same year, Pike moved his store up the hill to 305 Jefferson Street and brought his son Stanley into the business with him. In 1916, Harley Gossett purchased the store and named it Gossett Book Store. In 1953, Gossett bought the building at 112 N. Washington Street and connected it to the rear of his store to provide space for a warehouse. In 1955, Harley's sons Thad and Wallace took over their father's business along with their sister Wilma Gossett Everhart, shown here at the counter. The store closed on June 7, 1997, after 156 years in business. It was recognized at the time as Highland County's oldest continuously operated business.

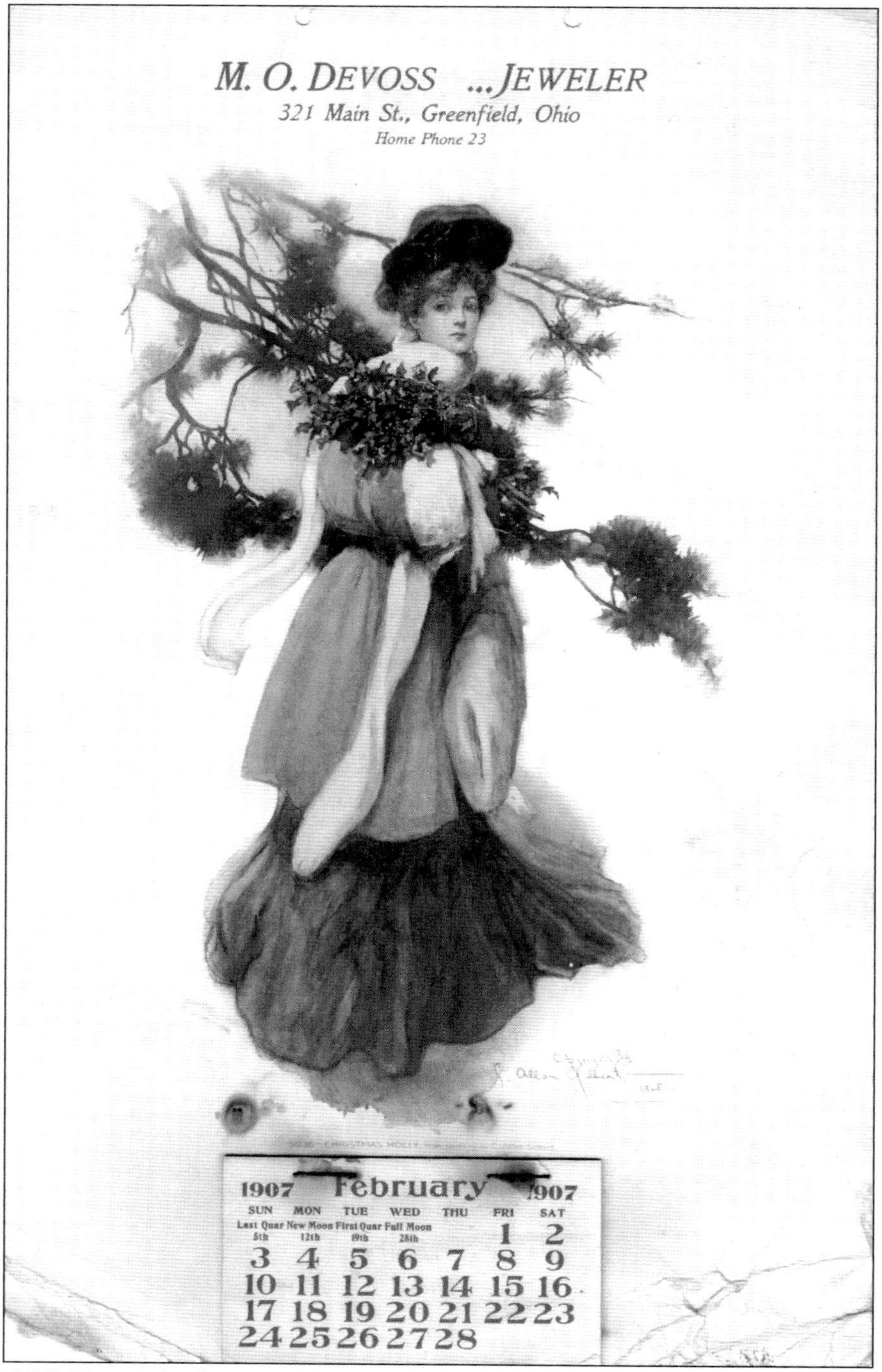

This 1907 DeVoss Calendar served as advertising for Milton Oscar DeVoss's jewelry business. A newspaper clipping from the era explains, "He carries a fine line of watches, clocks, rings, silverware, novelties, etc." DeVoss also repaired watches at his shop at 321 Main Street, now Jefferson Street. DeVoss Jewelers operated for 15 years.

Two

Services in Town

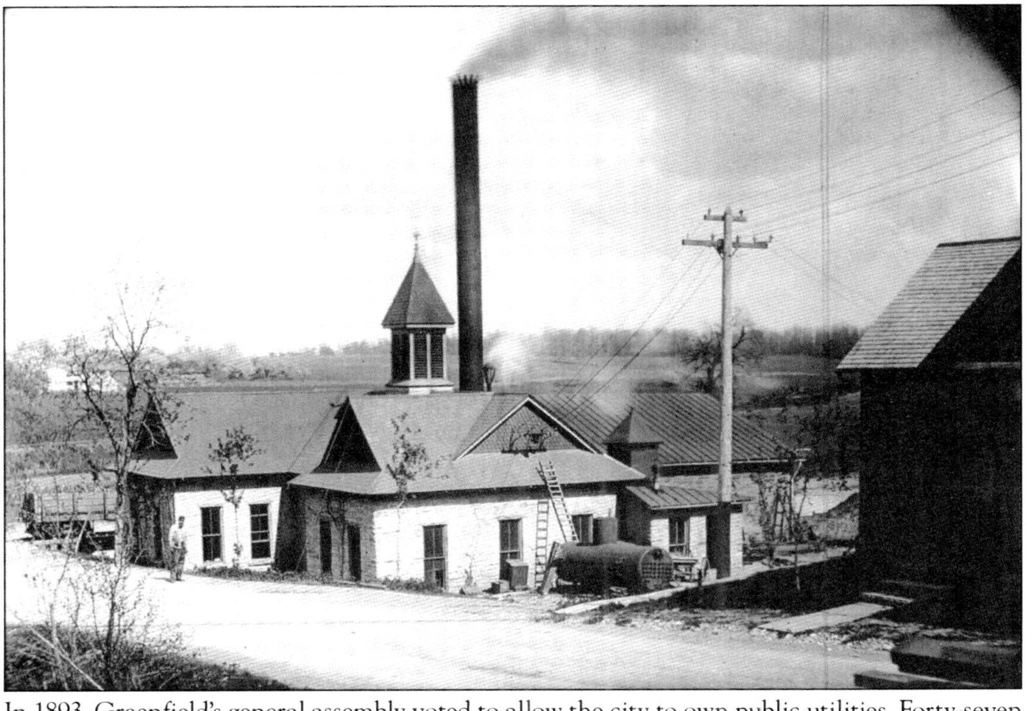

In 1893, Greenfield's general assembly voted to allow the city to own public utilities. Forty-seven arc streetlights that used carbon rods were installed at street intersections. The dangers of electricity were little known; a Mr. Taylor, hired to replace carbon rods, was electrocuted when he poked his umbrella into a malfunctioning arc light at Mirabeau and Second Streets. (Courtesy of Susan Thompson.)

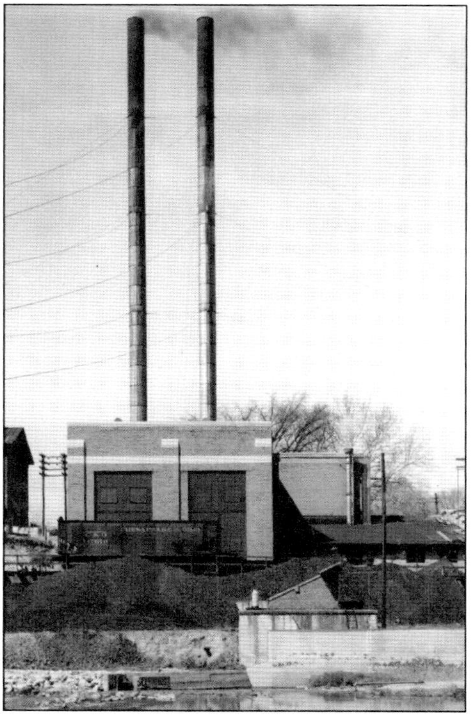

The original power plant was built with a $20,000 bond approved by a vote of 176 to 7 in 1893. Instead of a lamplighter making nightly rounds to light streetlamps, the electric arc lights needed daily replacing of carbon rods. The power plant was remodeled in the 1950s, and in 1963, Greenfield's power plant was sold to Dayton Power and Light. The building is now used for city services.

The power plant on the south side of the State Route 28 bridge over Paint Creek supplied electricity to Greenfield and Thrifton. Harry E. Sollars worked as a licensed engineer. Lora A. Holiday was the superintendent in charge of the power plant. These engines produced electricity equivalent to 50 horsepower.

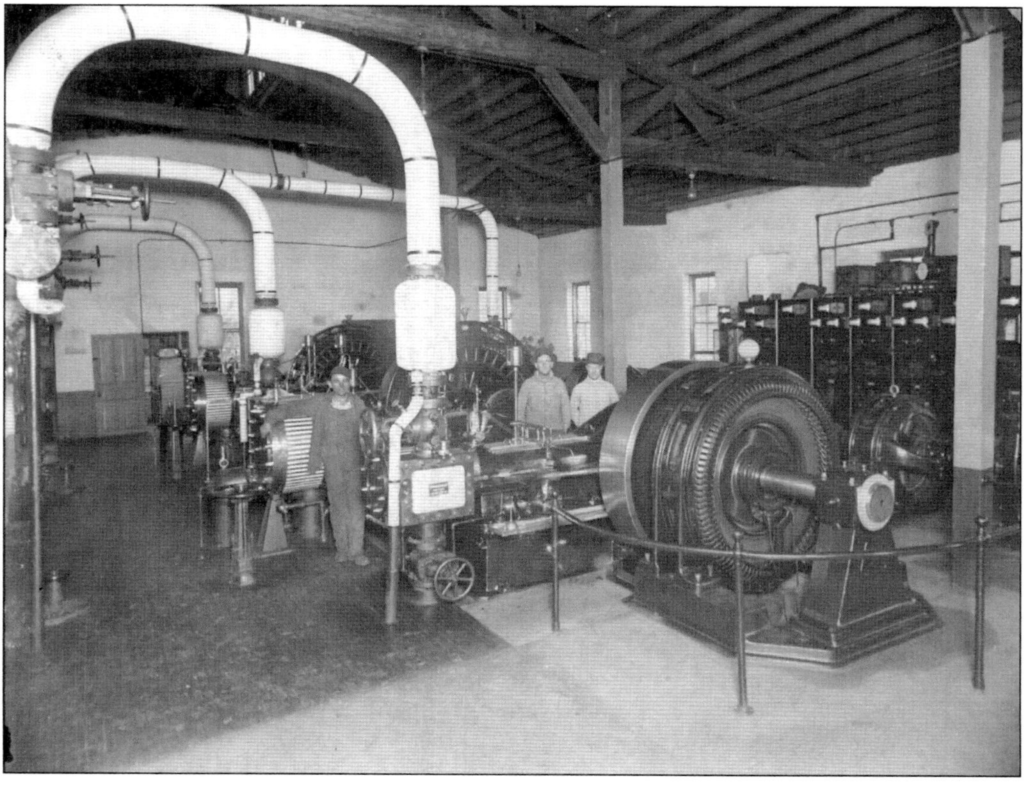

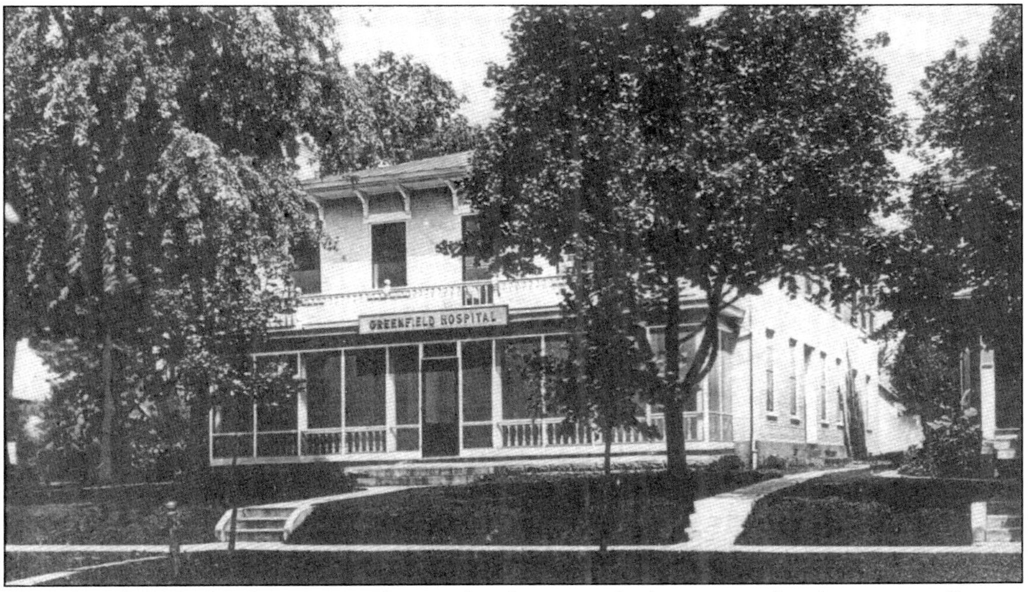

Daniel Hull built this house in 1859 outside of town with the intent of its being a roadhouse. Judge John Eckman bought it before it was finished, however, and it remained the Eckman family home for 40 years. Around 1900, it became known as the Boggess home. In 1918, the building was sold and began its 74-year service as the Greenfield Hospital. It was torn down to make way for the present Adena/Greenfield Medical Hospital.

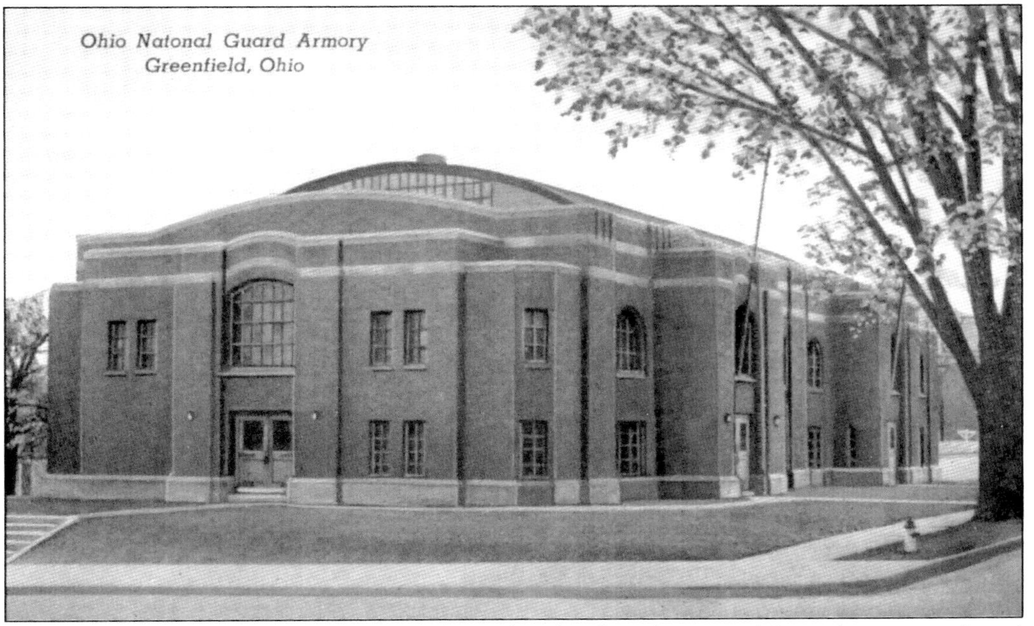

In 1928, the Greenfield Armory was dedicated. It has long been used for military, social, and athletic events. In 1972, it was made into a city recreation center and later became officially known as the Ralph Phillips Recreational Center. (Courtesy of Susan Thompson.)

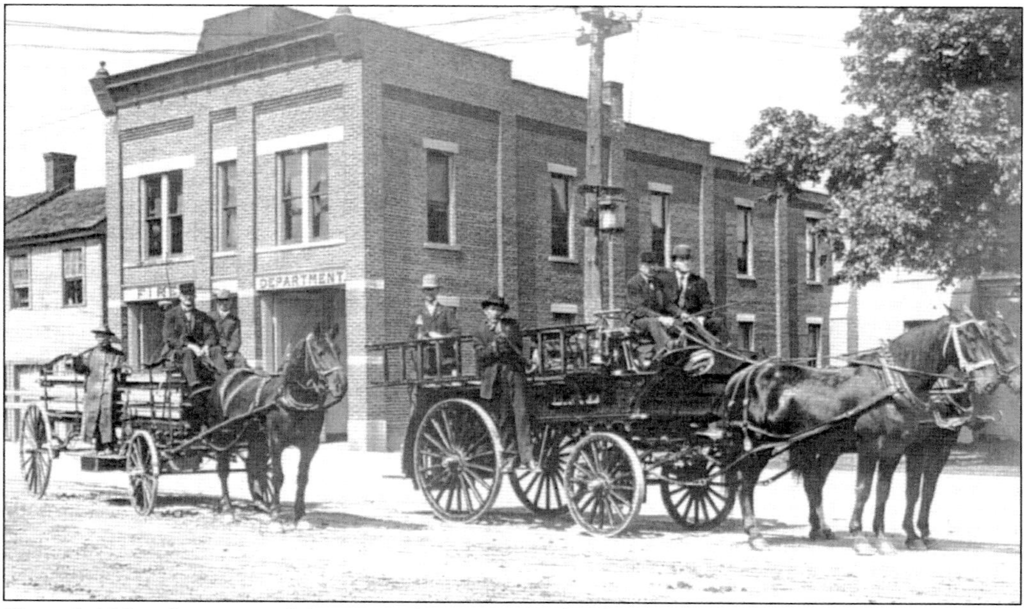

Greenfield fire department's horses and wagons stand in front of the fire station in 1907. In 1848, a volunteer fire department was organized with a hook and ladder. Several wells were established at various intersections, and when the town hall was built, a fire bell was installed. In 1898, the first full-time fire department was established with 20 firefighters, a team of horses, and a chemical hose wagon.

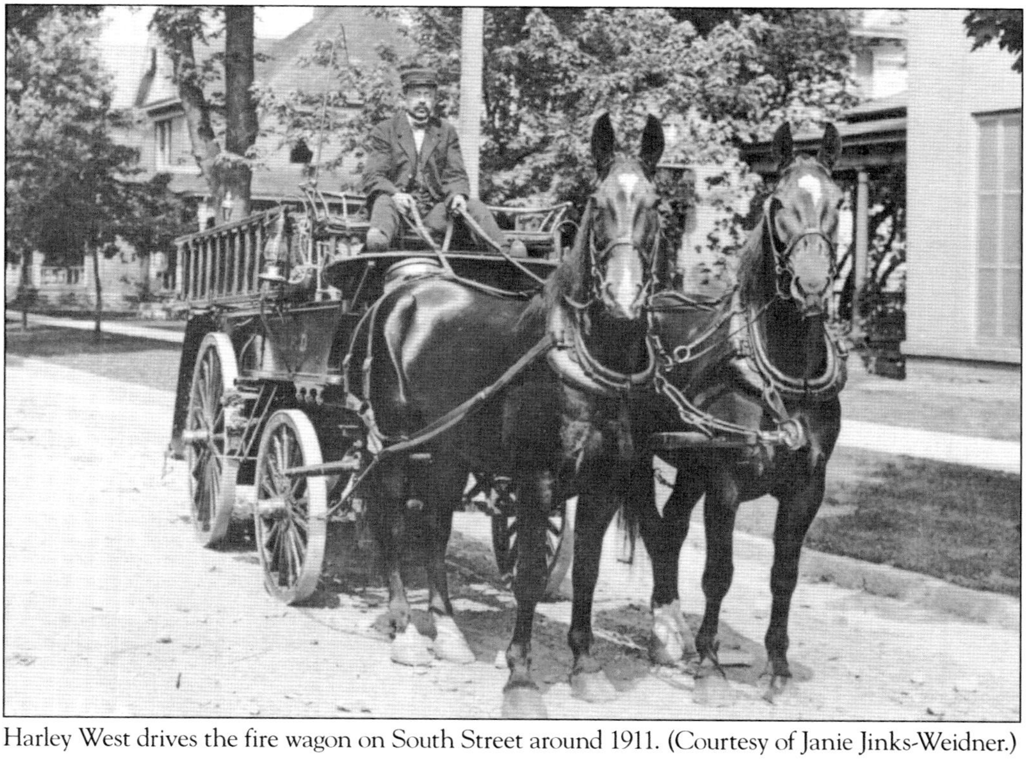

Harley West drives the fire wagon on South Street around 1911. (Courtesy of Janie Jinks-Weidner.)

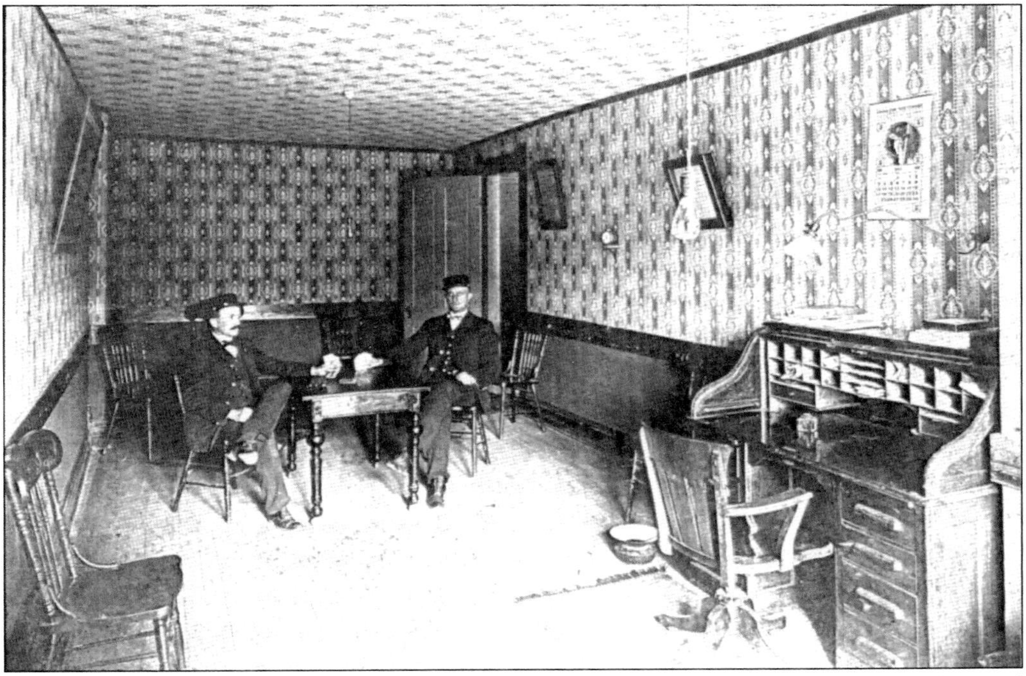

In 1907, the interior of the newly built firehouse afforded firefighters a spacious office and meeting room.

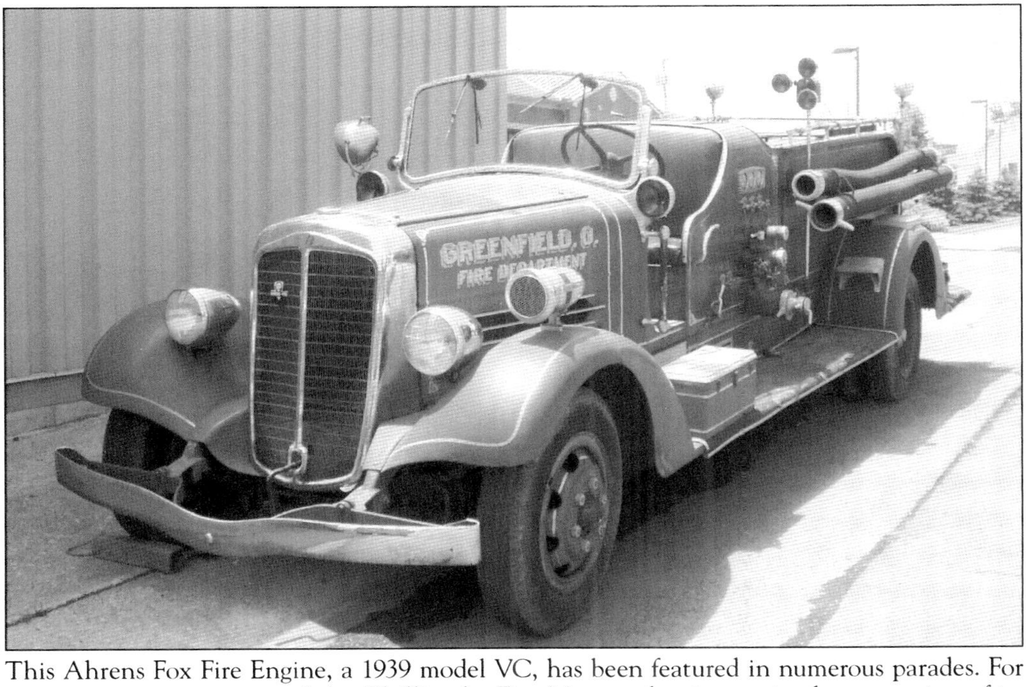

This Ahrens Fox Fire Engine, a 1939 model VC, has been featured in numerous parades. For many years, it was a part of the Chillicothe Fire Museum but is now in the possession of its original owner, the Greenfield Fire Department. It is stored in a building owned by the Greenfield Historical Society.

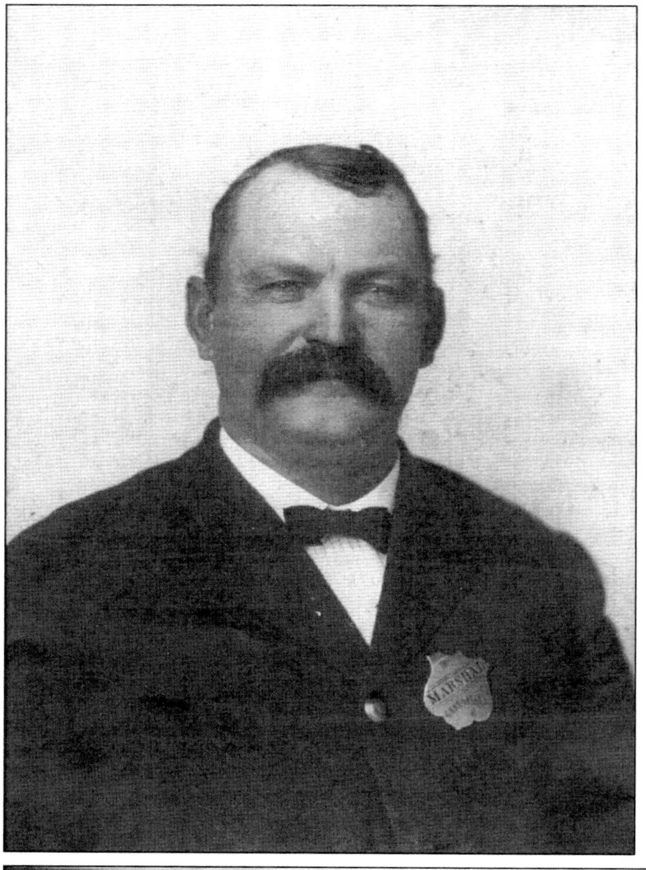

Marshal Silas Rooks came to Greenfield from Clinton County in approximately 1905. For a time, he worked in the drayage business; afterward, he served on the police force for 16 months. In 1908, he was elected to the position of marshal. This photograph dates to 1909. (Courtesy of the Greenfield Police Department.)

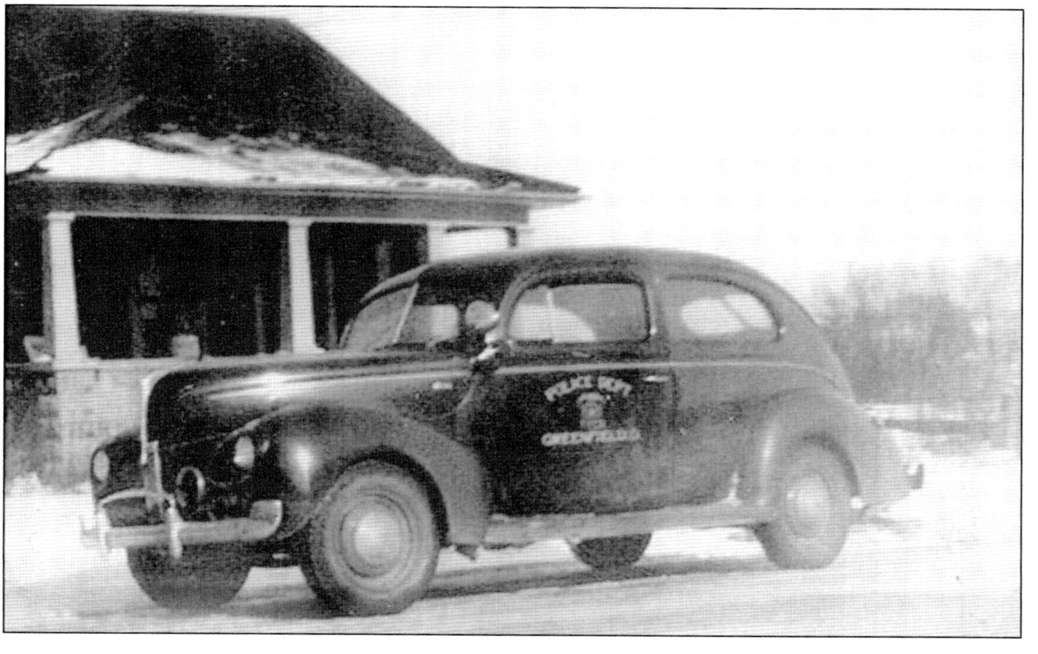

Officer George Jolly drove this 1939 Ford police department vehicle home for lunch when neighbor Kathleen Taylor Everhart took this snapshot of the new cruiser parked in front of Jolly's home on Lafayette Street and McArthur Way (then Front Street). Jolly served Greenfield as a police officer for nearly 40 years. (Courtesy of the Greenfield Police Department.)

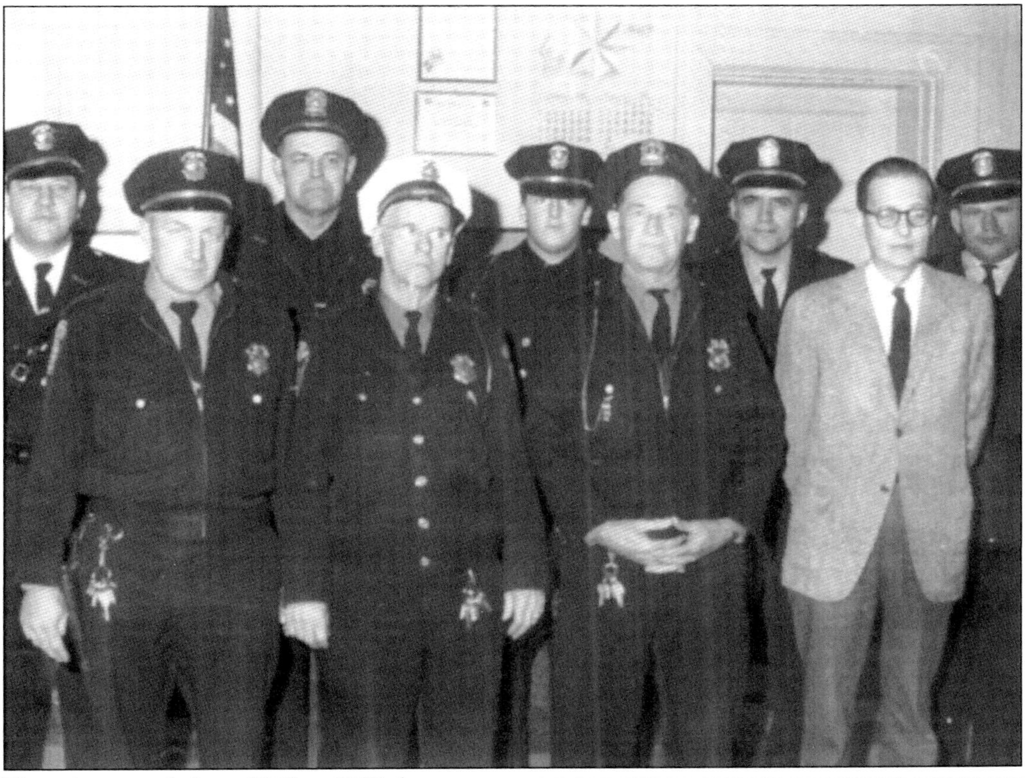

This photograph from 1966 or 1967 shows the police department with Mayor John T. Mains. The department included, from left to right, William Clay, Guy Hunter, Eldon Newlan, Floyd Matlack, Officer Poole, George Jolly, Bill Wisecup, Mayor Mains, and Hugh "Diz" Oyer. (Courtesy of the Greenfield Police Department.)

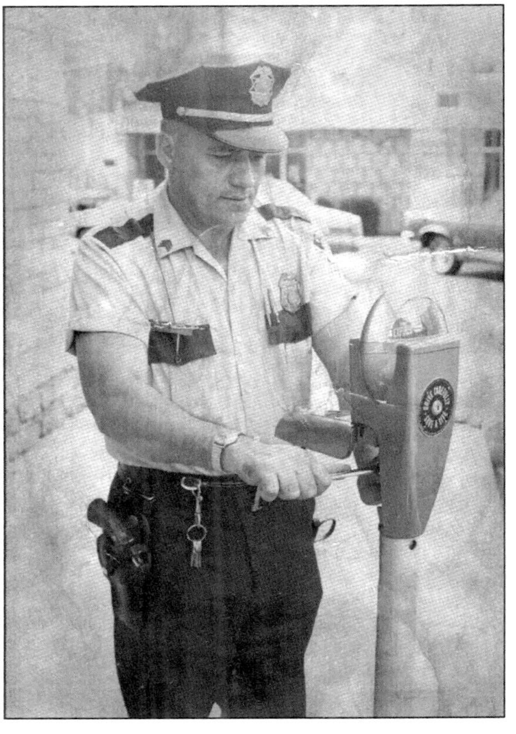

William B. Wisecup empties a parking meter. He served Greenfield as a police officer before becoming mayor from 1984 to 1987. (Courtesy of Mildred Wisecup.)

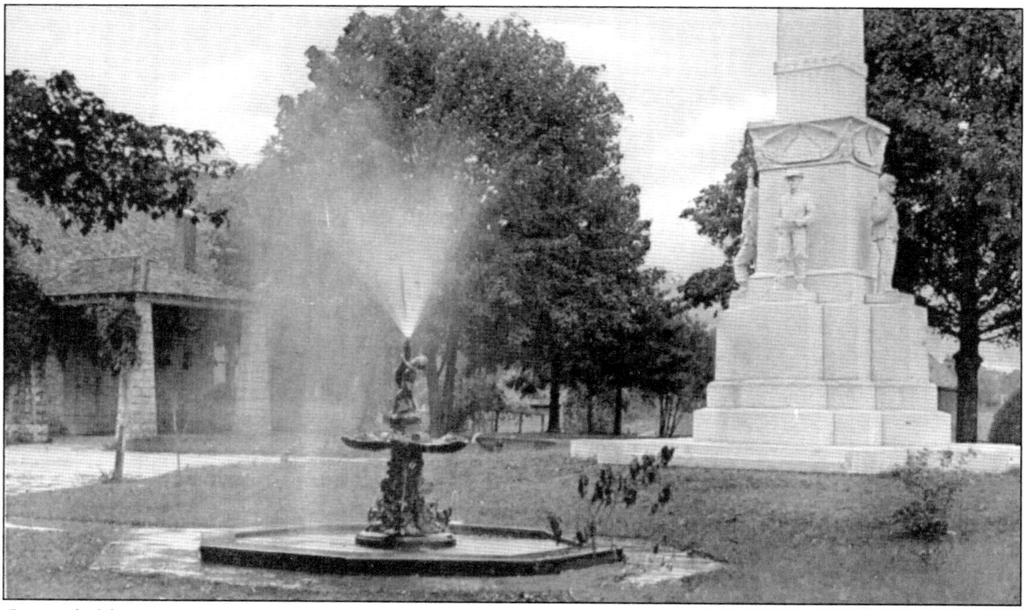

Greenfield Cemetery was laid out in 1868 by Leo Weltz on 26 acres after a bond issue was approved in the amount of $3,875. Weltz was a prominent landscape designer; many of his cemeteries are currently listed in the National Register of Historic Places. This view of the cemetery features a fountain, the Freshour Monument, and the chapel. (Courtesy of Susan Thompson.)

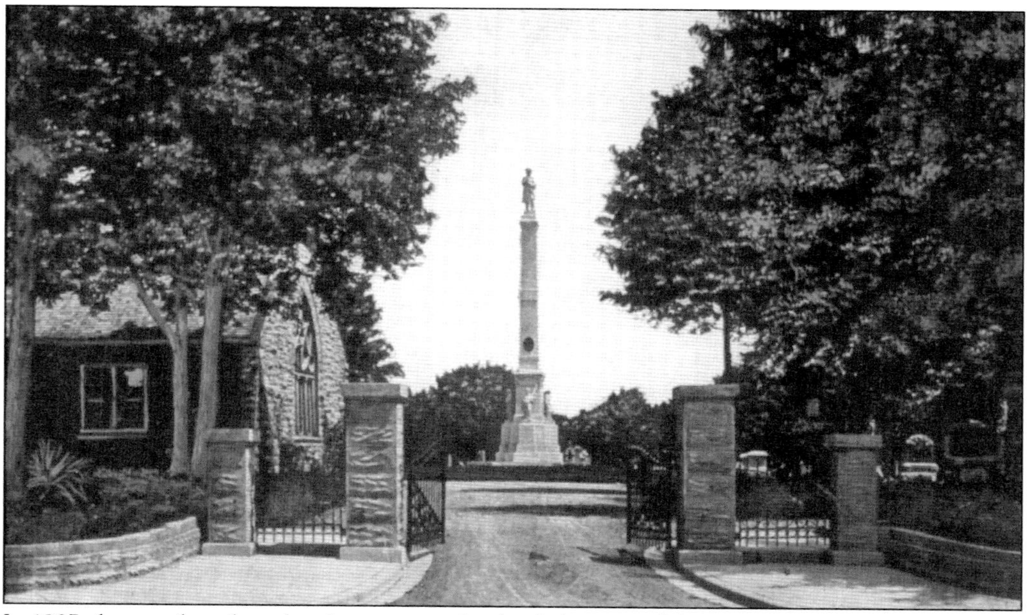

In 1907, thousands gathered at the cemetery for the dedication of the Civil War Soldiers' Monument donated by James H. Freshour, his sister Hortense Freshour, and their family. The monument is made with 198 tons of granite and stands 56 feet high with the top soldier measuring 8.5 feet tall. The base showcases four figures representing infantry, cavalry, artillery, and flag bearers/color guard. The sculpting was done by James Brown King.

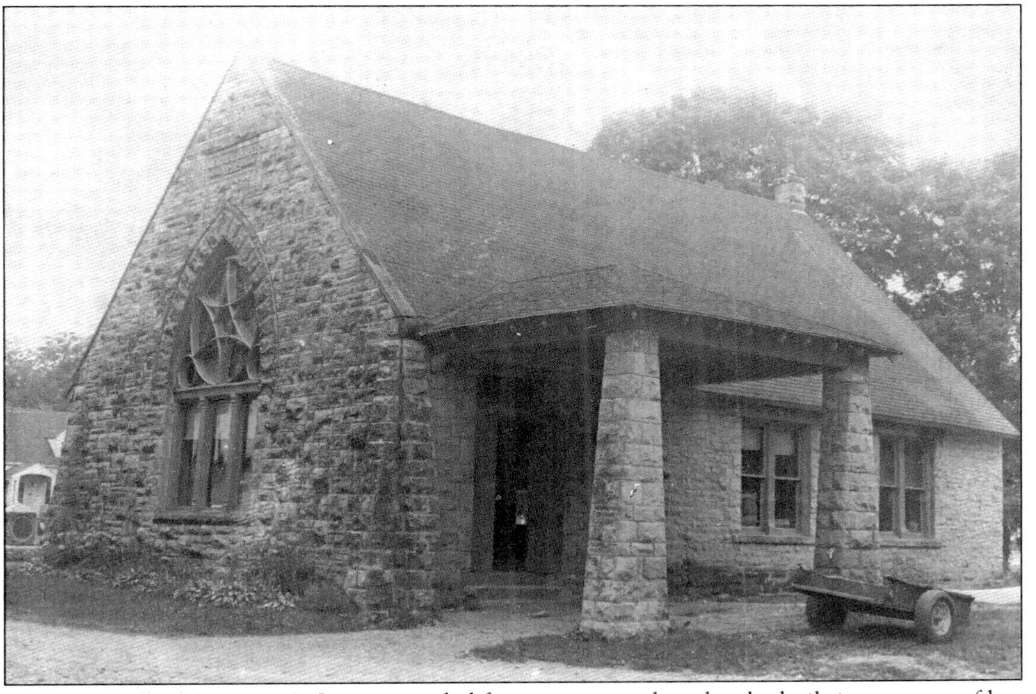

The 1896 will of Augusta A. Jones provided for a cemetery chapel to be built in memory of her husband, Benjamin. James Hallam supervised construction, which exceeded the $2,000 budget. A fundraiser provided the additional $350 needed to install windows and buy furniture. The chapel has been used for funerals and for public gatherings. In 1992, a group called Friends of the Chapel formed to make necessary repairs.

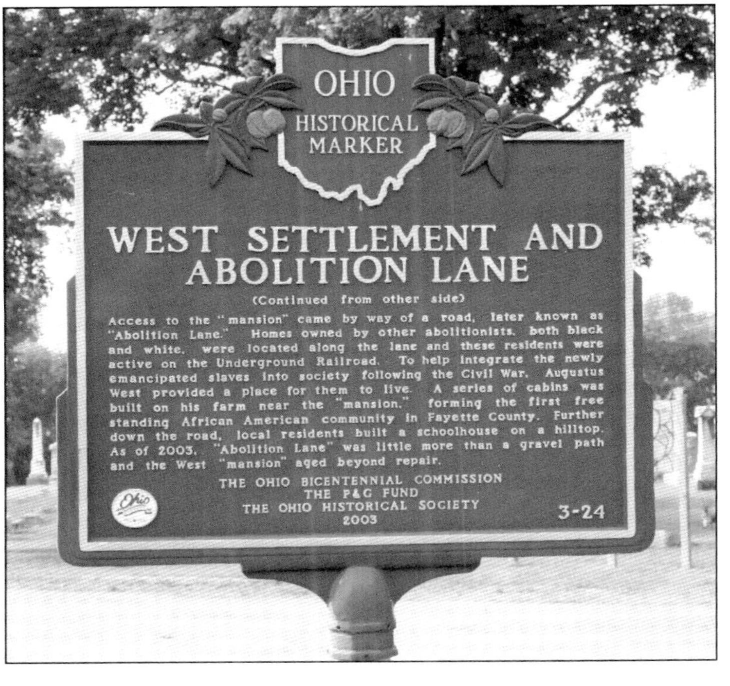

This West Settlement historical marker stands in the cemetery and recognizes Augustus West, a free black man who settled in Fayette County near the Alexander Beatty farm. Beatty and West engaged in an ingenious, yet dangerous, enterprise. Beatty would falsely sell West to southern plantation owners, then later return to help West and other slaves escape to freedom. With the profits from this repeated endeavor, West purchased land and created West Settlement.

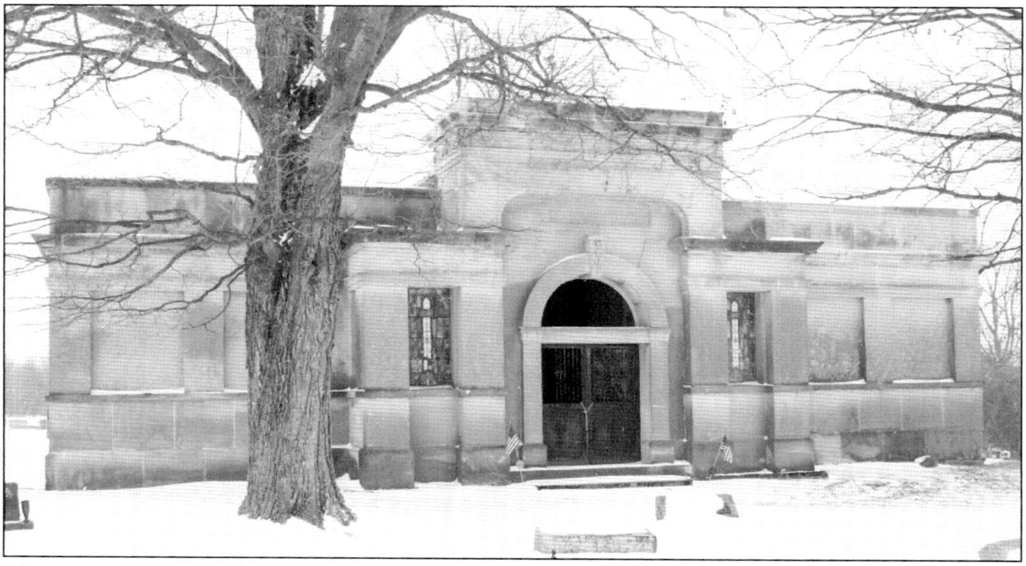

The cemetery's mausoleum construction began in 1917 and was finished with the generous gifts of the Christopher family and Lycurgus Cole. Christopher was a druggist, and Cole owned a furniture store. No human remains are housed here currently, and the structure is scheduled for demolition.

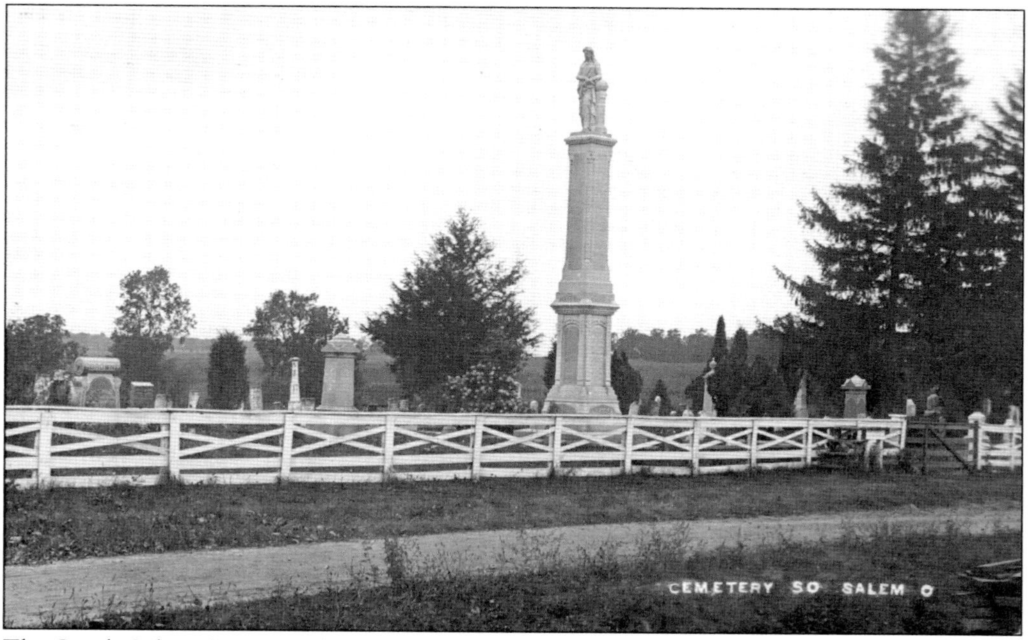

The South Salem Cemetery features the tall Diggs Monument. A well-known figure buried in this cemetery is Mary Morter, the half sister of Queen Victoria. Mary's ill-fated marriage to Blyth Morter, a commoner, resulted in her loss of royal status. Her husband carved her headstone after her untimely death from tuberculosis.

Three

FACES AROUND TOWN

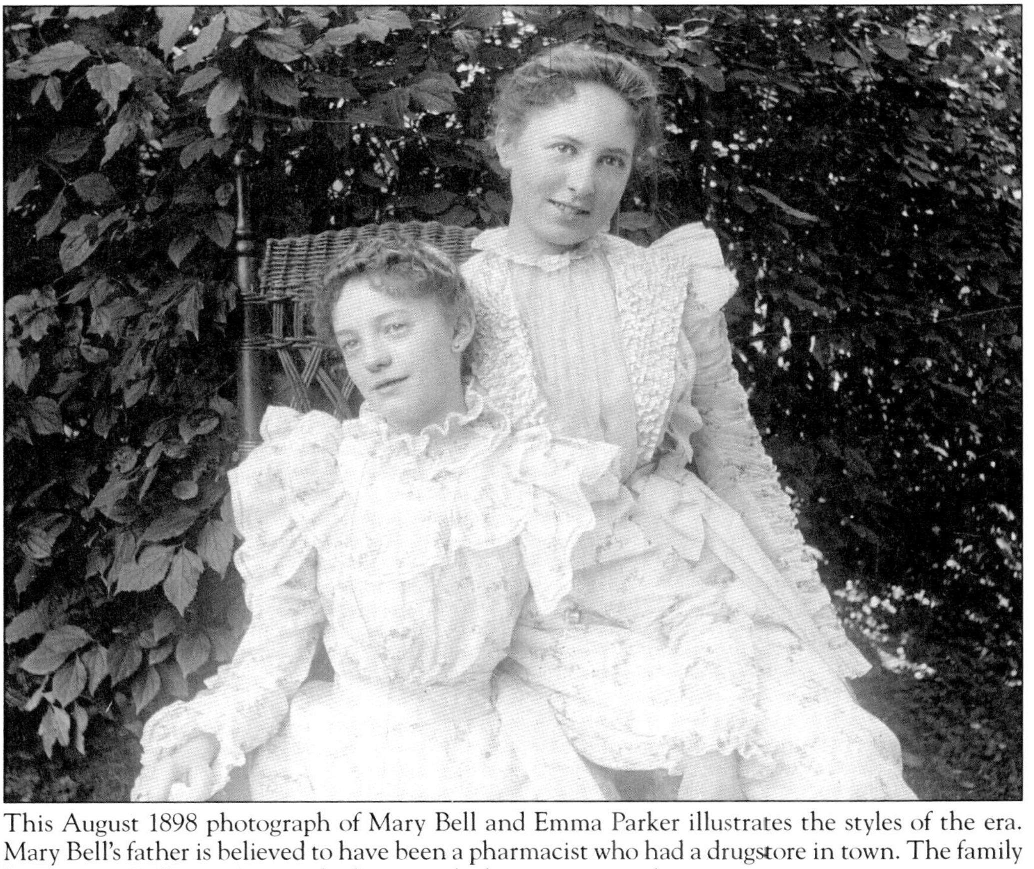

This August 1898 photograph of Mary Bell and Emma Parker illustrates the styles of the era. Mary Bell's father is believed to have been a pharmacist who had a drugstore in town. The family lived at 424 Jefferson Street, the home with the upstairs porch.

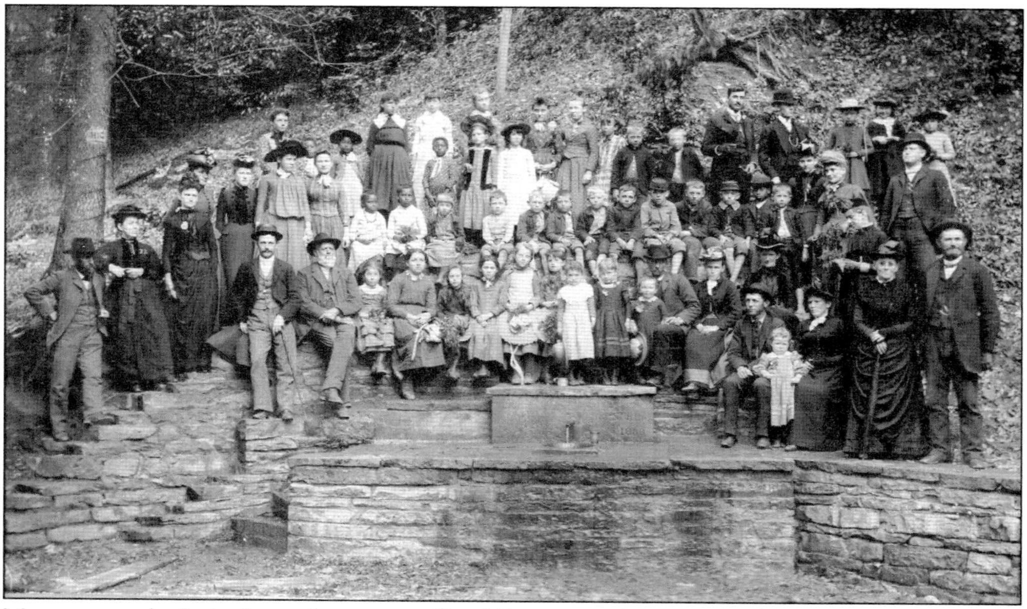

Many groups had picnics and outings at Pearl Springs on Morton Road outside of South Salem on the Willard Anderson farm. (Courtesy of Lew Speakman.)

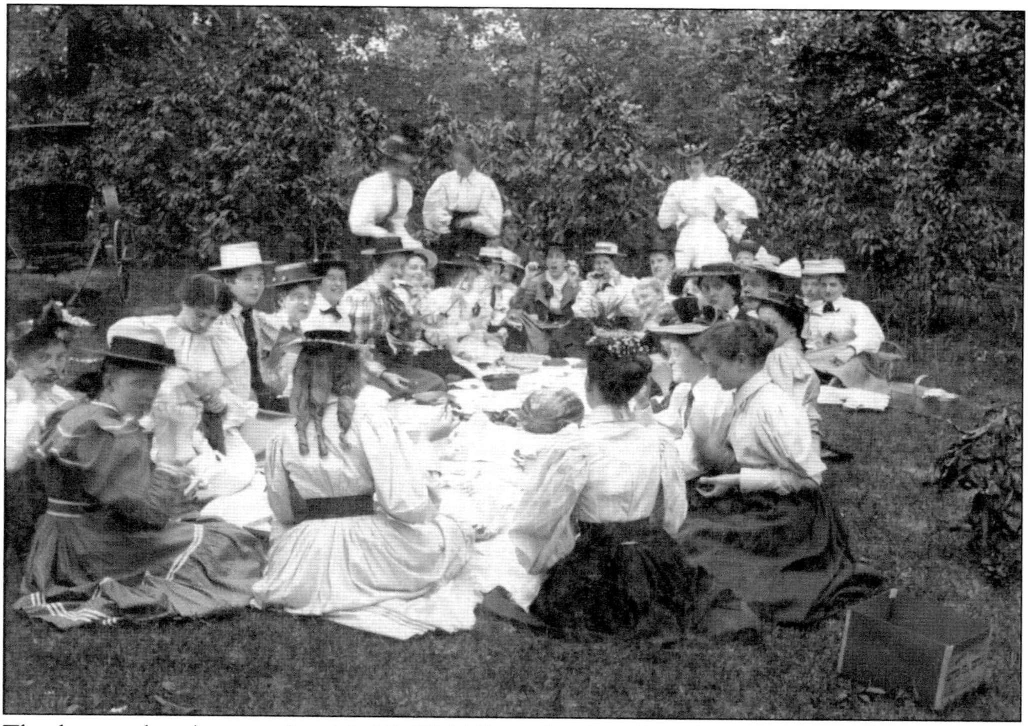

The date on this photograph is July 27, 1895. The only other identification on it reads "Cliff Party." It is believed that this women's picnic occurred on a cliff near Paint Creek. While little is known about this group and the occasion, it is interesting to note the formal nature of dress for a picnic on the grass. Also, notice the long sleeves and high necklines worn on a July afternoon.

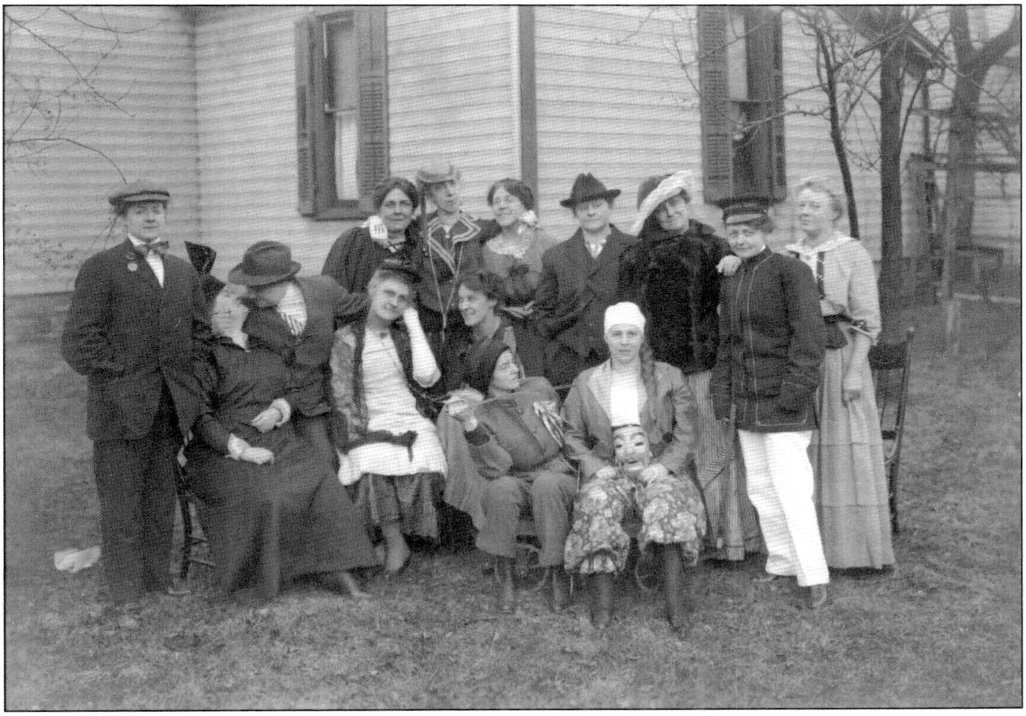

In this early 1900s photograph is a group of women dressed in Halloween costumes. The photograph, part of the collection of the Greenfield Historical Society, only reveals a few legible names: Mrs. Walter Dunlap, Mrs. Lou Waddell, Mrs. James Simons, Mrs. Renick, and Mrs. C.H. Rucker.

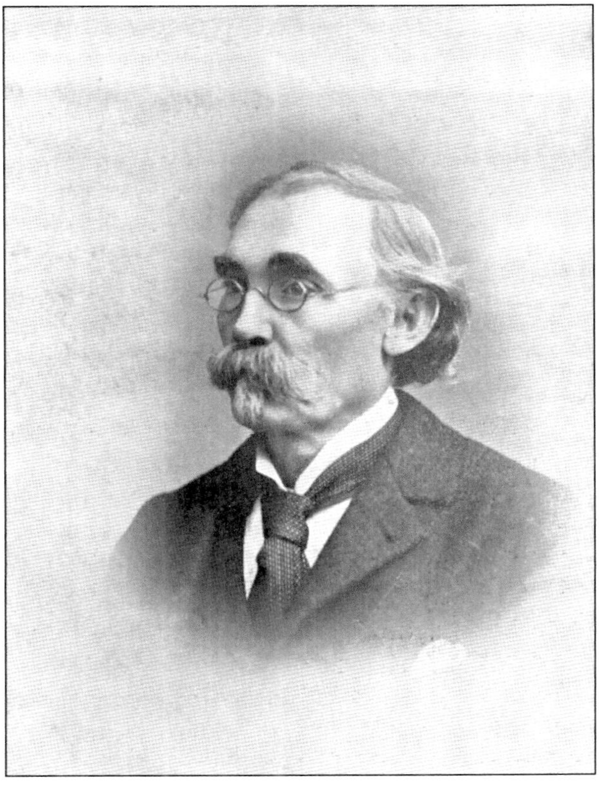

Henry Luther Dickey (1832–1910) represented Greenfield in many capacities. He trained initially to be an engineer and, later, a lawyer. His political career spanned 20 years from 1861 to 1881, serving in both branches of the Ohio General Assembly and the US House of Representatives. Locally, he was a bank president and builder of the Harper House, and lived in the grand home known as Avalon at 618 Dickey Avenue with his wife, Mary.

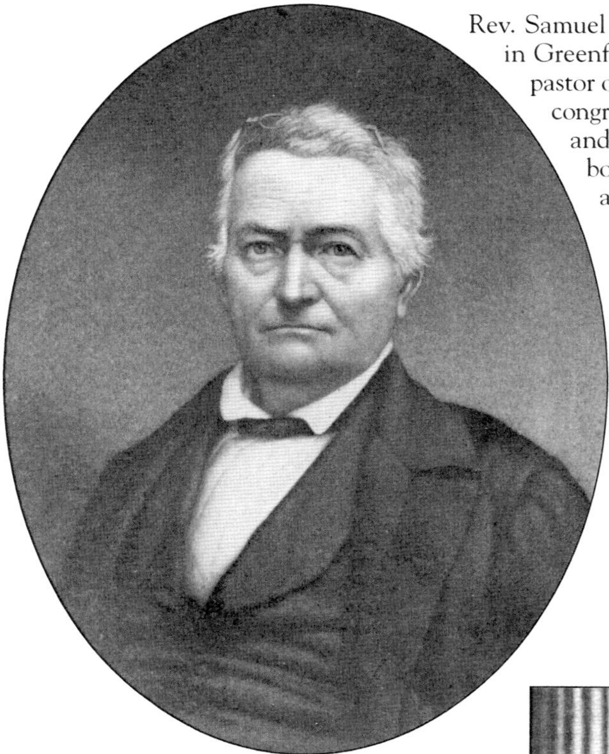

Rev. Samuel Crothers, DD, was a pioneer preacher in Greenfield. In 1820, Crothers became the first pastor of the newly organized First Presbyterian congregation. He wrote many anti-slavery books and pamphlets and was an active member of both the Greenfield Anti-Slavery Society and the Ohio Anti-Slavery Society.

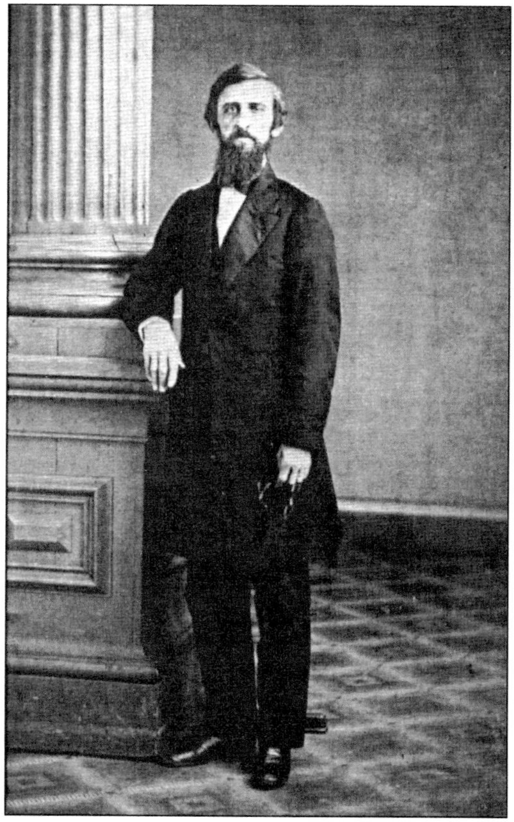

Prof. J.A. Lowes, a graduate of Miami University, became the third principal of the Salem Academy in 1848, following the Reverend James Fullerton and the Reverend John Thompson. Lowes resigned his position in 1858 and was re-elected principal in 1859. He then served until 1870. Lowes, familiar with the Mississippi River as a boy, was given a riverboat bell that is in the Academy today. (Courtesy of Lew Speakman.)

Noble Edward Irwin is one of Greenfield's most highly decorated servicemen. He was born just west of Greenfield on a farm along Sugar Run and attended the US Naval Academy. Upon graduation in 1891, he was commissioned as an ensign on the USS *Newark* and saw action in several conflicts, including the Spanish-American War and the Boxer Rebellion. His military career spanned 46 years before retiring as a rear admiral in 1924. (Courtesy of Library of Congress.)

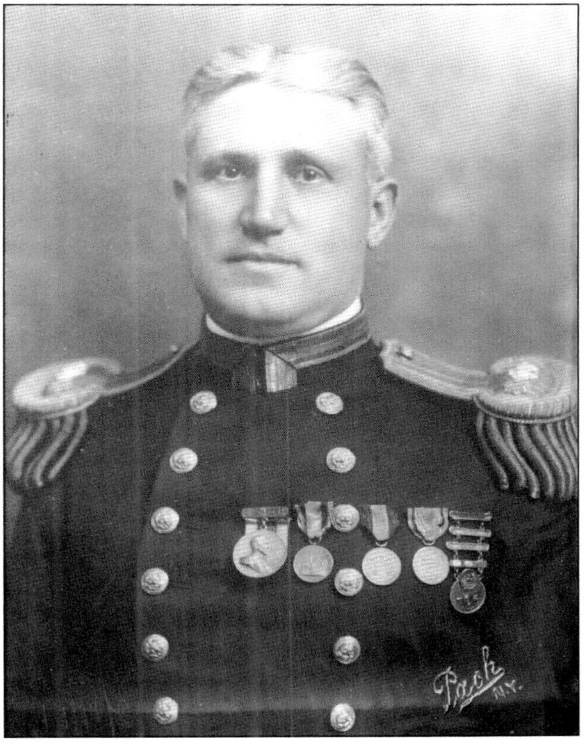

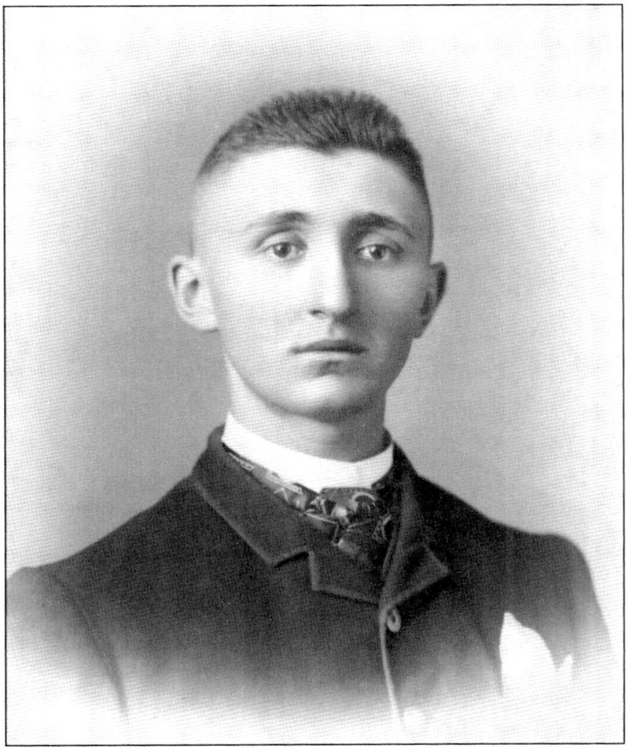

In 1913, Charles M. Mains took over management of TAPATCO when E.L. McClain retired. Mains's sons Charles F. and John T. later joined him in management. Charles T. Mains became the first vice president of the Greenfield Rotary Club in 1922. J.A. Harps served as president. (Courtesy of Janie Jinks-Weidner.)

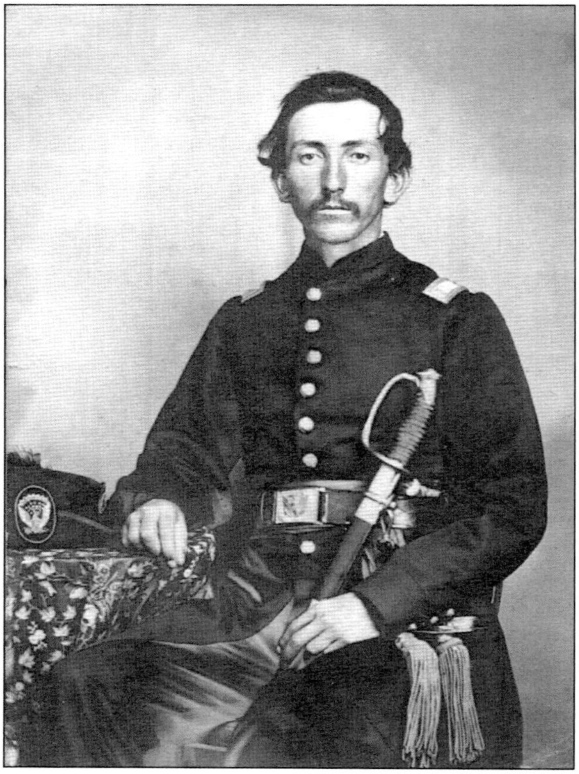

Highland County native Edward Hamilton Miller (1838–1921) was a Civil War first lieutenant in the 73rd Ohio Volunteer Infantry. Reported dead in the Battle of Bull Run, his brother R.H. Miller and Dr. Milton Dunlap went to retrieve the body but instead found him alive in a military hospital. In 1868, after a year as cashier at the Highland County Bank, he bought out the stockholders and became president.

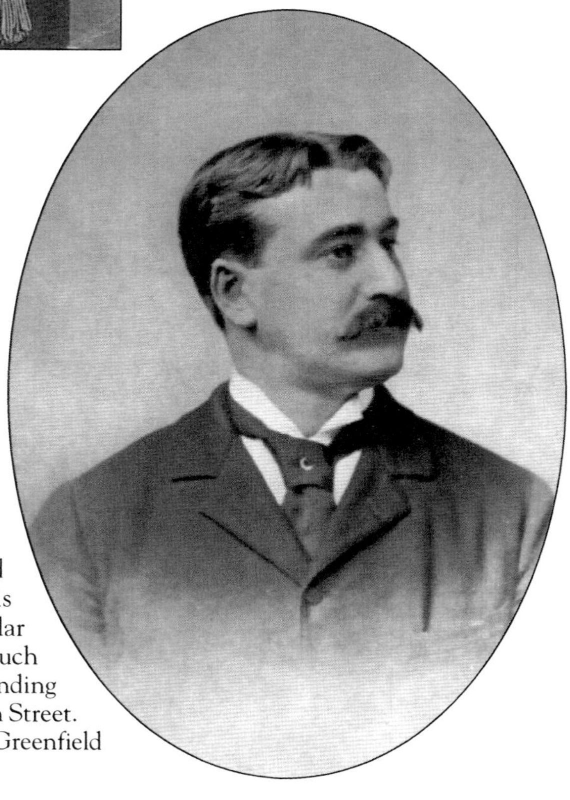

Edward Lee McClain, shown here in 1892, was born in May 1861 and raised in Greenfield at 546 Jefferson Street. His 1881 invention of a revolutionary horse collar pad that he manufactured afforded him much wealth, and in 1914, he donated land and funding for a new high school to be built on Jefferson Street. McClain's factory, TAPATCO, was a major Greenfield business for over 80 years.

Emma Gore Miller (1840–1917) married Edward H. Miller on May 6, 1863. Her parents were Joshua Gore from Frederick County, Maryland, and Rebecca Jane Hughes Gore from Springfield, Ohio. The Greenfield Historical Society has a brown beaded dress belonging to Emma Miller that was made in the 1870s.

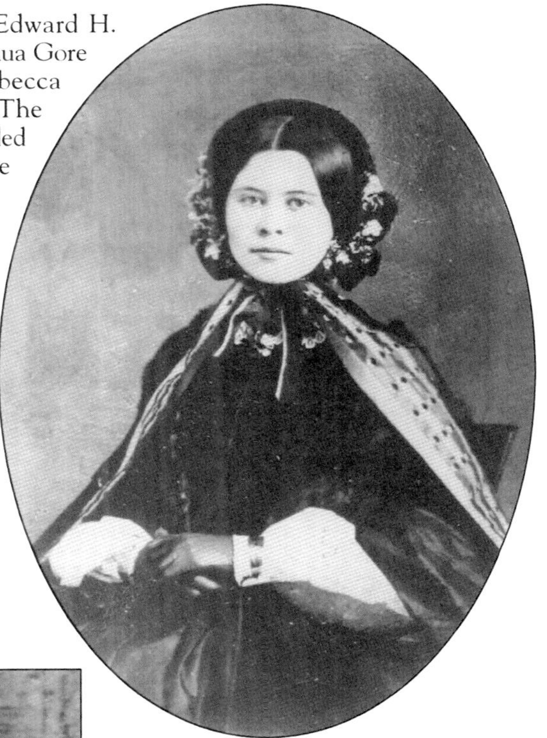

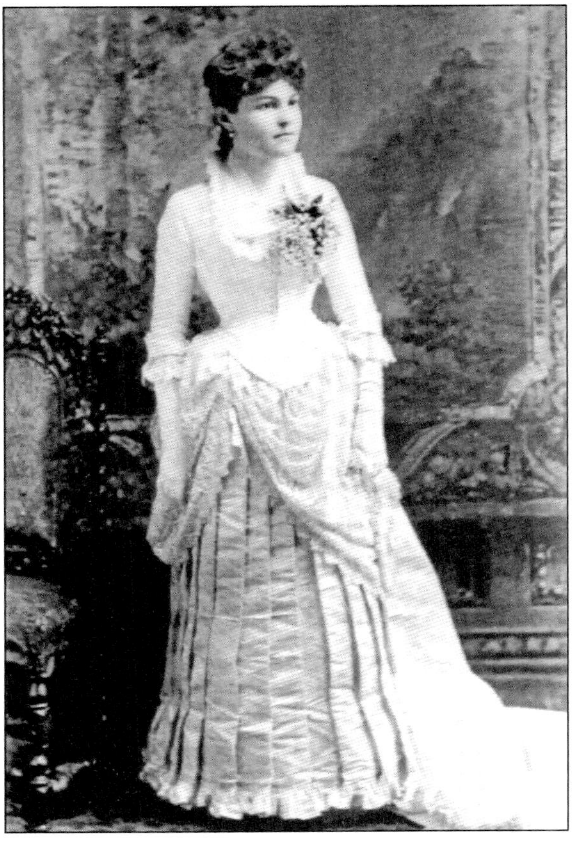

Lulu Theodosia Johnson McClain supervised the installation of the artwork in the new high school that she and her husband, Edward Lee, donated to Greenfield. Lulu McClain was born and raised in Cincinnati and met her husband when she was visiting Greenfield in 1884. They married on December 17, 1885, and after a short stay in Cincinnati while their home was being built, moved permanently to Greenfield in August 1887.

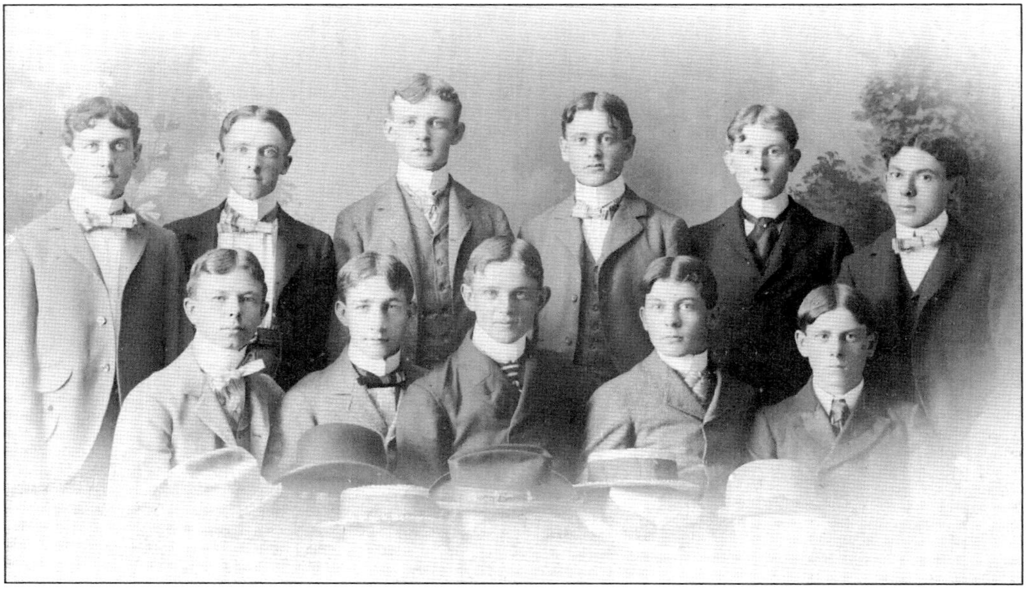

A group of young Greenfield friends are pictured in this c. 1890s photograph; only a few of the names are known. From left to right, they are (first row) unidentified, Frank Harvey, Frank or Charlie Head, and two unidentified; (second row) unidentified, Neil Waddell, Frank or Charlie Head, and three unidentified.

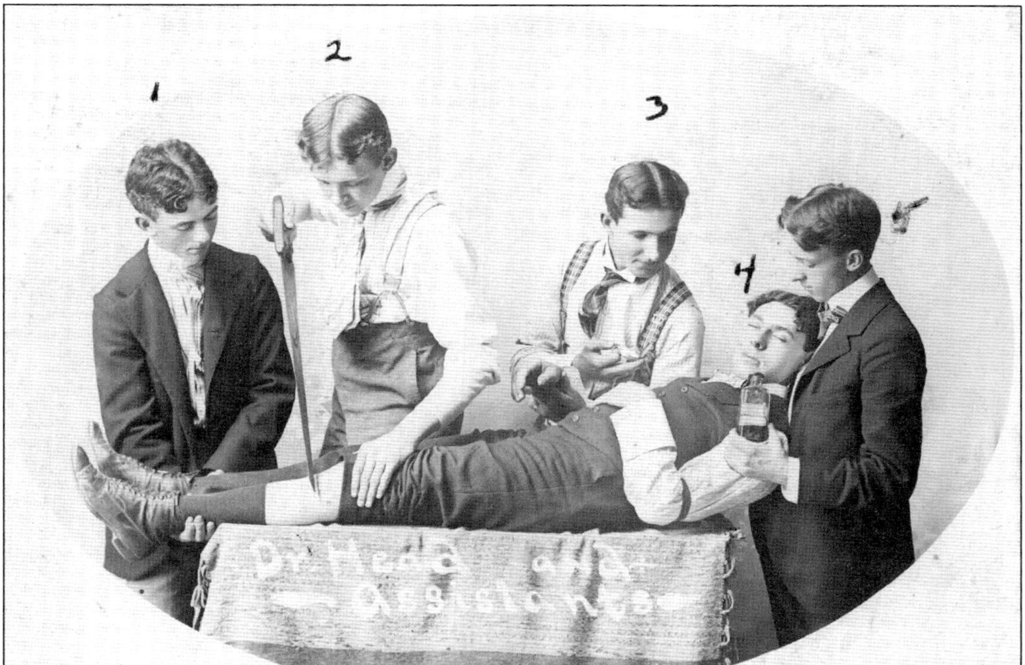

One can only imagine the occasion for the apparent spoof portrayed in this picture. Lads involved are, from left to right, Walter Gray, Frank Head, two unidentified, and Frank Harvey—the same boys pictured above.

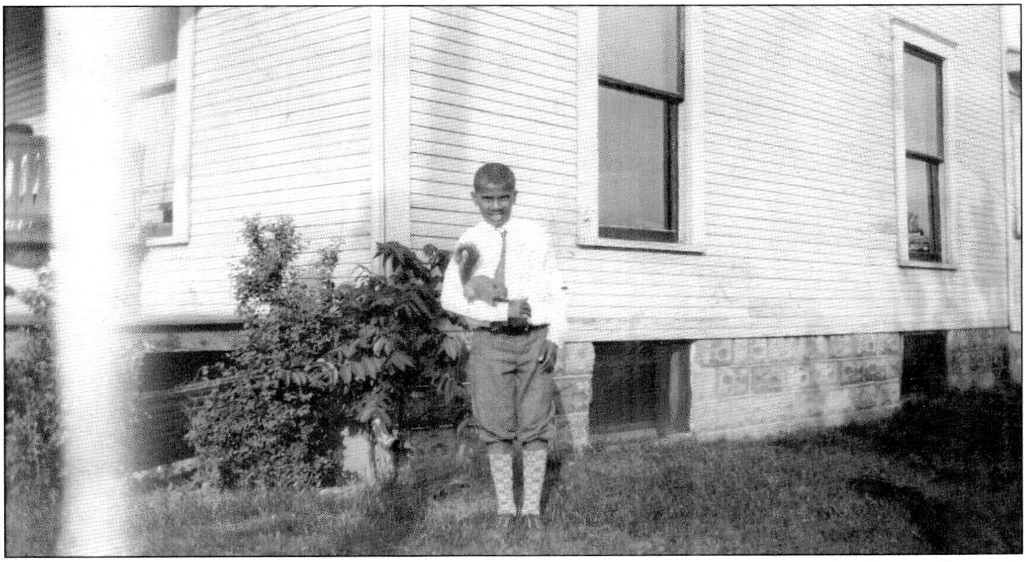

William Henry "Bill" Byrd holds a squirrel in front of a house at 902 Carford Pike that still stands today. Byrd's grandmother, Bessie E. Payne Byrd, was a deaf woman who loved animals and seemed to attract them. (Courtesy of Constance Ford.)

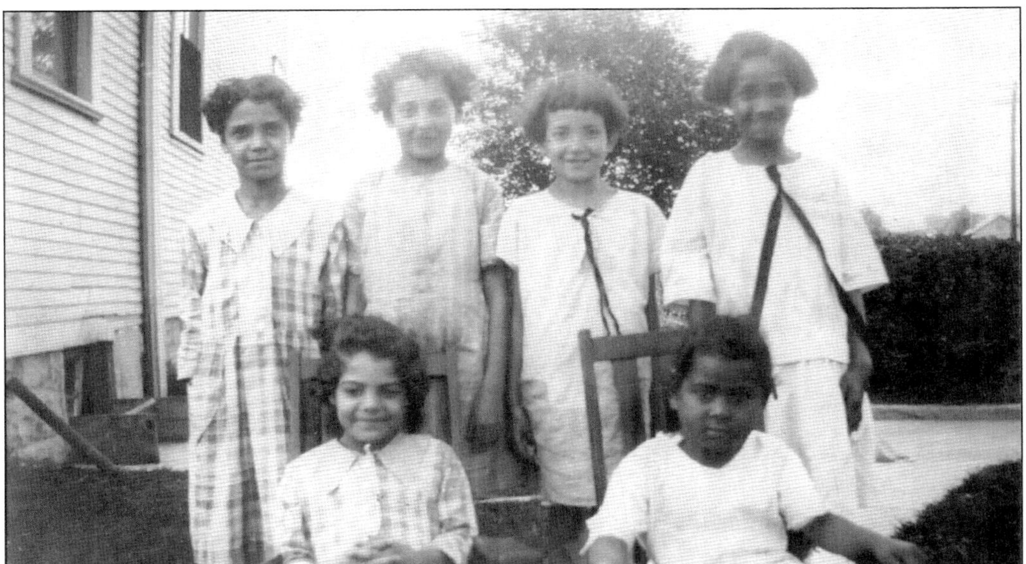

This group of eight-year-old girls went to school together in the 1920s. They are, from left to right, (first row) Mabel Seldon Stodgel Seward and Alice Steward; (second row) Alice May Pettiford, Ann Pettiford, Mary Seldon Berryman, and Mabel Byrd. (Courtesy of Constance Ford.)

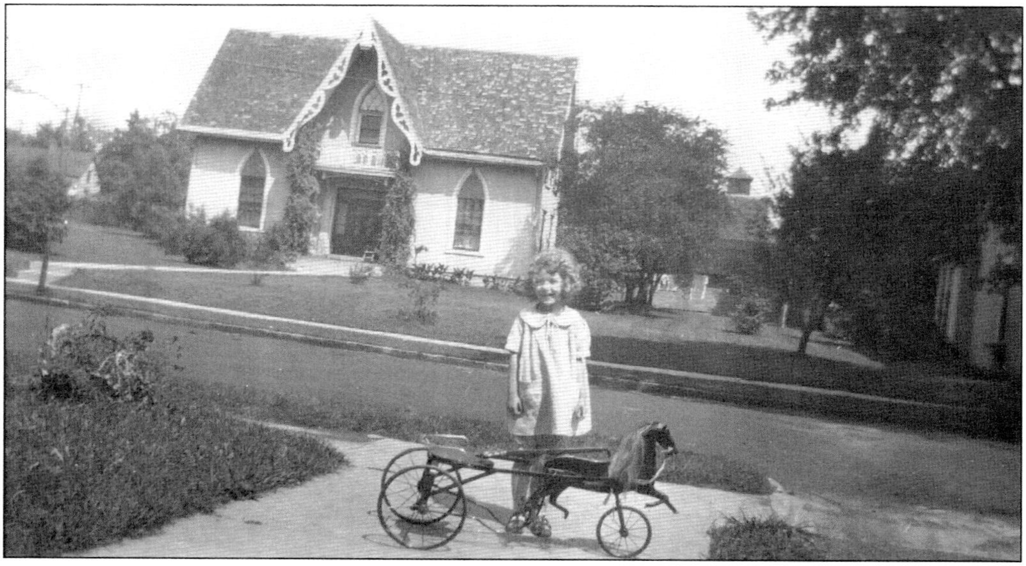

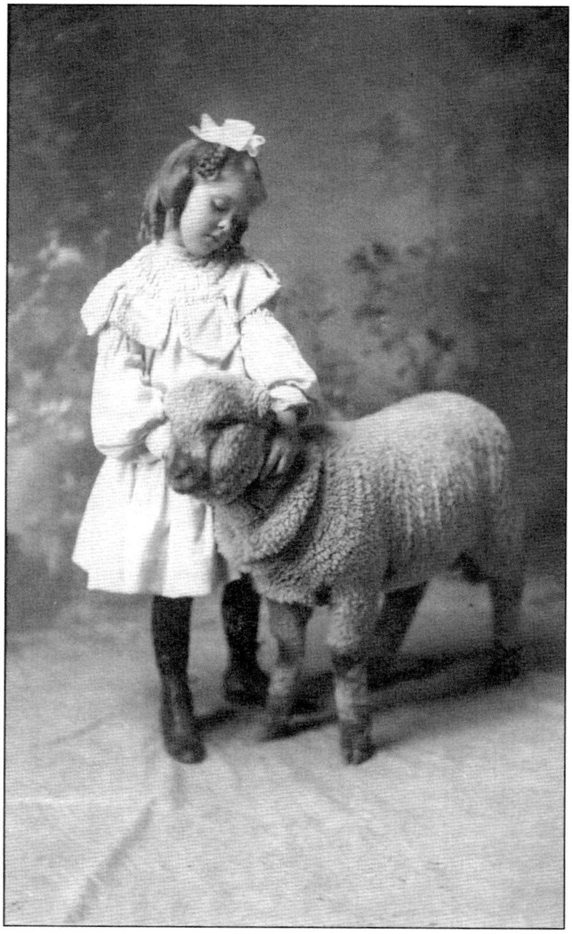

Becky Jeanne Woodmansee is shown here with her toy horse carriage. Becky is the daughter of Forrest Woodmansee, owner of Woodmansee's Ice Cream Factory. This picture was taken on South Street at the factory; in the background is Judge Alfred Dickey's 1859 home, which still stands behind the South Street Market.

Louise Lohr, daughter of Frank and Sarah Harvey Lohr, is shown with her pet lamb, Bill. Louise is posing with the lamb for ceremonies dedicating the then-new Methodist Church. Born in Greenfield in 1898, Louise attended Greenfield schools through eighth grade.

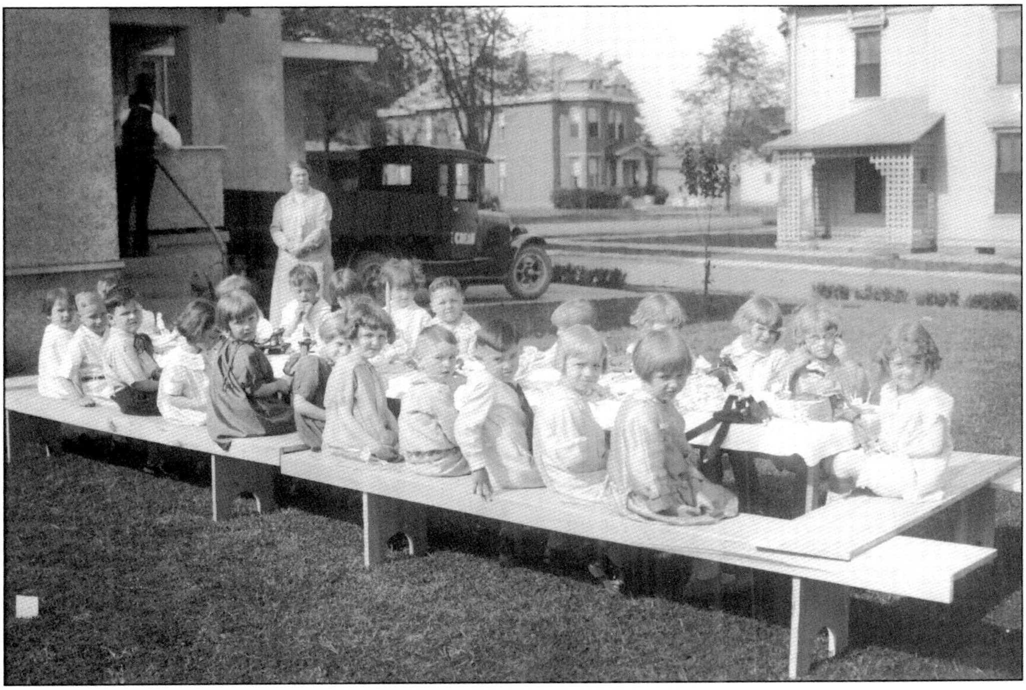

Pictured is Becky Woodmansee's sixth birthday party at South and Fourth Streets. An ice cream maker's daughter would naturally have a well-attended celebration. Children attending were, counterclockwise from the left, Margot Noble, Dean Messick Waddell, Curtis Mosley, Elizabeth Ann Slavens, Rose Ann Fairley, Carletta Uhl, Elizabeth Ann Wilson, John Thomas Steward, Lowell Cherry, Mary Jane Shinner, Mary Louise Stultz, Becky Jeanne Woodmansee, Jean Ann Spargur, Elizabeth Gray, Betty Miller, Betty McGhee, Robert Spargur, Shirley Rhodes, Mary Ellen Davis, James Allen, Jackie Kerr, and Boyd Cleveland.

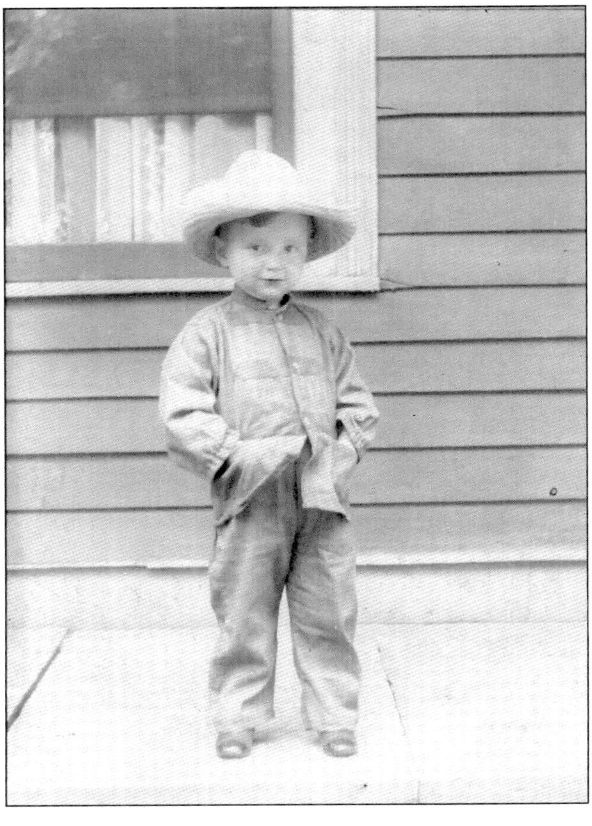

Howard Martindill was the son of W.C. and Ruth Martindill. W.C. was a local doctor. As an adult, Howard "Doc" worked as a foreman at the US Shoe Factory and was a member of the Greenfield Lions Club.

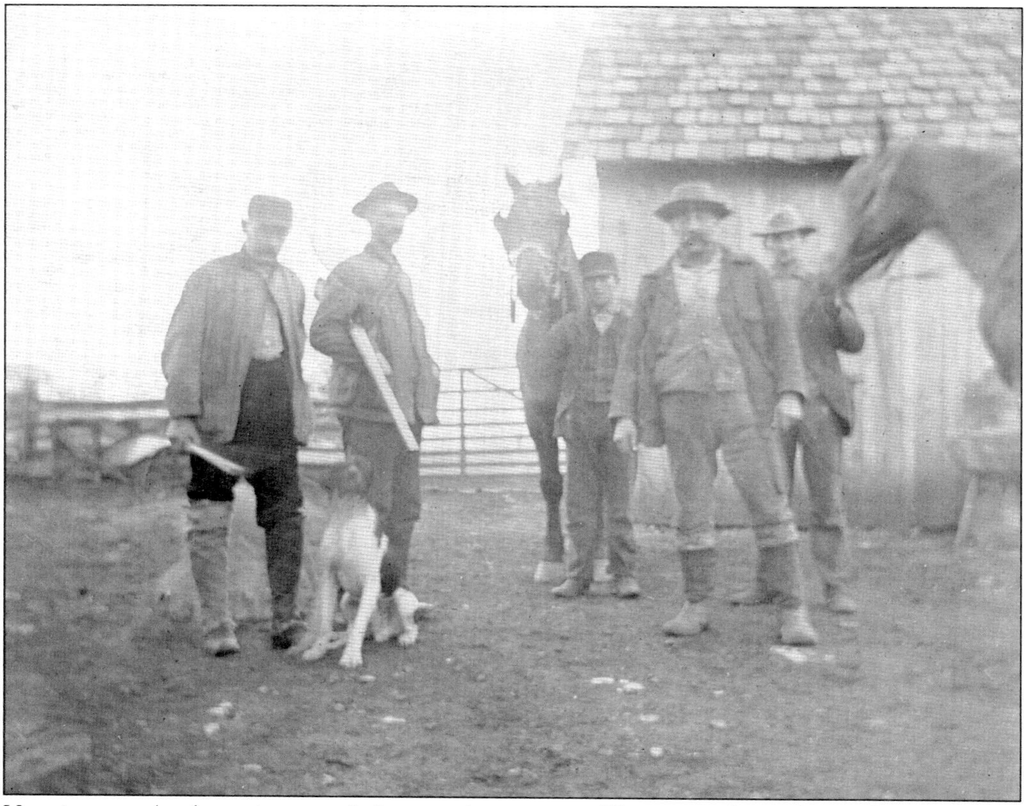

Hunting was (and continues to be) a popular pastime. These men have their rifles ready and, along with their dogs and horses, appear to be set for a bountiful day.

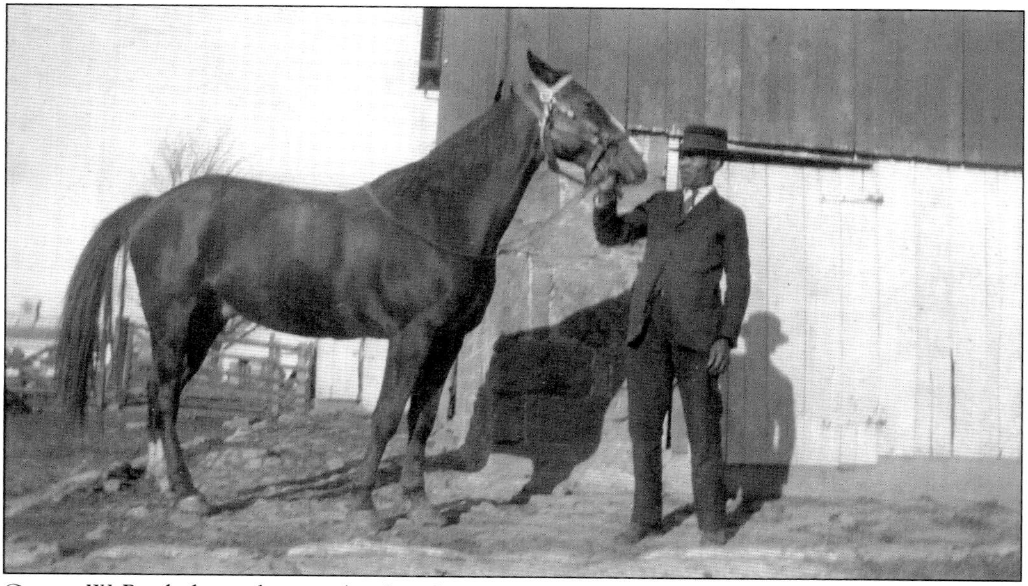

George W. Byrd, shown here with a farm horse, visited friends at the Hudson farm near Leesburg. (Courtesy of Constance Ford.)

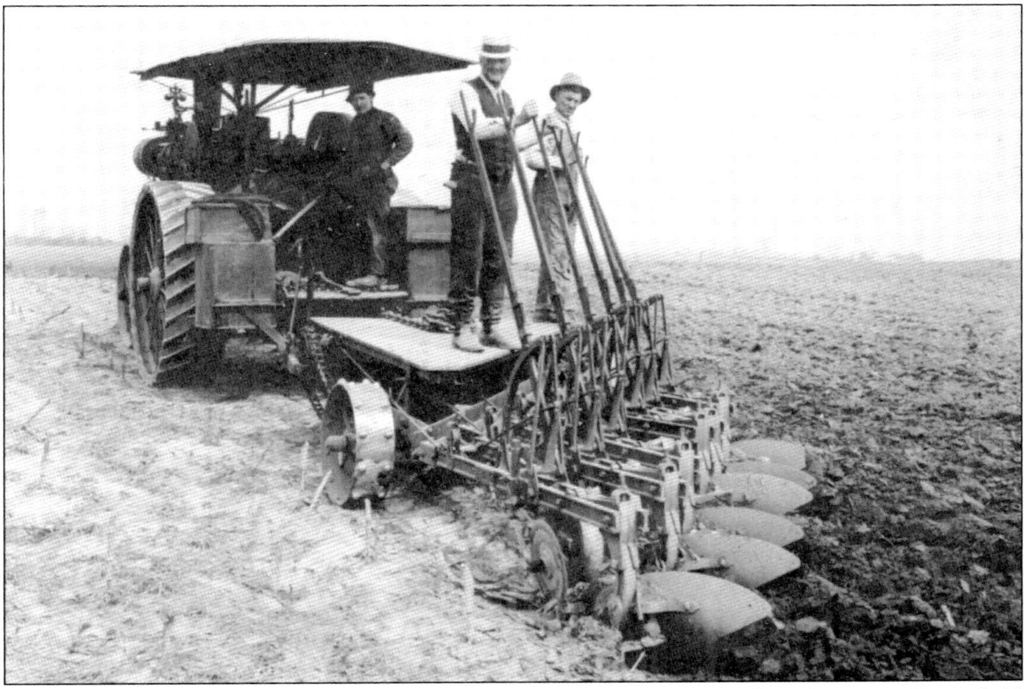

This gasoline-powered tractor is pulling a plow on the Dan Coyner farm between Greenfield and Lyndon. The crew consists of, from left to right, Earl Howard, Dan Coyner, and Ron Moore. (Courtesy of Lew Speakman.)

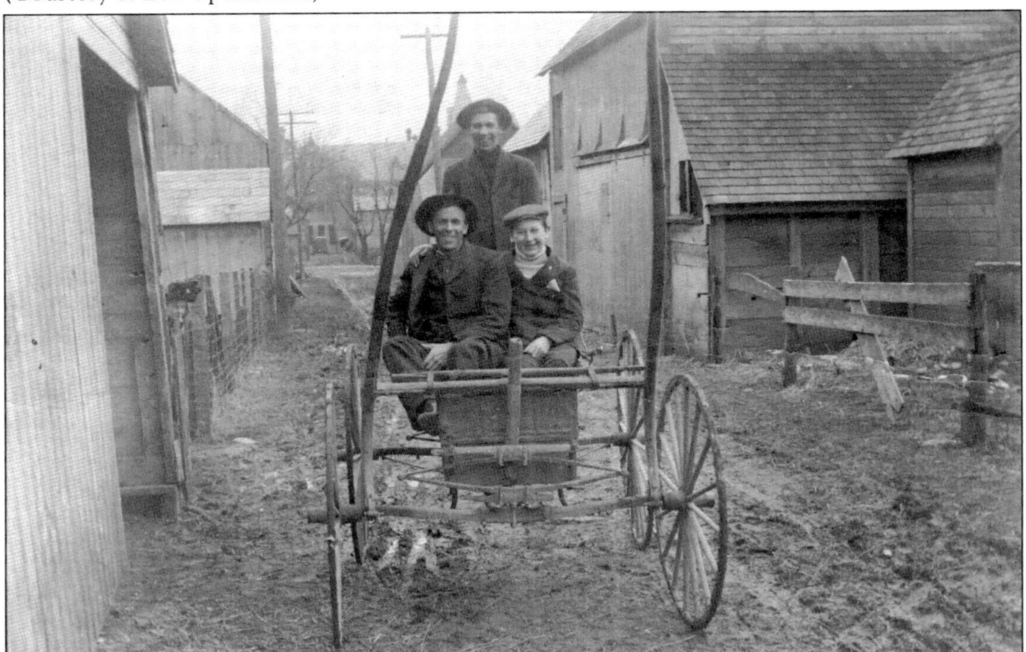

This picture, taken in an alley, shows Raymond Harvey, Walter Harvey, and Roy Ashley in a wagon. The building at the end of the alley is a grade school.

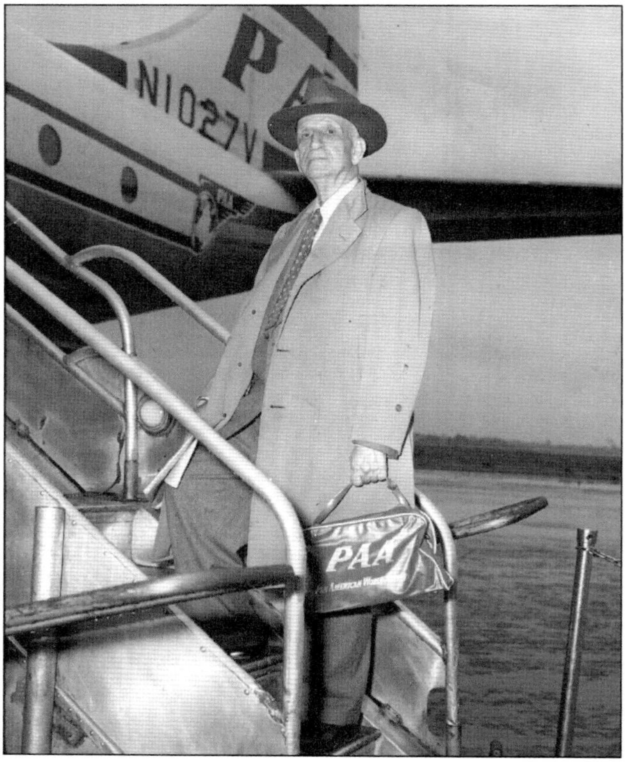

Frank Raymond Harris (1880–1965) is a well-known Greenfield educator, historian, writer, and world traveler. Born in Greenfield, he attended Ohio Wesleyan University and Harvard University, returning home to become principal and superintendent. He traveled extensively, accumulating over 100,000 miles and visiting 128 countries. He also traveled on the Hindenburg. He authored numerous newspaper articles and four books, *A Greene Countrie Towne*, *Hometown Chronicles*, *Itchin' Feet*, and *Roses in December*.

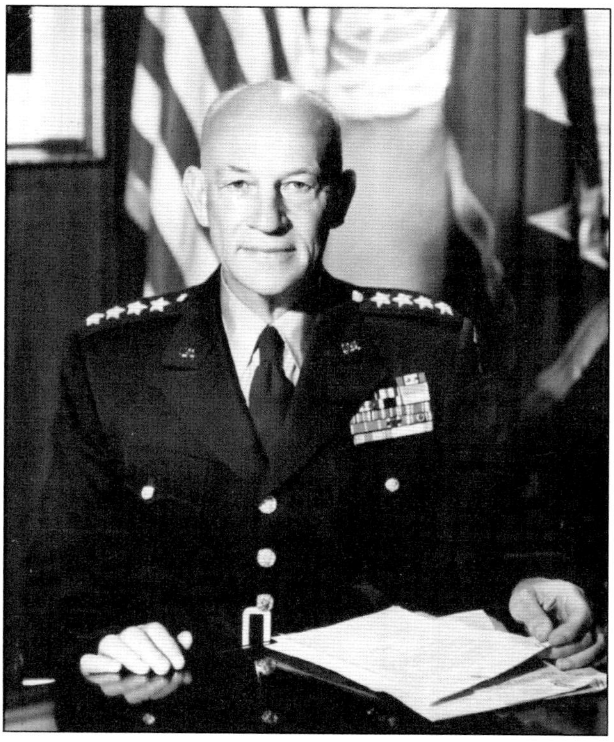

Four-star general John Edwin Hull (1895–1975), a local sports and military hero, played football at Greenfield and at Miami University, where he played every minute of every game during his four years there. He was a captain in World War I; in World War II, he served in France, was a general staffer under General Marshall, and became chief of operations under General Eisenhower. He retired from the military in 1955.

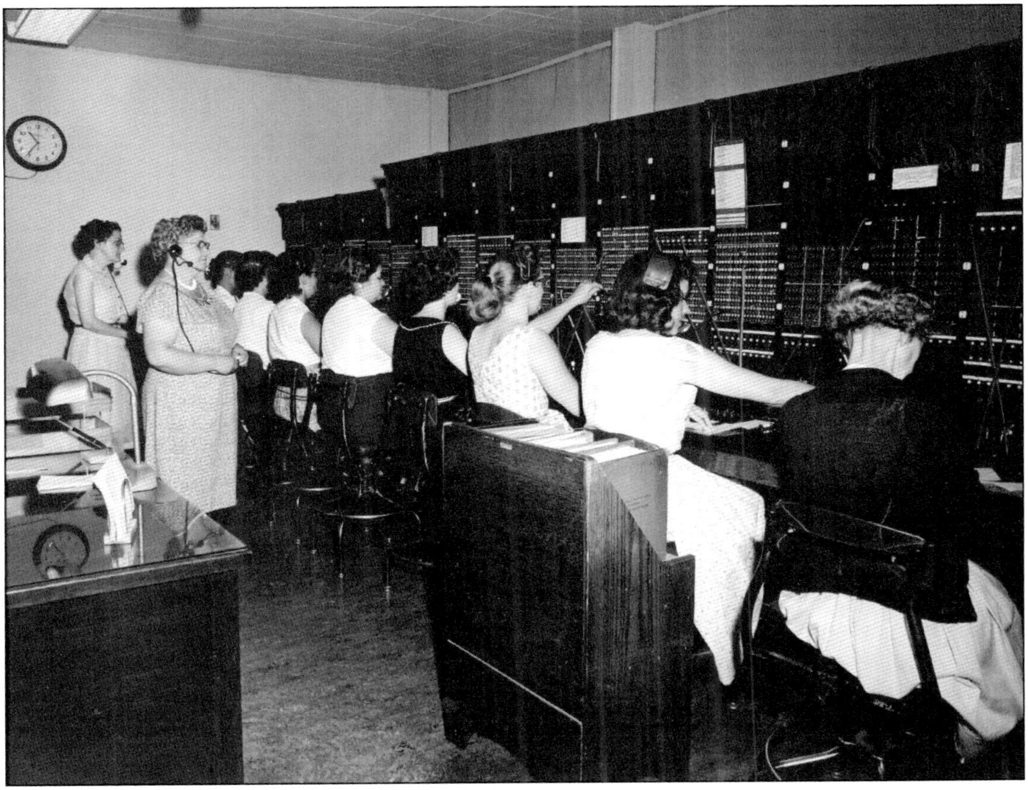

Employment opportunities for women grew significantly with the advent of the telephone. Operators at work at the General Telephone Company of Ohio in 1960 are, from left to right, (sitting at the board) Olive Wheaton, Catherine Clouser, Helen Whitley, Judy Frazier, Mary Satterfield, Roberta Hakes, unidentified, and Mary Runyon; (standing) Dorothy Woodruff and Carrie Duncanson.

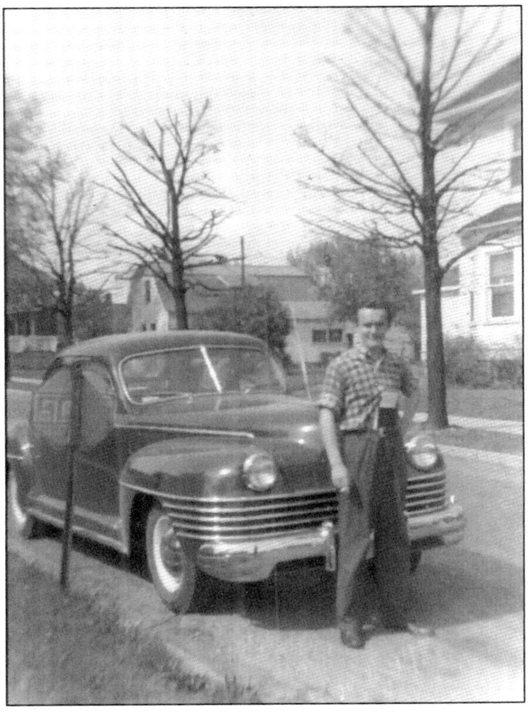

Ronald Yankee stands proudly in front of his automobile in 1942. (Courtesy of Kenneth Eltzroth.)

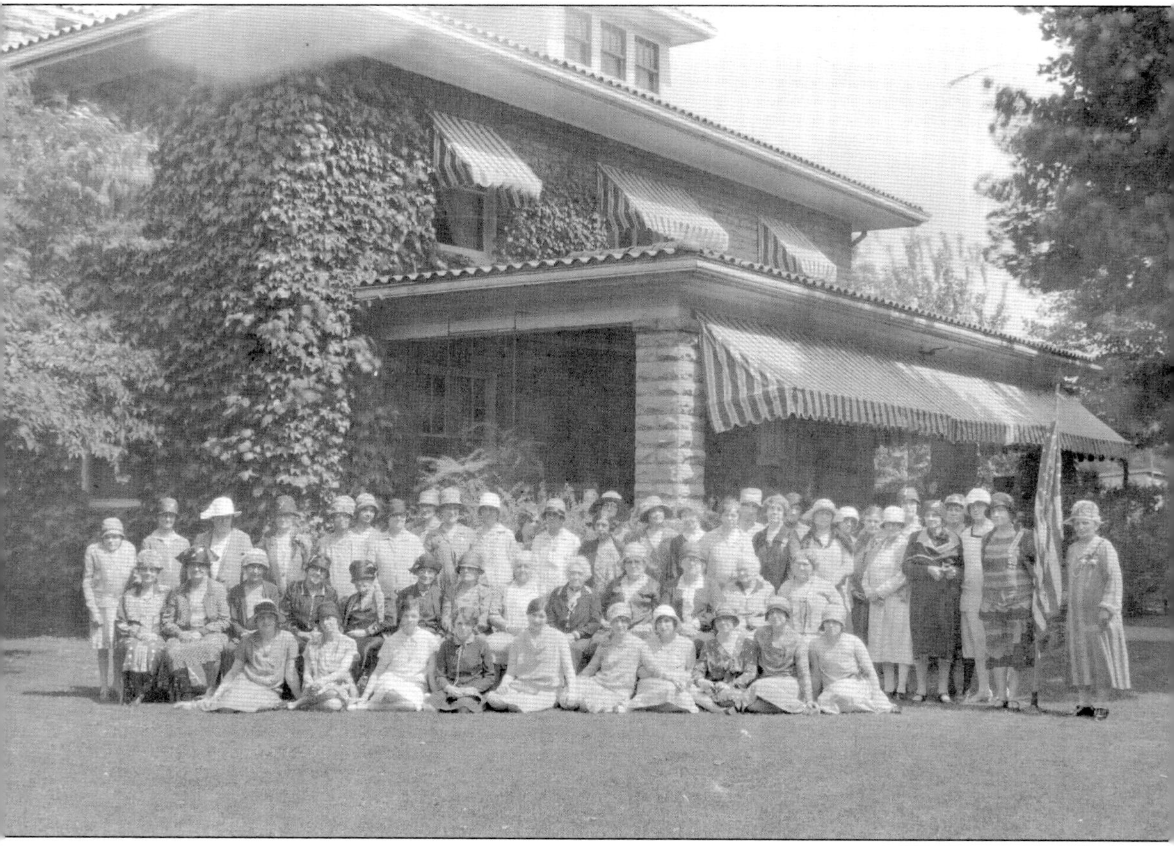

Juliana White Freshour was Greenfield's only real Daughter of the American Revolution (DAR). The local DAR was organized as the Juliana White Chapter by her daughter Hortense Freshour, who became its first regent in December 1920. This c. 1930s DAR group poses in front of 543 S. Washington Street.

Four

Faith and Worship

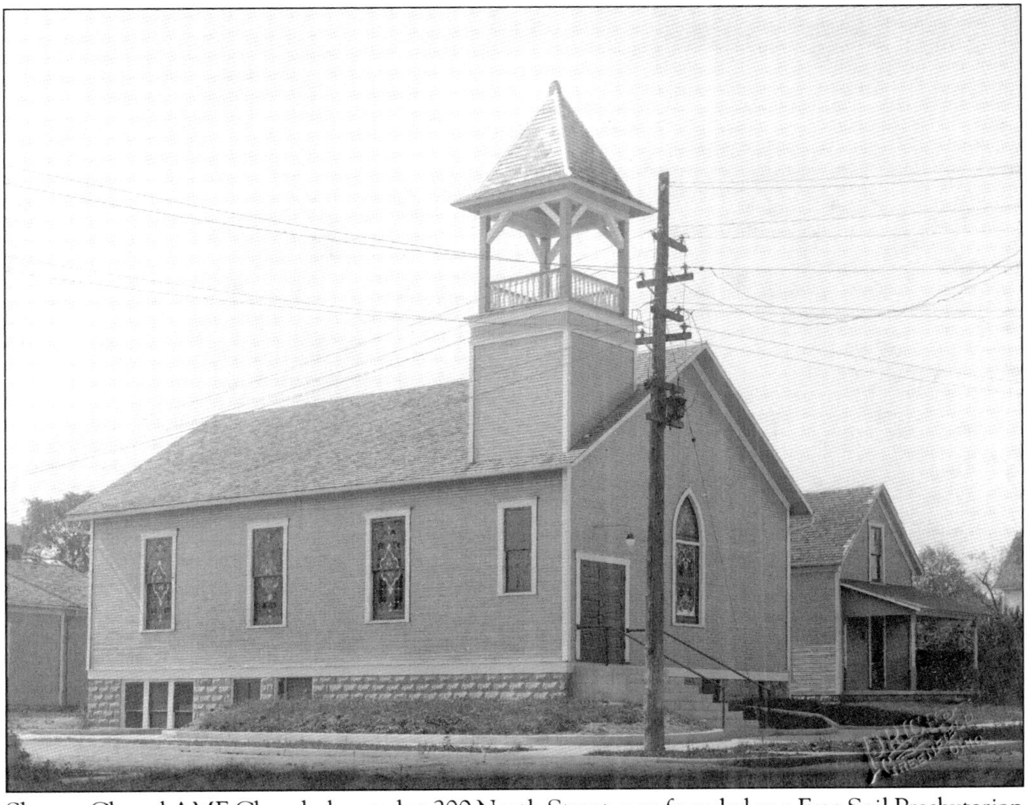

Shorter Chapel AME Church, located at 200 North Street, was founded as a Free Soil Presbyterian Church by Adam Lowry Rankin. After the Civil War, it was sold to the AME congregation. The original building was torn down, and this building was erected in its place.

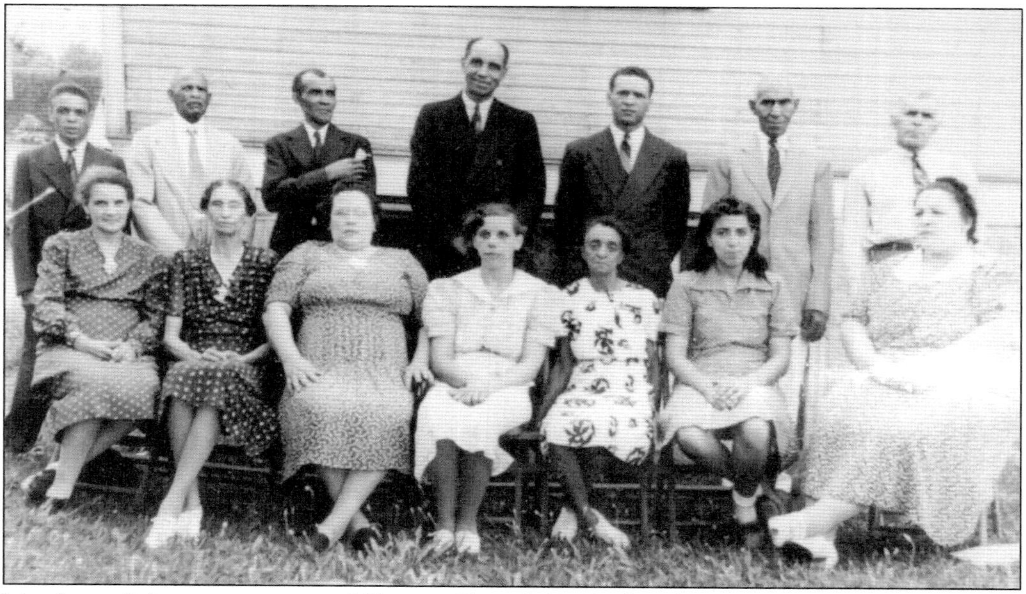

Members of the congregation of Shorter Chapel AME Church in roughly the 1930s or 1940s included, from left to right, (first row) Bessie Payne Byrd, Carrie Bell Byrd, Ida Richardson, Opal Greene, unidentified, Mary Ford, and Wilda Bailey; (second row) Walter Greene, Mr. Simms, Arliss Bailey, LaVelle Ford, Joseph Richardson, and John Ford. (Courtesy of Constance Ford.)

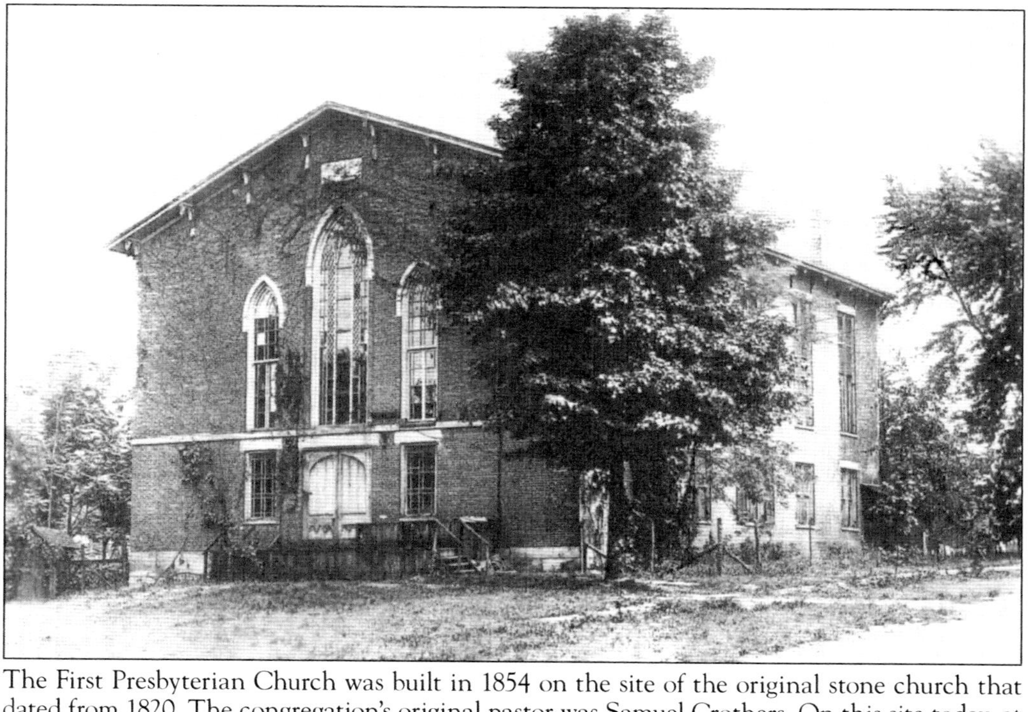

The First Presbyterian Church was built in 1854 on the site of the original stone church that dated from 1820. The congregation's original pastor was Samuel Crothers. On this site today, at the corner of McArthur Way and Jefferson Street, is the Travellers Rest.

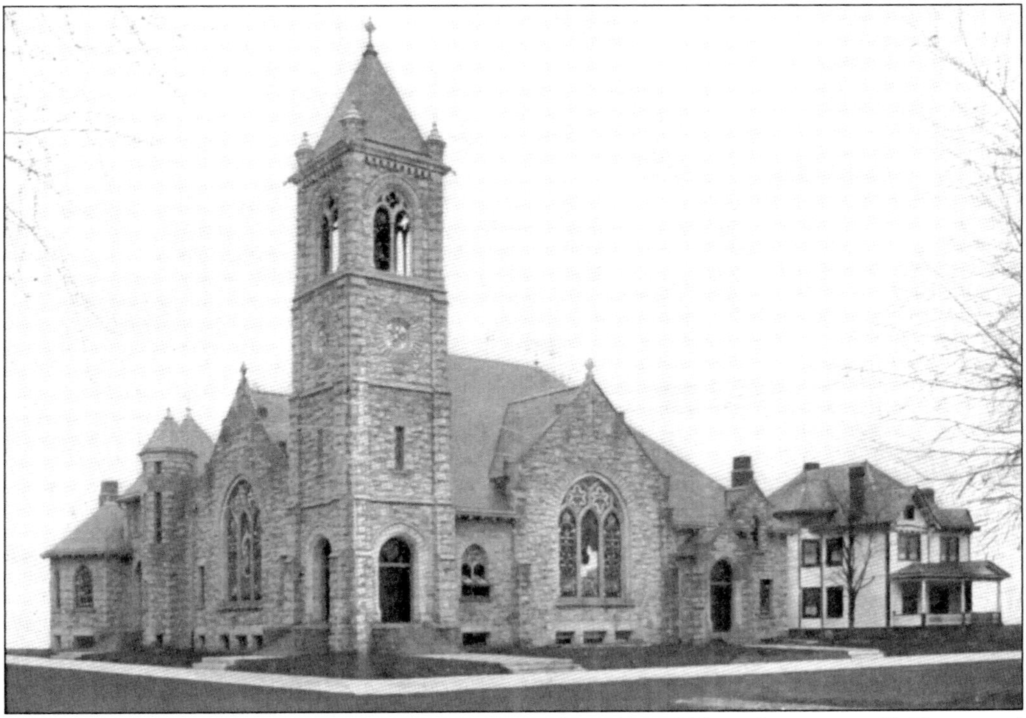

The First Presbyterian Church and Manse was erected in 1901–1903 on the corner of Jefferson and Fifth Streets. In the early 1800s, a woolen mill owned by David Bonner occupied this site, which was then considered outside of town. Later, it was the Odd Fellows Hall, and then it was rented out for use as a school. This congregation's former location was Jefferson Street and McArthur Way (then Front Street).

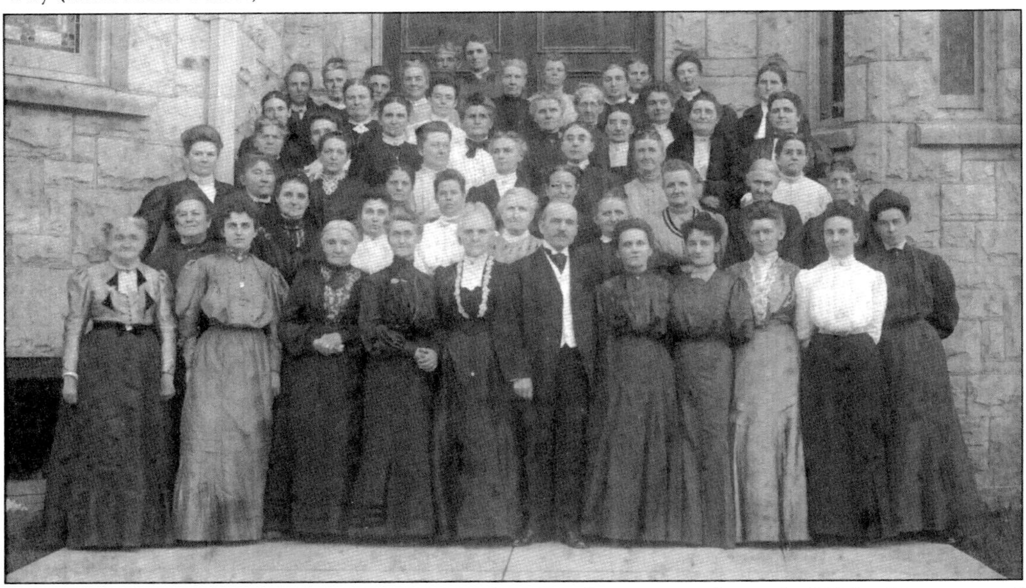

The Presbyterian Women's group poses on the church steps in the early 1900s. (Courtesy of Patricia Smith.)

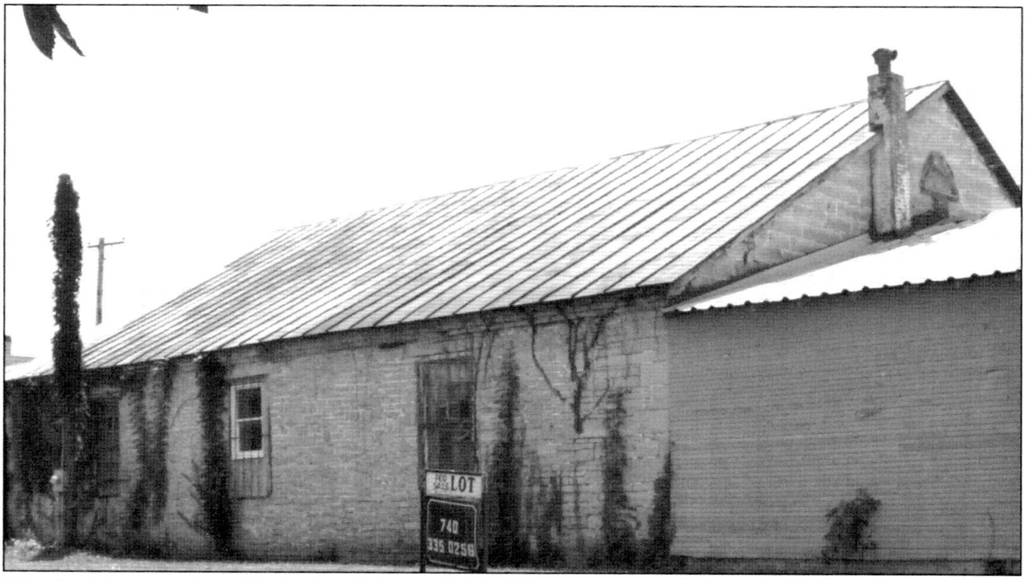

This building in the 100 block of Mirabeau Street is an old Methodist church dating from 1833. The Methodists organized in 1822 and had a prior building on this site as early as 1828. This structure has since been used as a garage, factory, gymnasium, and skating rink.

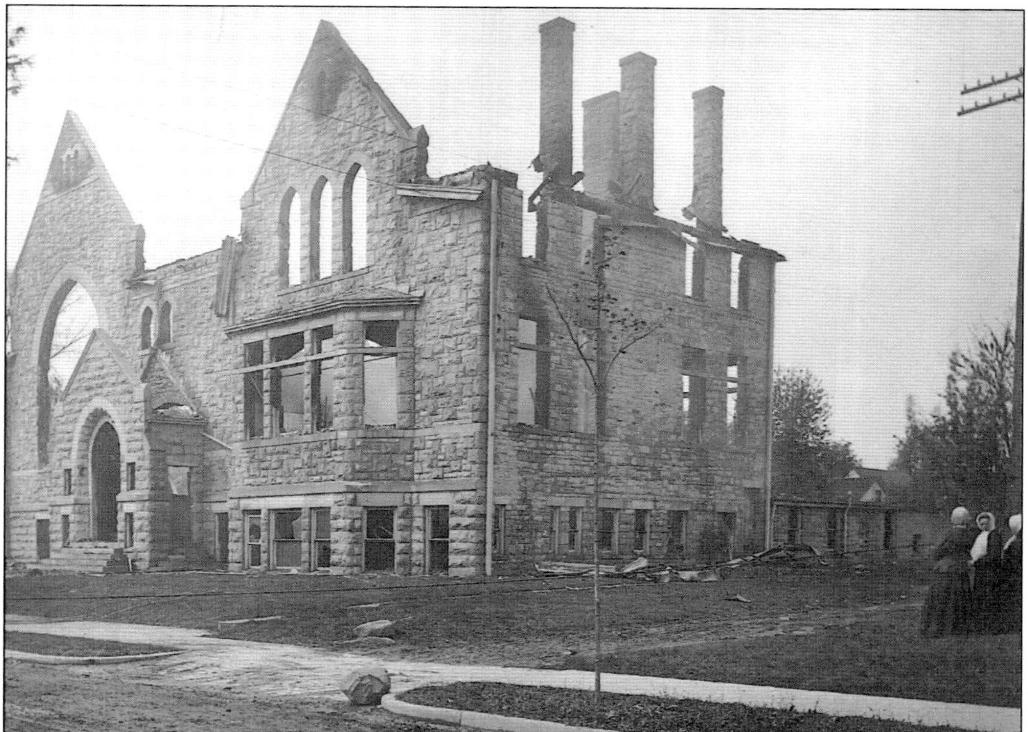

The Methodist church suffered a great catastrophe in 1910 when a massive fire destroyed it. Located at the corner of South and Fourth Streets, the structure was only six years old when it burned.

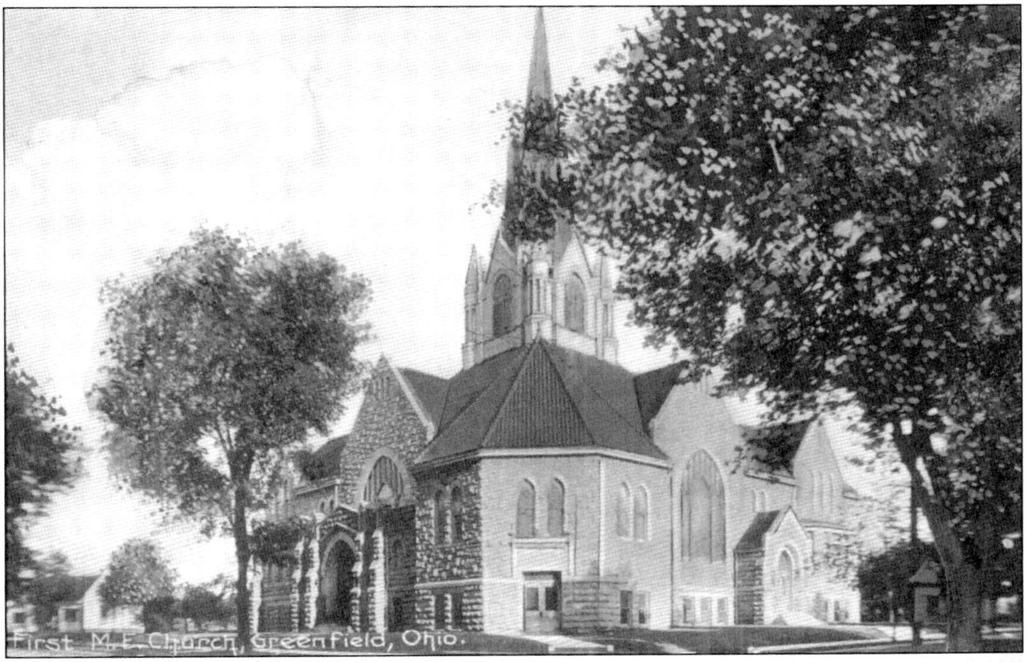

In the early 1900s, prevailing thought embraced the idea of a church providing activities to fulfill all facets of social life. The Methodist church housed a gymnasium, a swimming facility, two fully equipped bathing departments, lockers, and dressing rooms. This church burned, as shown on the previous page.

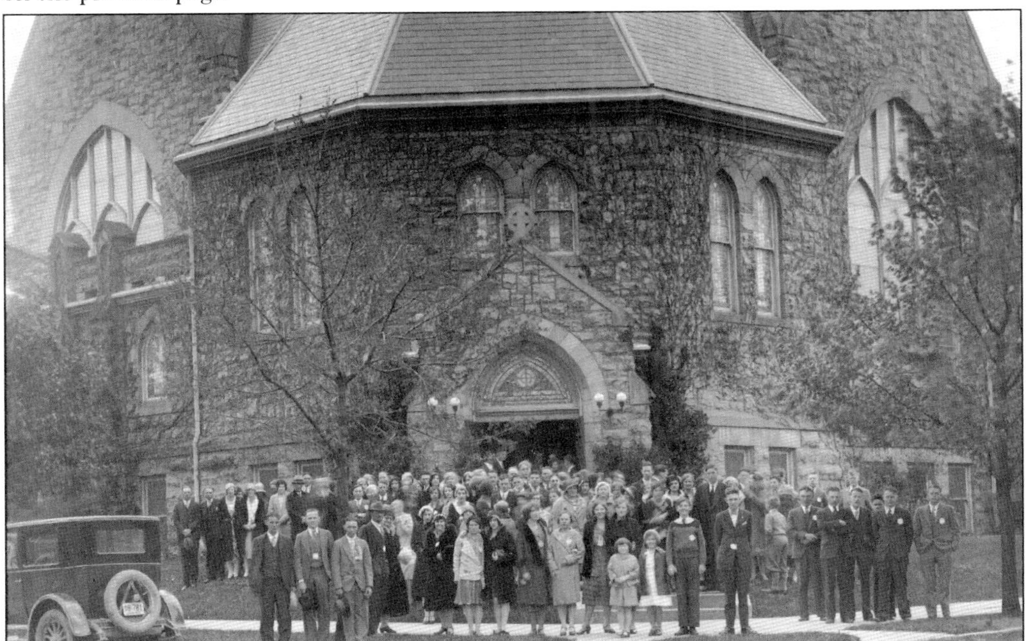

Members of the Methodist congregation are standing in front of the rebuilt church in about 1930. (Courtesy of Susan Thompson.)

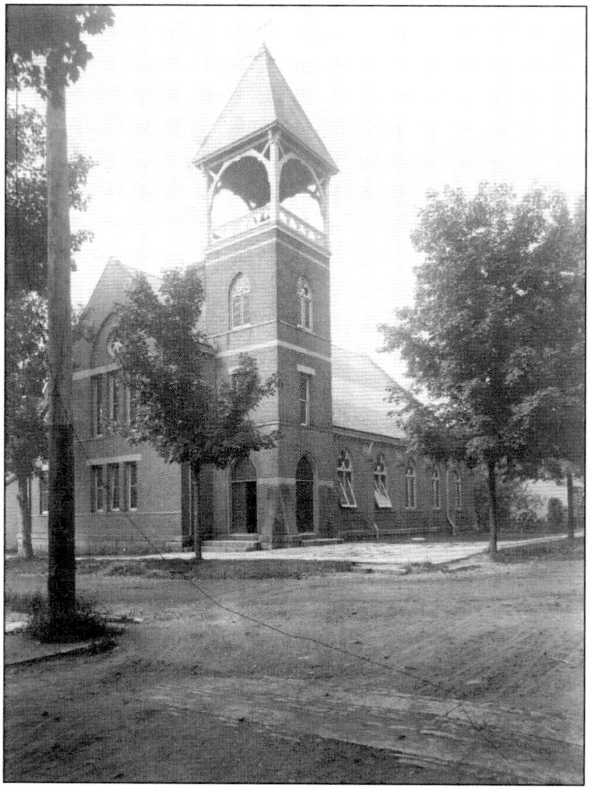

St. Benignus Catholic Church is located at Mirabeau and Second Streets. The original building on this site was owned by the Methodist Church, which suffered a tornado in 1863 and a fire in 1880. This building was erected in 1882 and sold to the Catholics in 1904.

Pictured here is the ornate interior of St. Benignus Church as it looked in the early 1900s. The Irish immigrants who came in the 1840s and 1850s, many of whom worked in the stone quarries, comprised the earliest Catholic congregation. (Courtesy of Susan Thompson.)

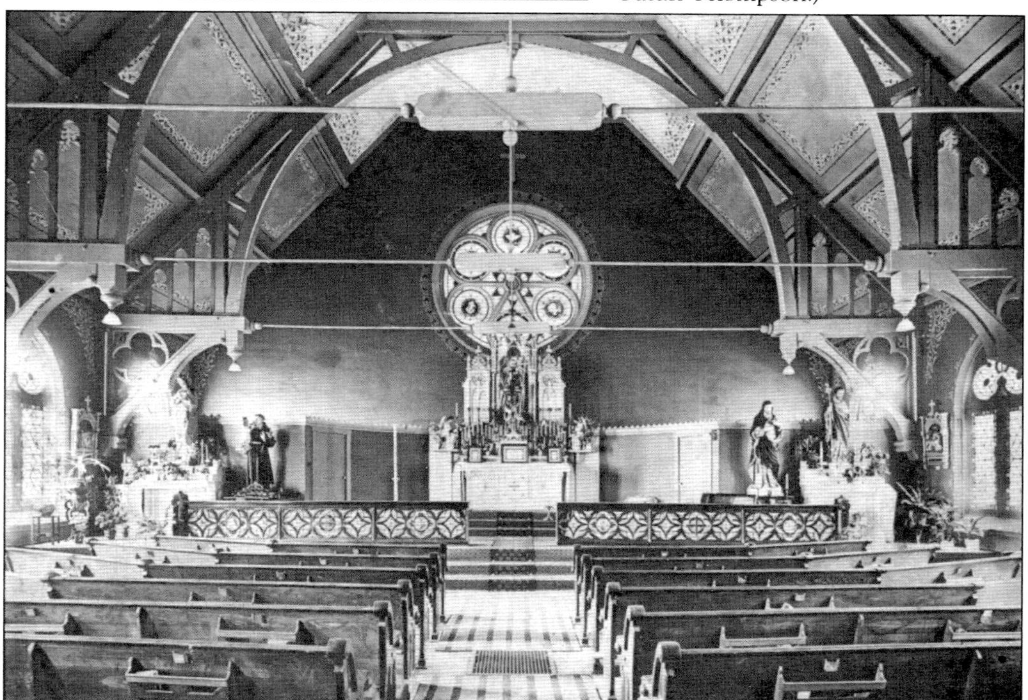

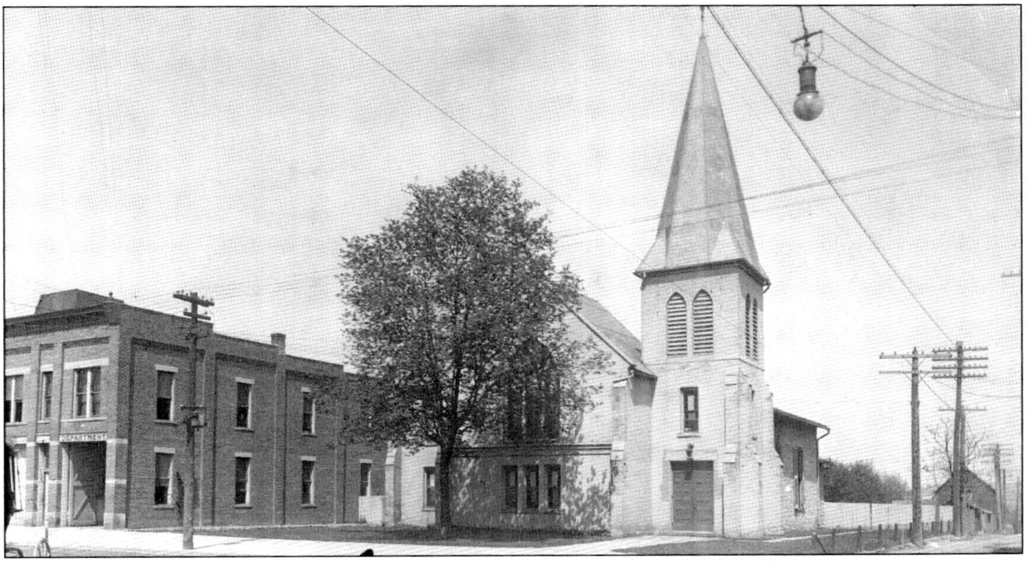

The Baptist congregation was established in 1829. Hugh Smart donated land for a church that was, at that time, outside of town to the west. The church was erected in 1830, with extensive renovations occurring in 1840 and 1883. In 1895, two rooms were added on to the east side of the church and seven memorial windows were installed.

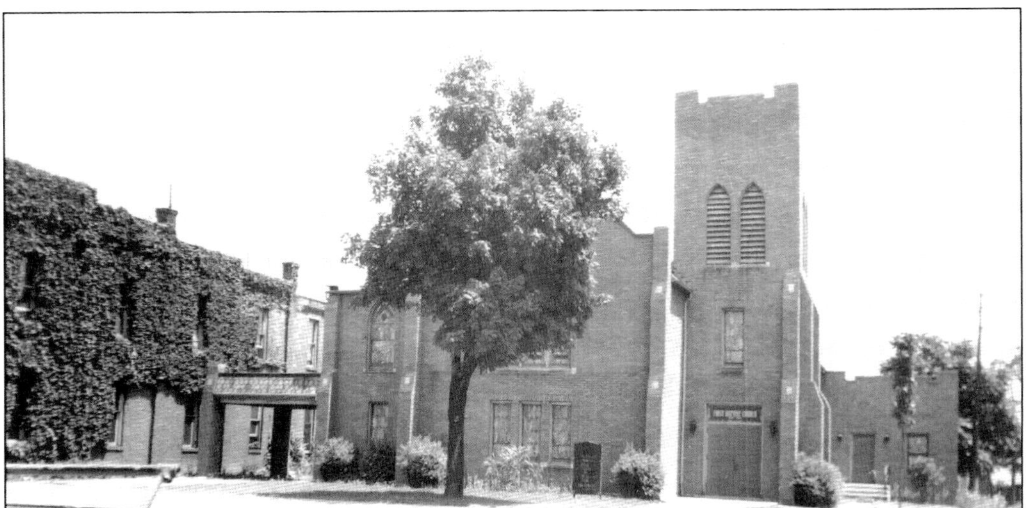

The First Baptist Church is shown here with its steeple removed. Several additions on the north and east side had also been made.

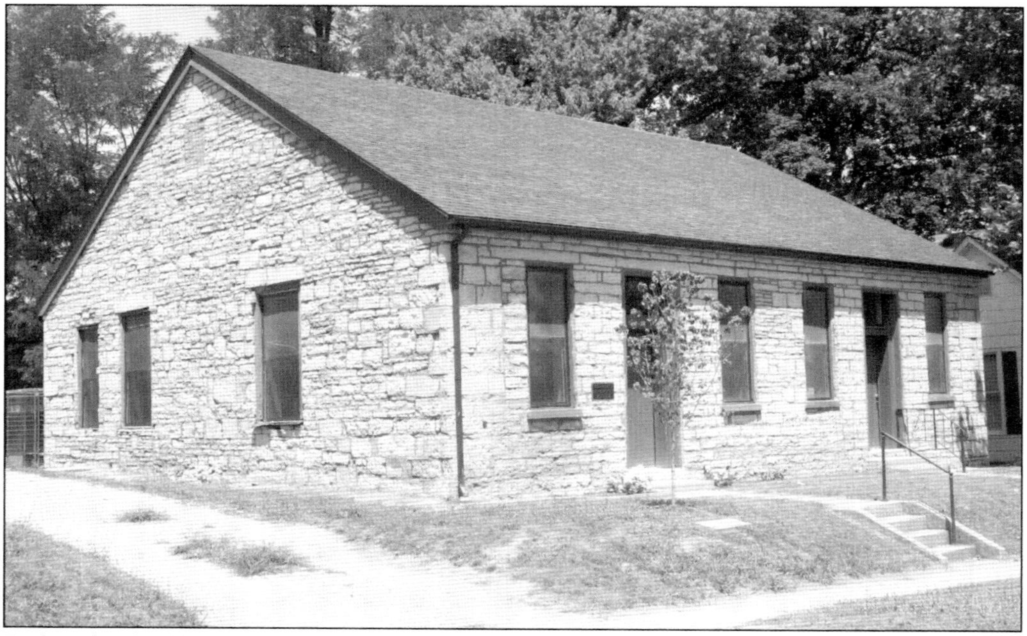

Today, this building is known as the Konneker Education Museum; however, it dates to 1835 or 1836 and has a varied history. Originally built by the Associate and Reformed Church, a Presbyterian branch, it was used as a church until 1867. It was then sold to the Greenfield Schools and served as a two-room school until 1884, when it was sold into private ownership. It was sold to the Greenfeld Historical Society in 2005.

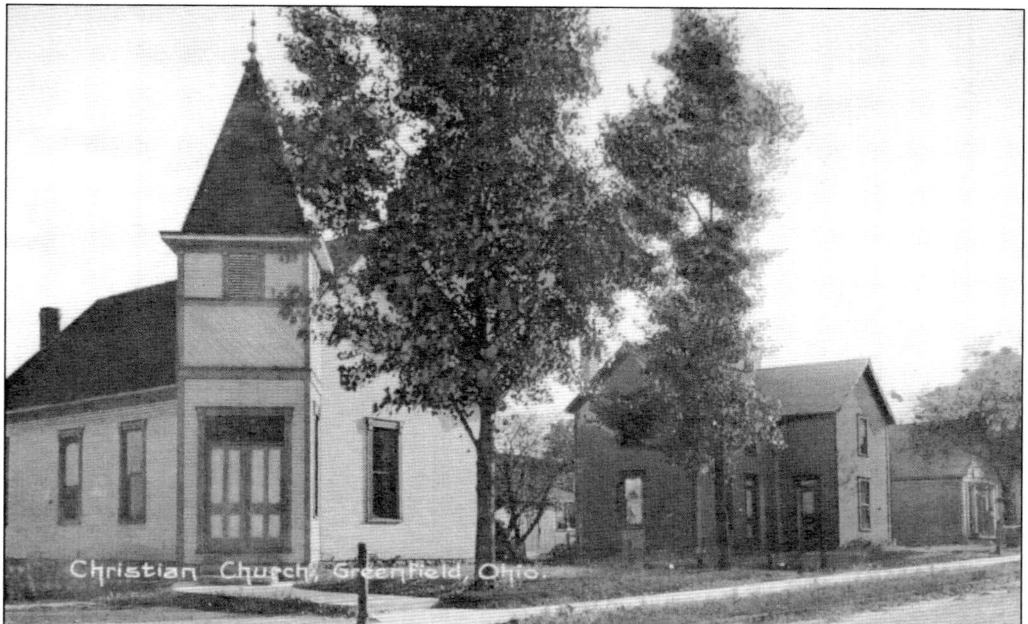

The Christian Church occupied this building on South Street near Seventh Street from 1900 to 1921 before moving to the old United Presbyterian building on S. Washington Street. This structure became the Woodmansee Ice Cream Factory and is presently three apartments.

The Masonic Temple at the northeast corner of S. Washington and South Streets has a long history in Greenfield. It was built in 1867 by the United Presbyterians. In 1921, it became the home of the Central Church of Christ. The photograph at right shows it as a church. In 1957, the Church of Christ moved to its new location at Jefferson Street and Edgewood Avenue. The Masons then bought the building to use as their lodge, as seen below.

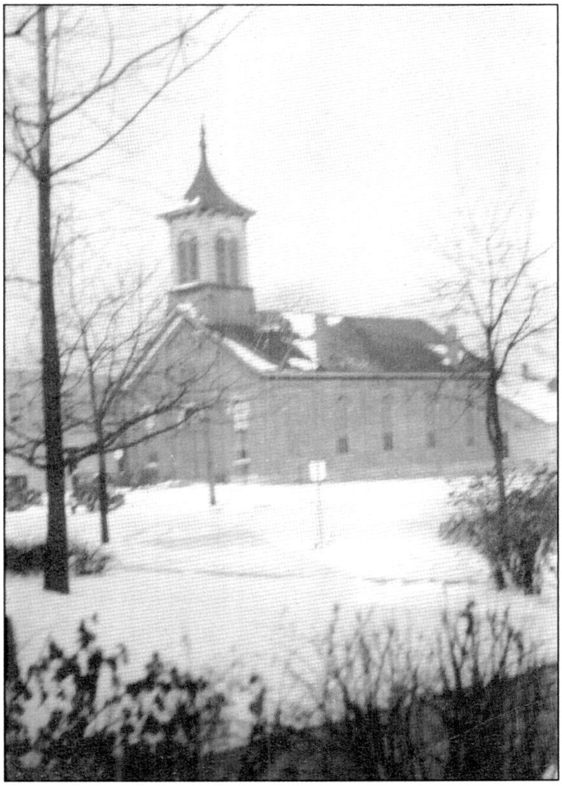

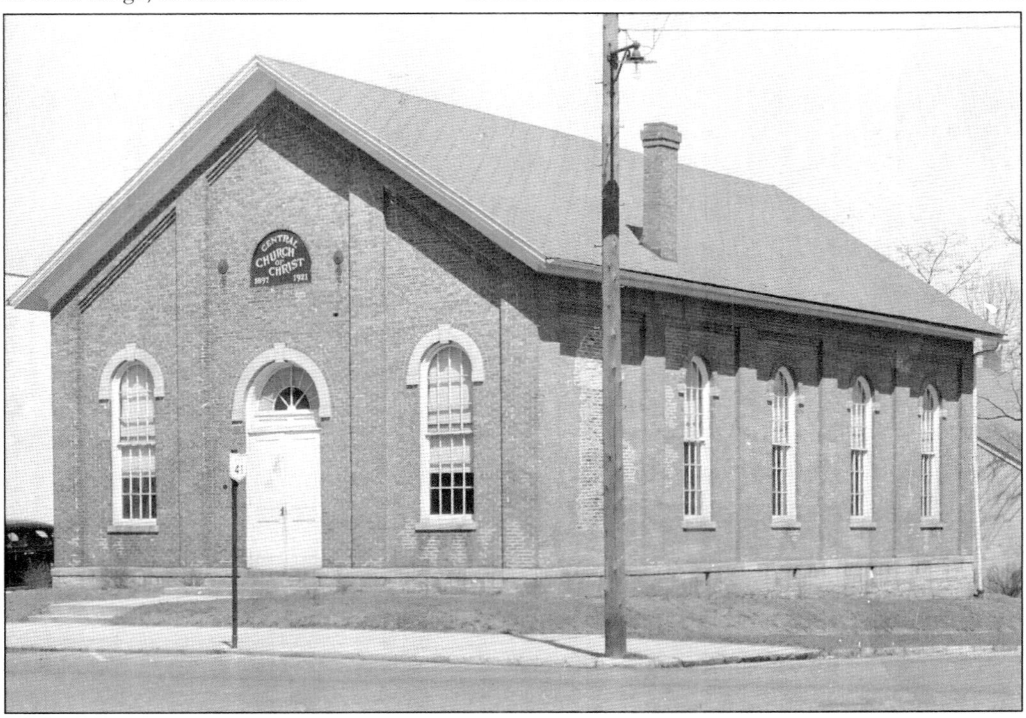

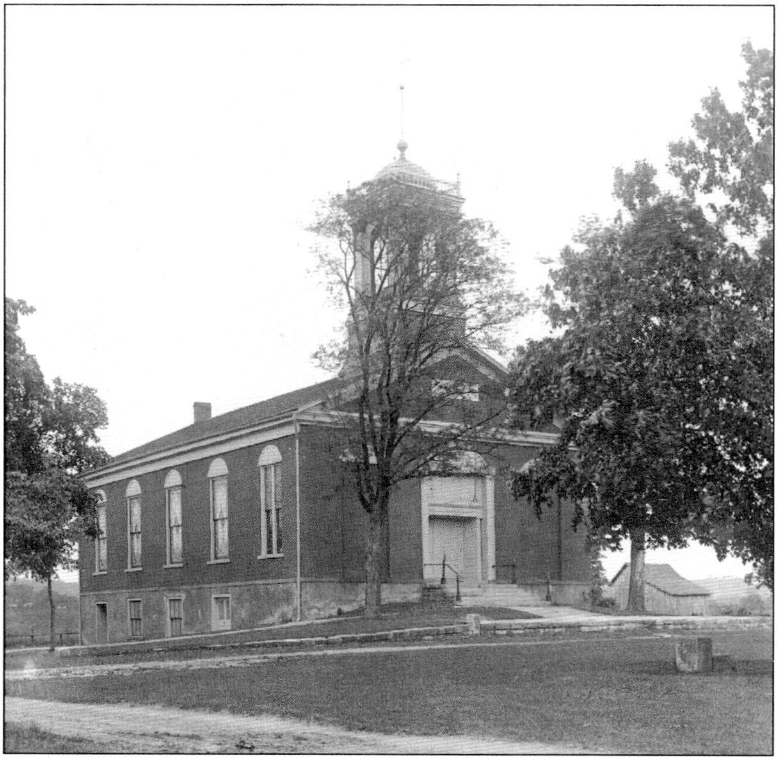

The South Salem Presbyterian Church was built in 1854–1856. Prior congregations had met as far back as 1802. The church suffered a split when differences concerning slavery arose in 1858, and a faction left to form the Free Soil Church of Greenfield. The group reunited after the Civil War. The church remains active today.

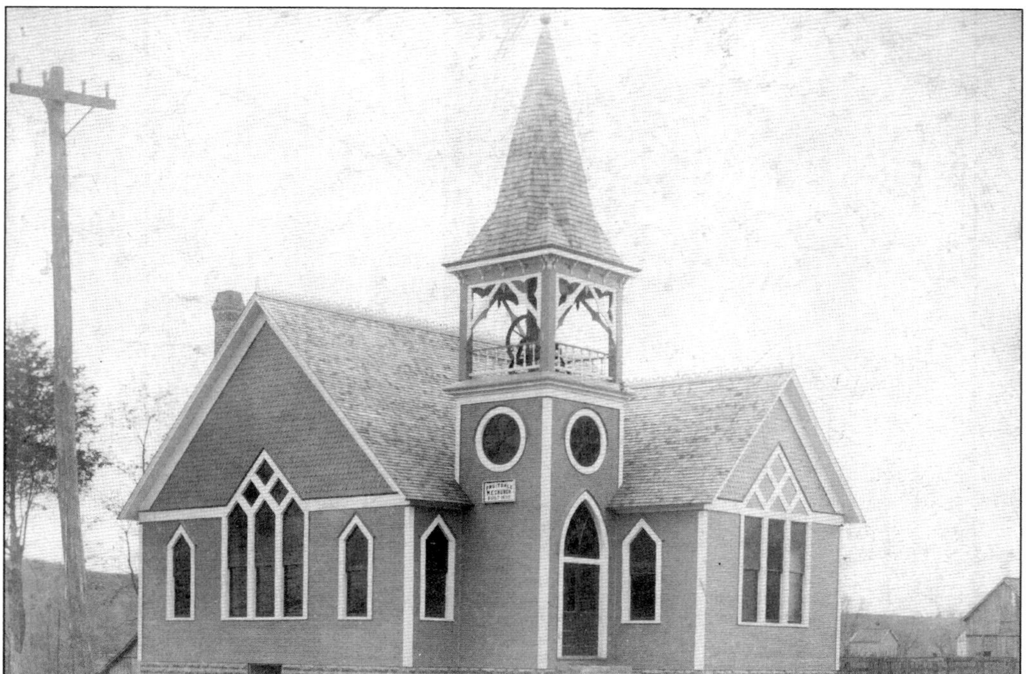

The Fruitdale Methodist Church is located south of Greenfield on State Route 41 in Fruitdale.

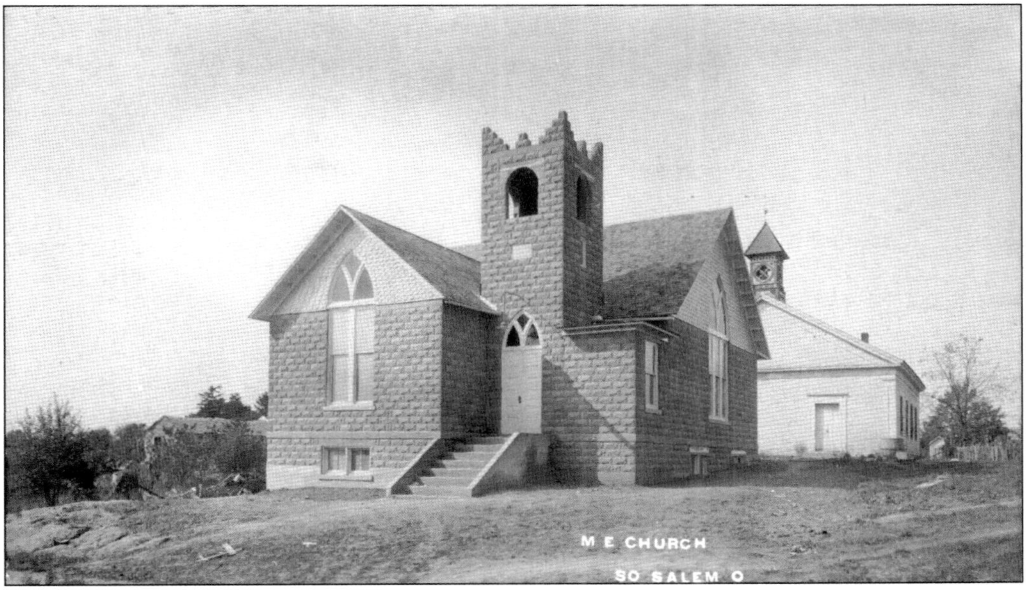

The South Salem Methodist Church is located on Broadway Street and continues operating today with an active congregation. Behind this church is the original church building. (Courtesy of Lew Speakman.)

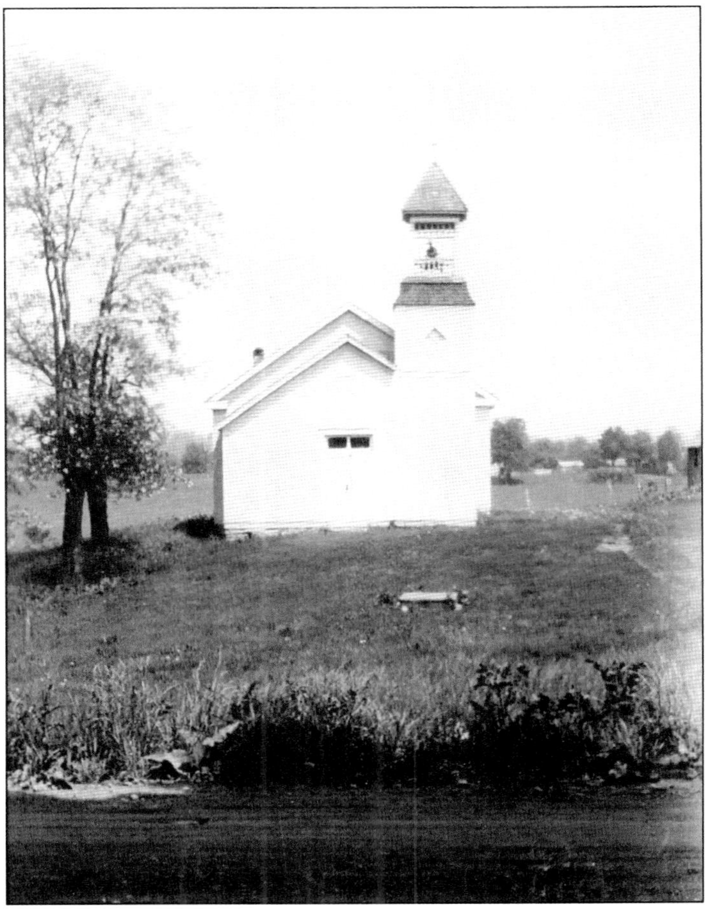

The Mt. Zion Baptist Church was built in 1851 by a Methodist congregation. It was purchased in 1878 by the Mt. Zion African American congregation. It was located on Main Street in South Salem. This building is now a private residence. (Courtesy of Lew Speakman.)

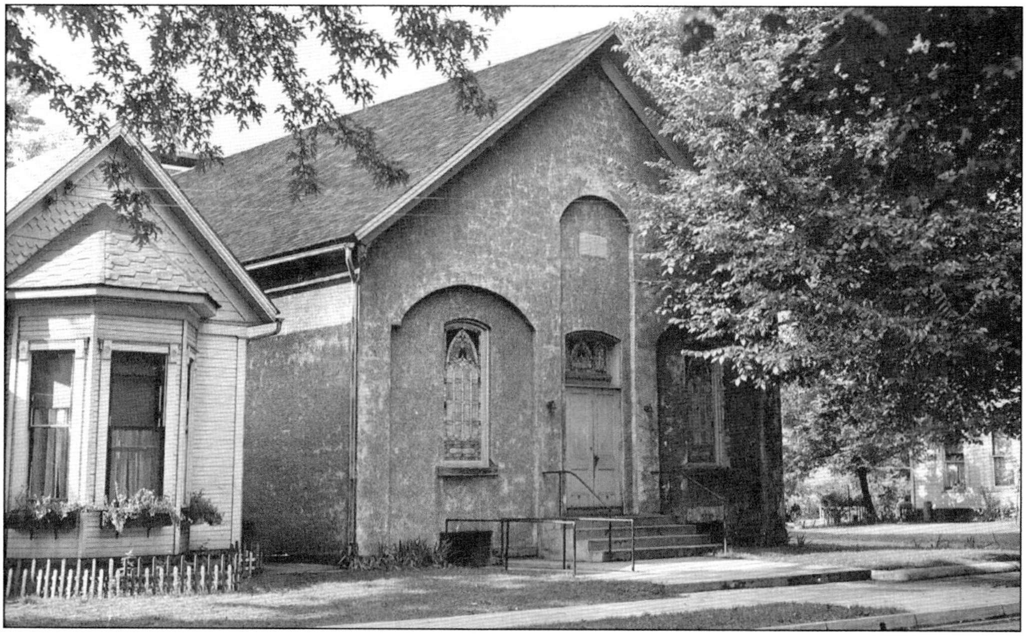

The Shiloh Baptist Church, located on Lafayette Street, was organized by black citizens on July 8, 1866, with Elder J. Powell as moderator and Elder J.M. Meek as clerk. Their initial meetings were held at a schoolhouse three miles north of Greenfield. This church was built in 1874. The building has been unused since around the 1980s.

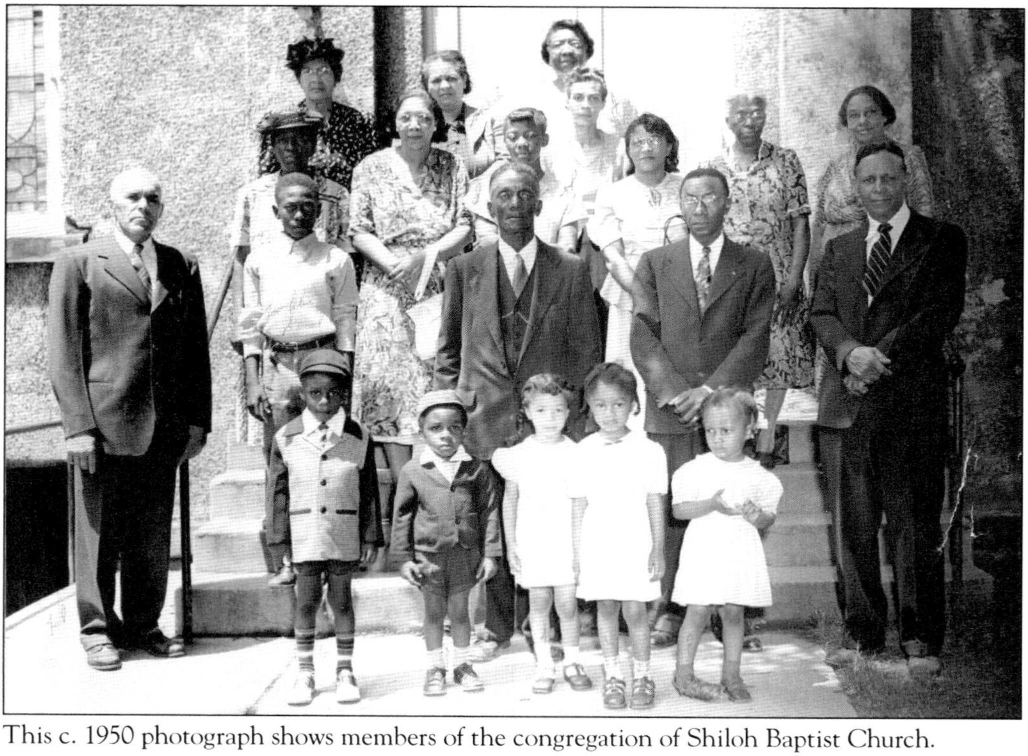

This c. 1950 photograph shows members of the congregation of Shiloh Baptist Church.

Five

Community Scenes

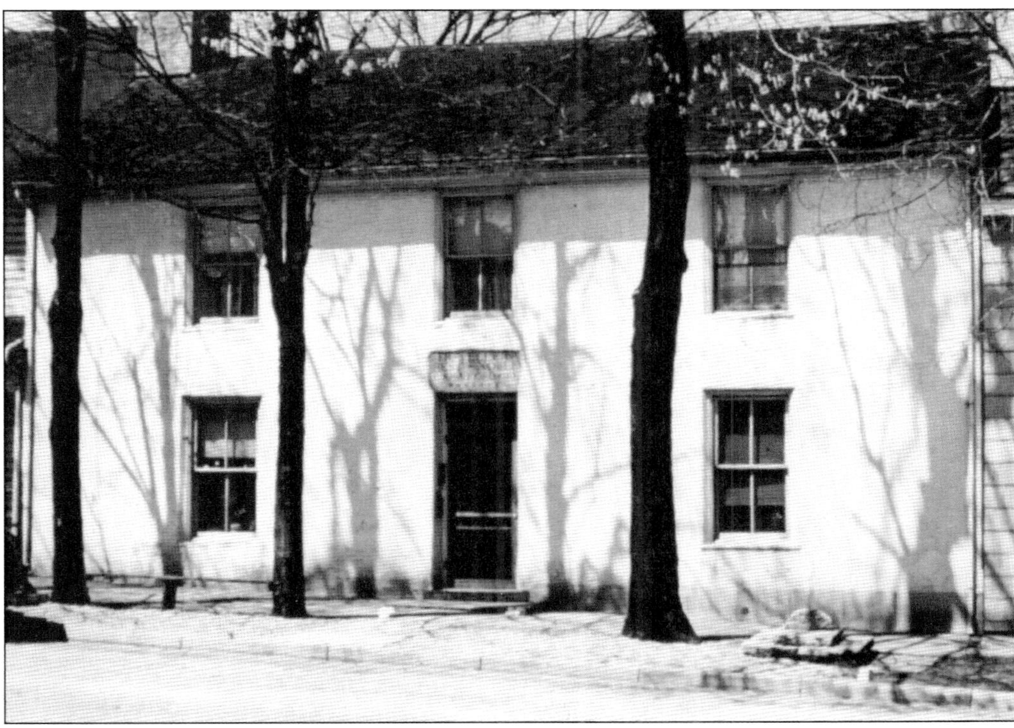

The Travellers Rest was built by Noble Crawford in 1812 on land currently occupied by a Burger King parking lot. The first stone house in Greenfield, the Travellers Rest was moved by the Greenfield Historical Society stone by stone and reassembled on its present spot at the southeast corner of Jefferson Street and McArthur Way. It was dedicated in 1974 and is one of the oldest inns still standing in Ohio. This image was captured prior to the 1974 move.

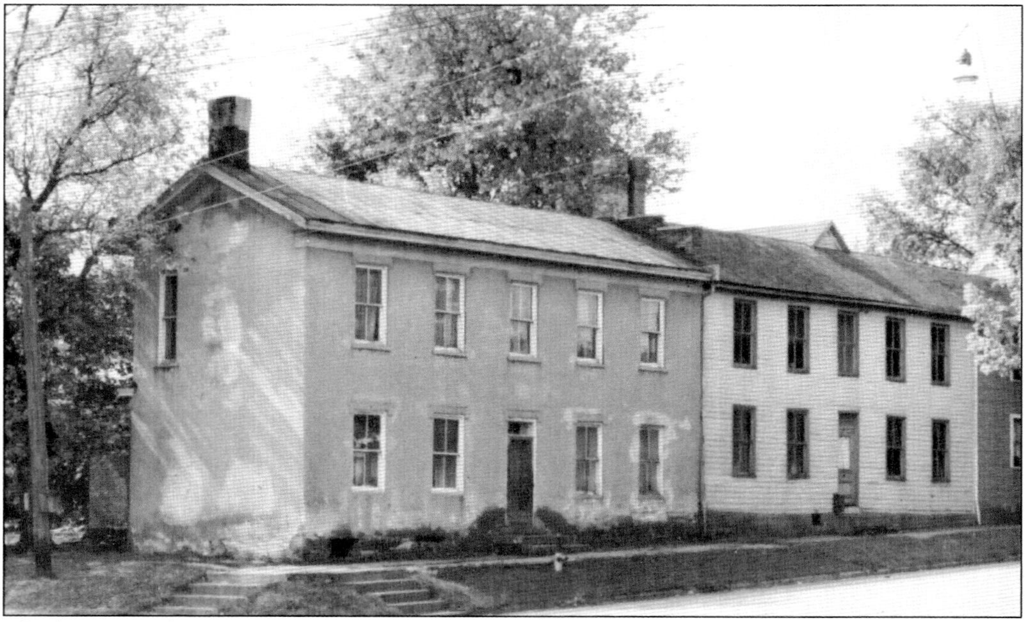

The house in the foreground was located on the current site of Merchants Drive-Thru Bank. Erected by James Boyd in the early 1820s, it imitated the design of Smith's Tannery across the street. The frame house next door, which was built later, was occupied by several generations of the Pommert family and served as an Underground Railroad stop. In 1880, Frank R. Harris was born here. Both buildings were demolished in 1962.

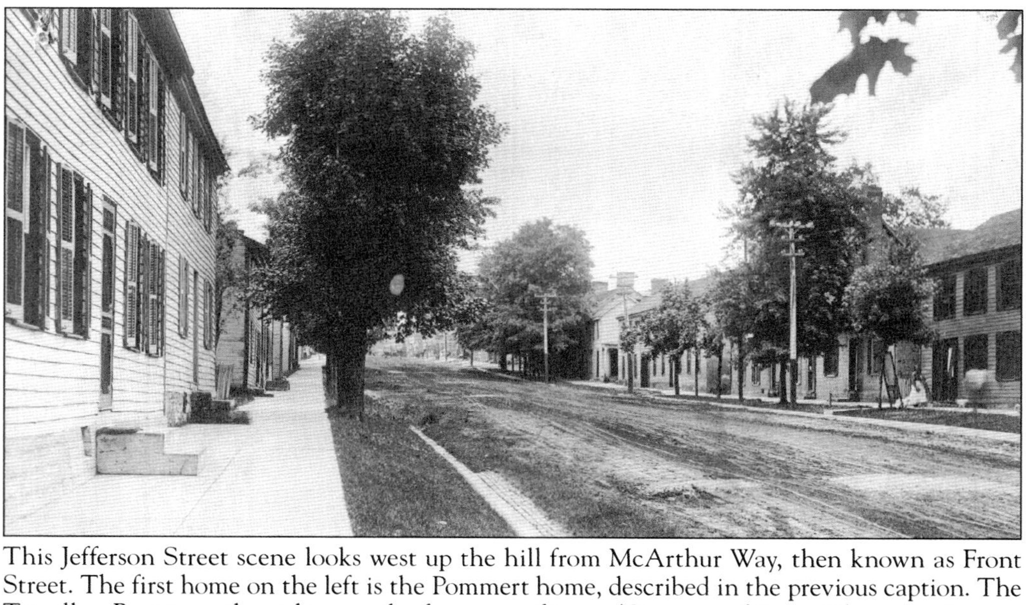

This Jefferson Street scene looks west up the hill from McArthur Way, then known as Front Street. The first home on the left is the Pommert home, described in the previous caption. The Travellers Rest is on the right near the far group of trees. (Courtesy of Susan Thompson.)

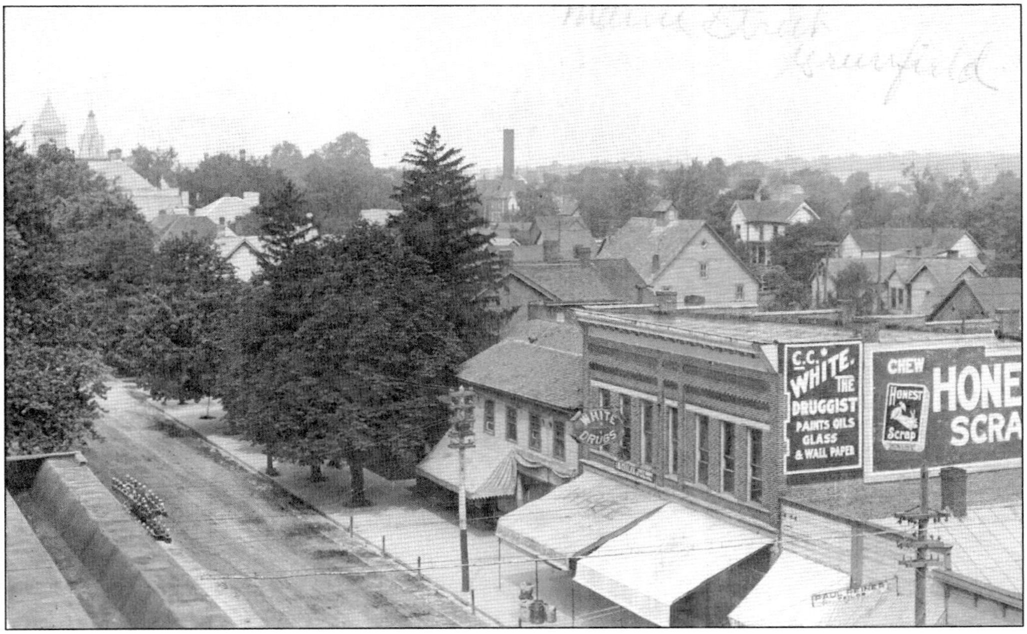

C.C. White Drug Store, at 339 Jefferson Street, dominates the foreground of this street scene. The billboard next to the White sign advertises Honest Scrap Chewing Tobacco. This building is occupied today by Scott's Pizza. The image dates to before 1923 when one of the structures with steeples, the Central School in the upper left, was removed to make way for the new elementary school.

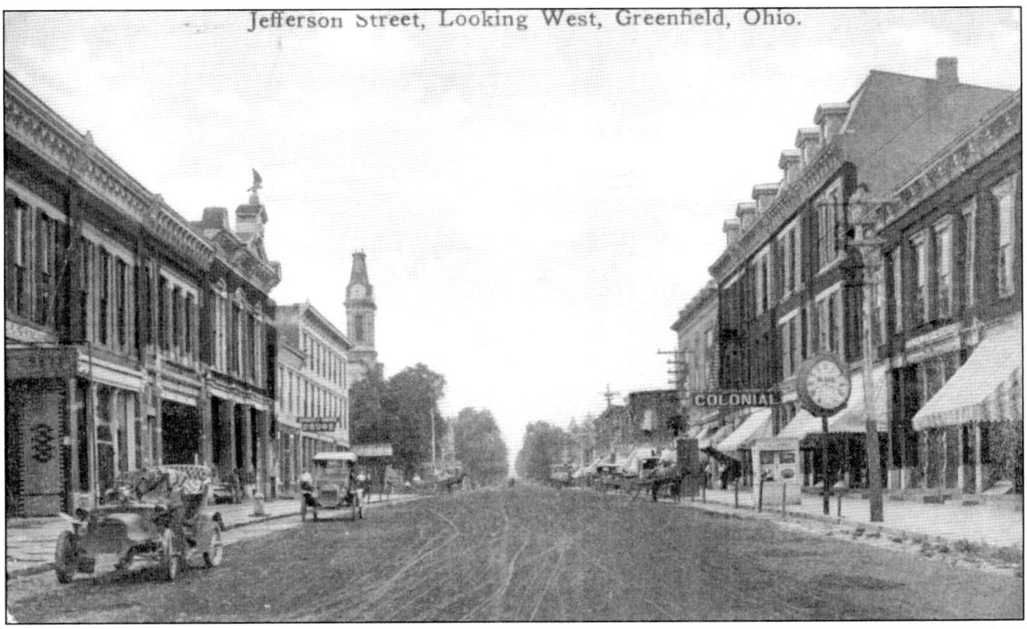

This view of the business district of Greenfield as it looked in the early 1900s shows a few landmarks that are still recognizable today. The Colonial Theater on the right operated through 1907. (Courtesy of Susan Thompson.)

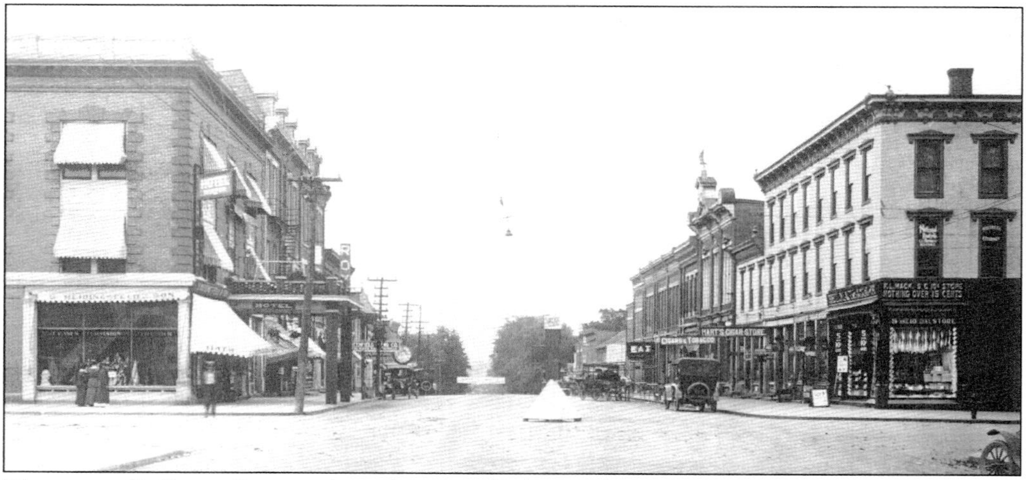

This view of Jefferson Street, taken after 1908, looks east from roughly the center of town. Careful examination of the store signs shows the Royal Theater now operating from the former site of the Colonial Theater mentioned in the previous caption. On the right, approximately three doors down from the corner, is Hart's Cigar Store. That building and the one to its west is now a gas station lot. (Courtesy of Susan Thompson.)

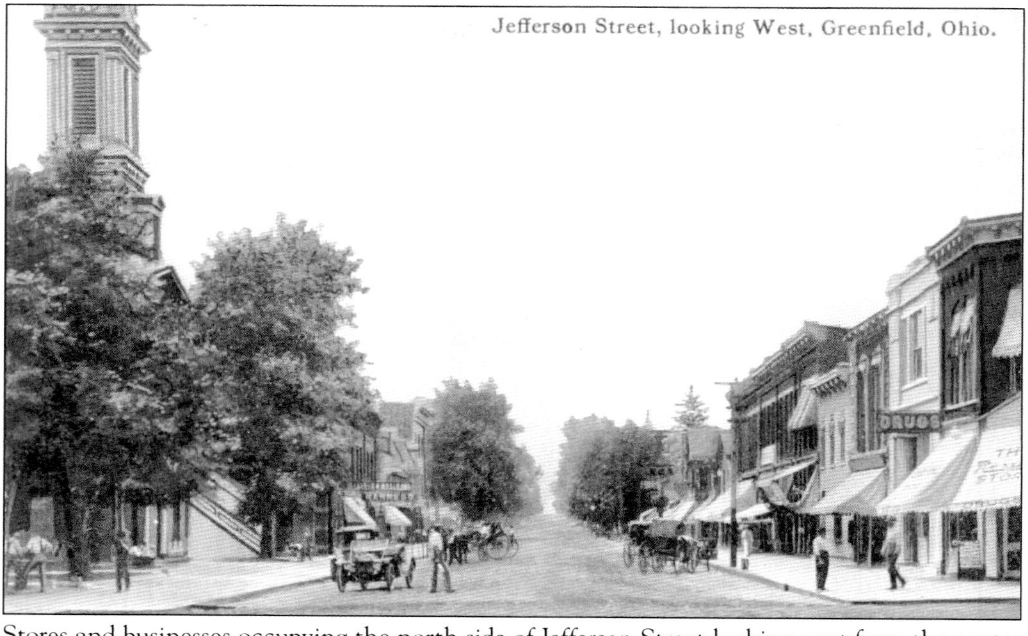

Stores and businesses occupying the north side of Jefferson Street looking west from the center of town include Christopher's Drug Store and Ice Cream Parlor, Peoples Bank, Pikes Book Store (later Gossett's), Dr. Jones' office, Jenaro Wolf's Grocery, and at the far end of the street, C.C. White Drugs. On the left, the town hall stands majestically above the trees. (Courtesy of Susan Thompson.)

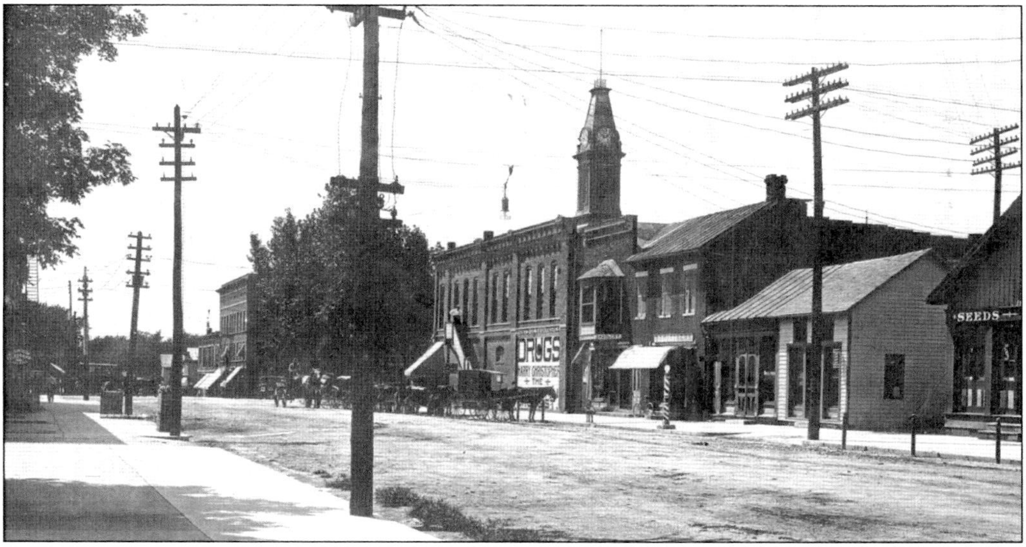

Looking south on N. Washington Street from approximately the current site of the fire department shows storefronts occupied by C.C. Norton Seeds, far right, which evolved over 100 years (1868–1968) from a general store to a wholesale and retail handler of seeds and feeds. Five generations of the Norton family operated the store. Other stores include Glenn Harris' Tailoring and Cleaning and Christopher Drug Store on the corner. (Courtesy of Susan Thompson.)

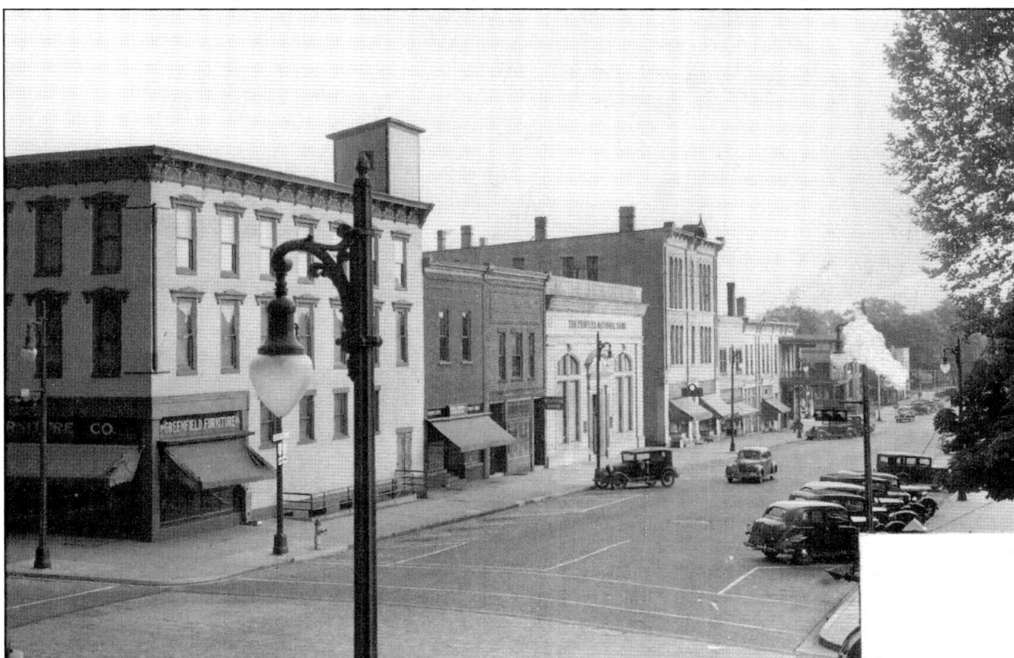

This photograph of S. Washington Street, taken in the 1930s or 1940s, features the Smart Building on the left corner, which housed Greenfield Furniture. The building with the rounded window tops was the location of the Peoples Bank, established in 1936. Today, it houses the Merchants Bank.

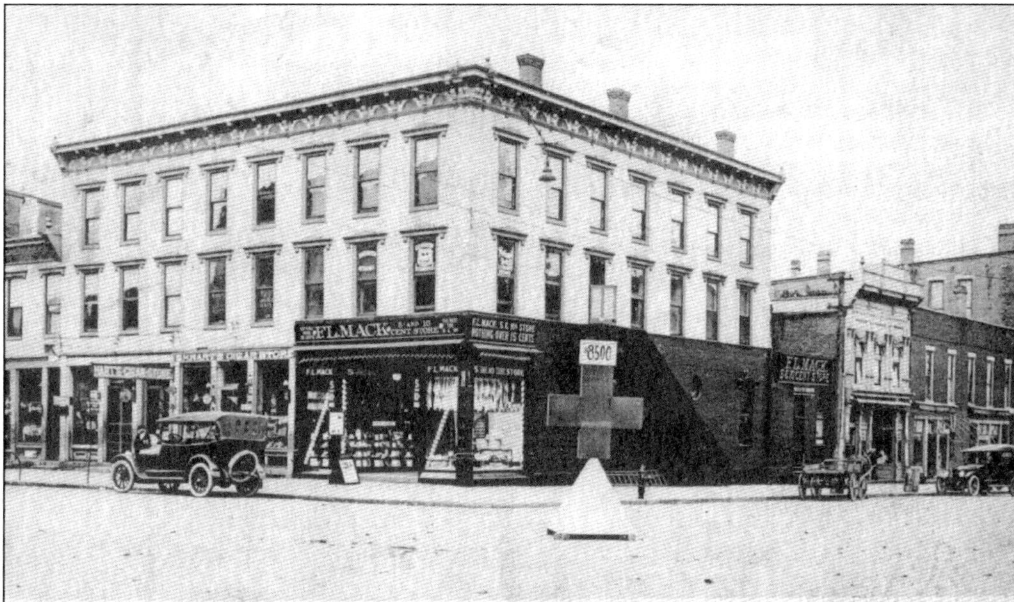

F. L. Mack, 5 & 10¢ Store, Corner Washington and Jefferson Street, Greenfield, Ohio.

The Smart Block occupied the southeast corner of Jefferson and Washington Streets. It provided space for a number of businesses over the years, including F.L. Mack 5 & 10 Cents Store, which operated on the first floor. In 1900, Otis Long jumped from the roof of this building to test the Browder Life Saving Net. The Smart Building was razed in 1967. (Courtesy of Susan Thompson.)

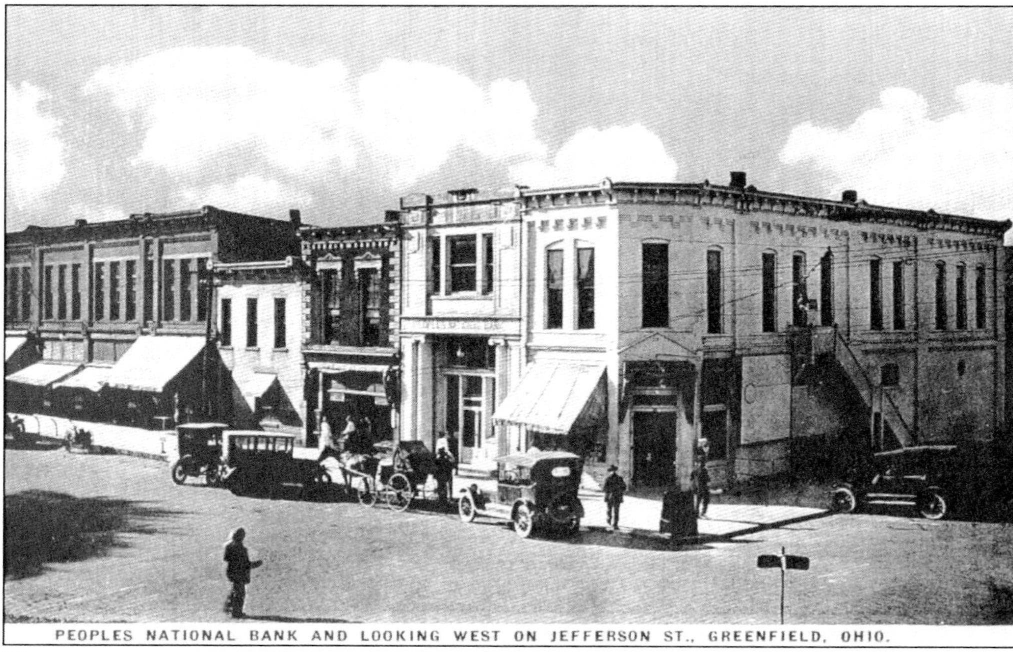

PEOPLES NATIONAL BANK AND LOOKING WEST ON JEFFERSON ST., GREENFIELD, OHIO.

The northwest corner of Jefferson and Washington Streets is known to some as the "Round Corner." Christopher's Drug Store occupied the corner store; Peoples National Bank was in the white building next to Christopher's. (Courtesy of Susan Thompson.)

The Pythian Castle was dedicated in 1894 with an impressive banquet hosted by H.G. Simons, master of ceremonies. The third floor was occupied by the McClain Lodge No. 262 of the Knights of Pythias, which had been organized in 1887. An old newspaper clipping reported, "this prosperous lodge has purchased elegant rooms . . . in the Pythian building . . . which they have furnished in fine style."

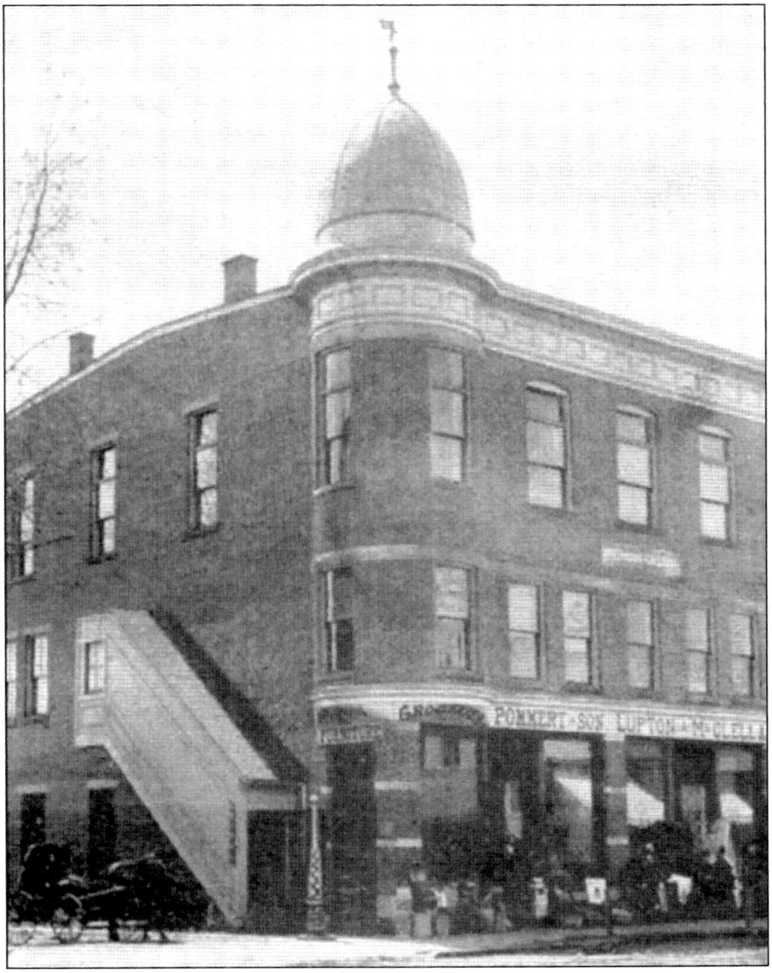

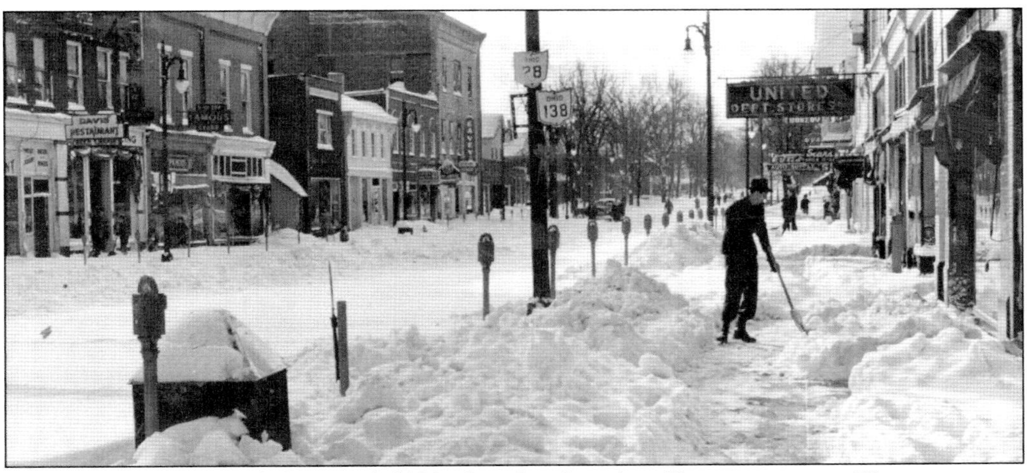

The great storm of 1950 left Greenfield blanketed under piles of heavy, wet snow. This snowstorm occurred the same weekend of the Snow Bowl, when Ohio State hosted Michigan.

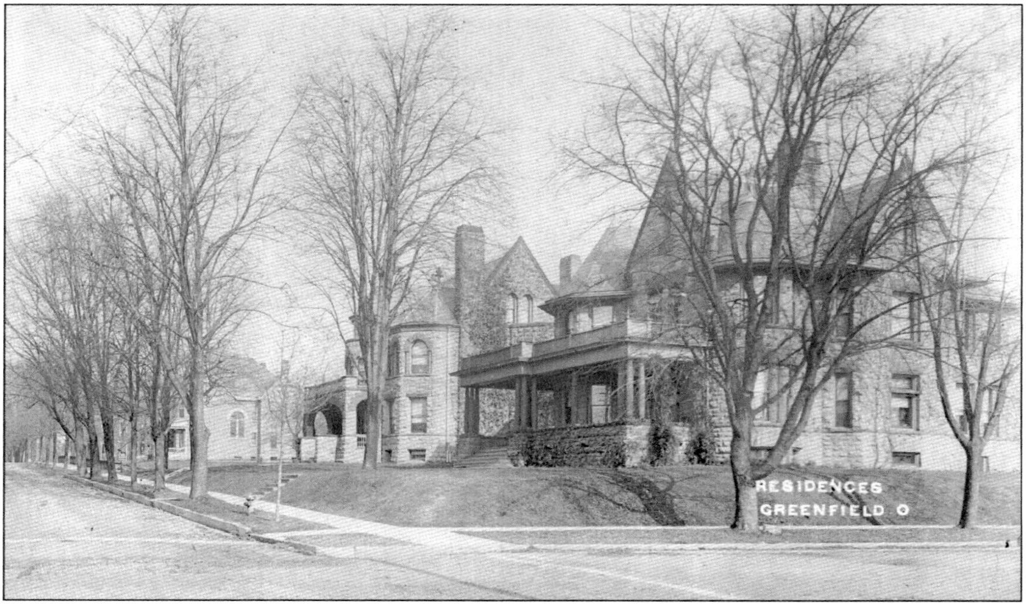

The three stone residences on S. Second Street were all built using stone from Rucker's Quarry. The home at 245 S. Second Street, in the foreground, was built in 1898 for Dwight O. and Madge Miller; he was a banker for Highland County Bank. (Courtesy of Tom Smith.)

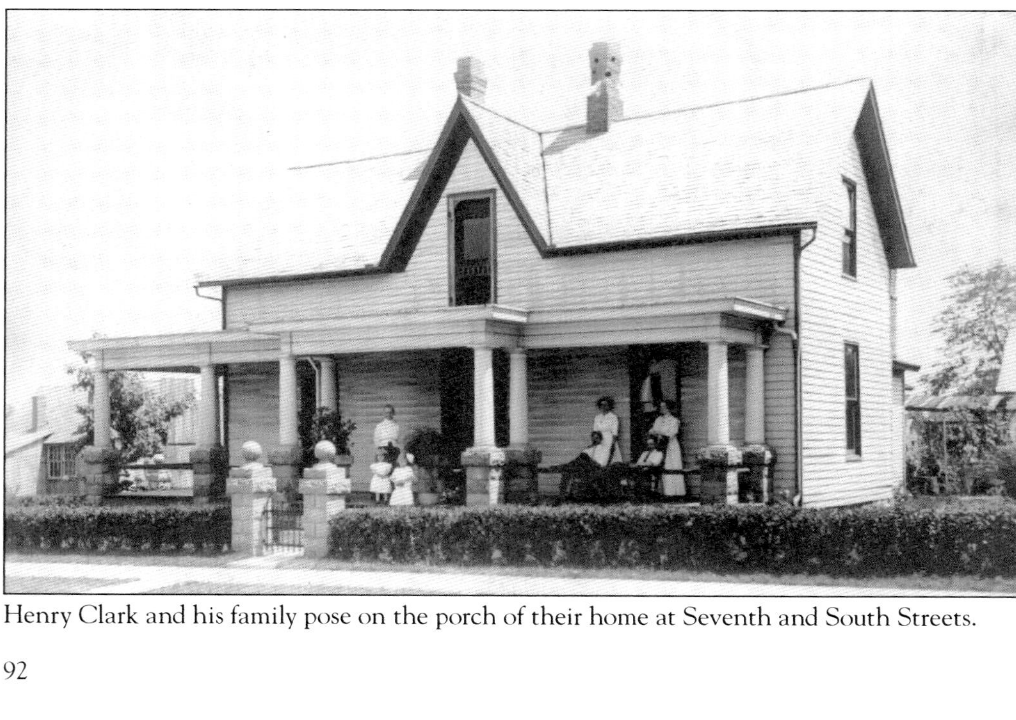

Henry Clark and his family pose on the porch of their home at Seventh and South Streets.

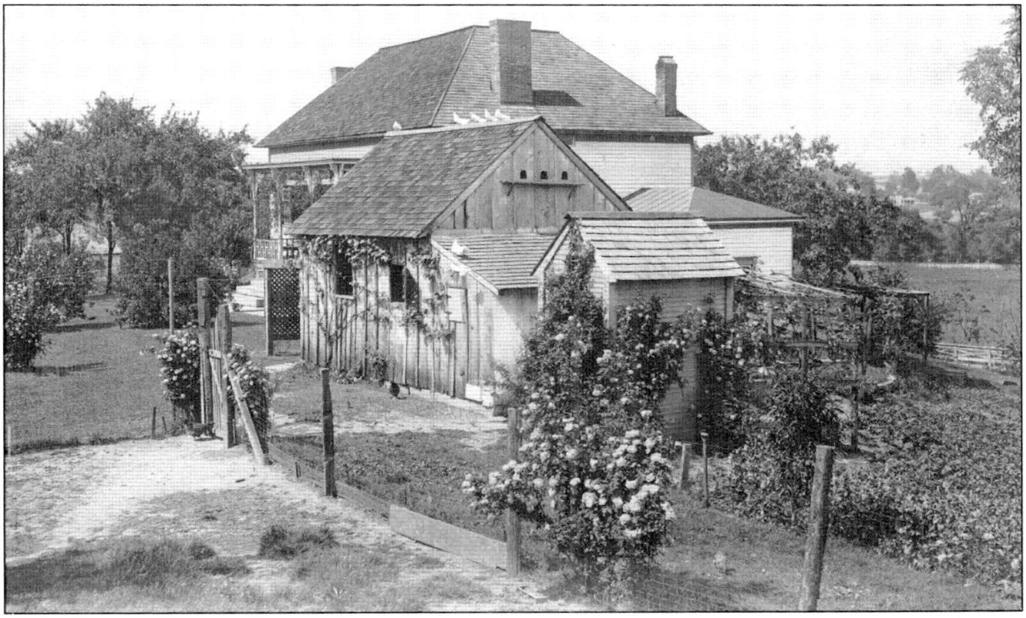

According to census records in 1900, this was the residence of Dr. F.P. Crowe on Paint Street; the house is still standing. Note the well-manicured gardens, arbors, and yard. The doctor's office was at 208 S. Washington Street.

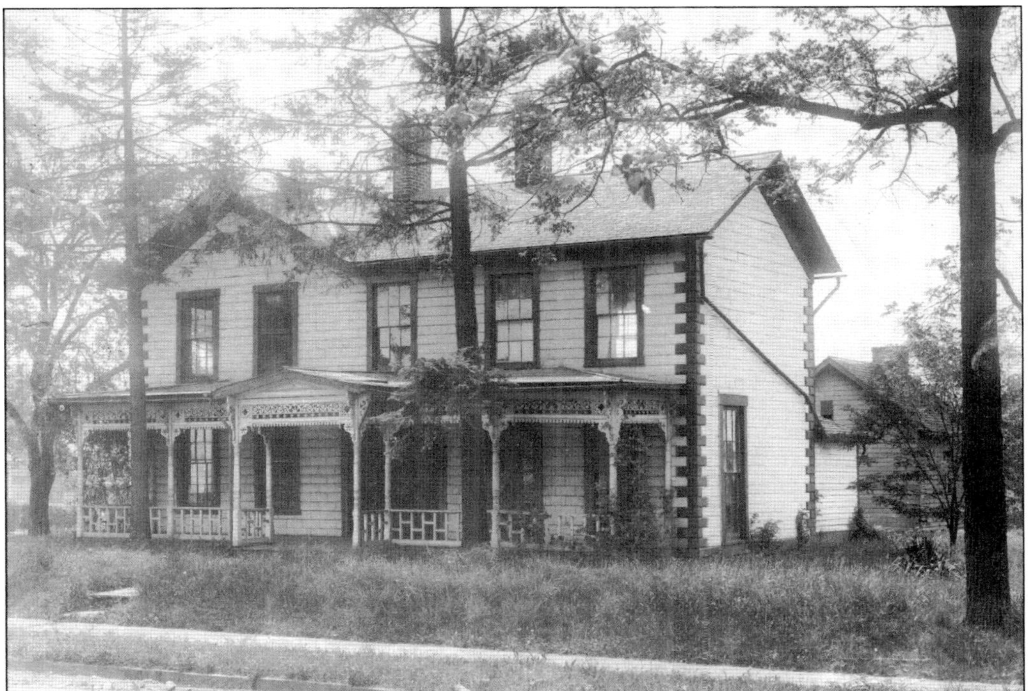

This ornately decorated Victorian home was located at 604 South Street; the hospital parking lot currently occupies this site.

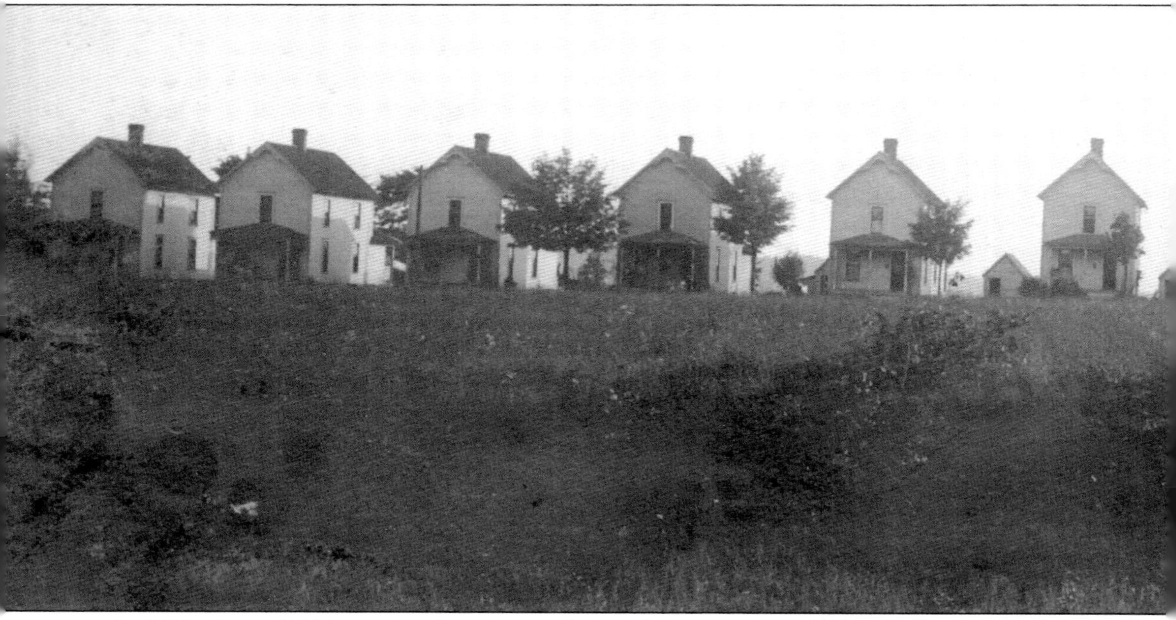

In 1890, Greenfield became a boomtown due to the expansion of E.L. McClain manufacturing Company (later TAPATCO). McClain's brother Arthur McClain built 12 two-story homes costing

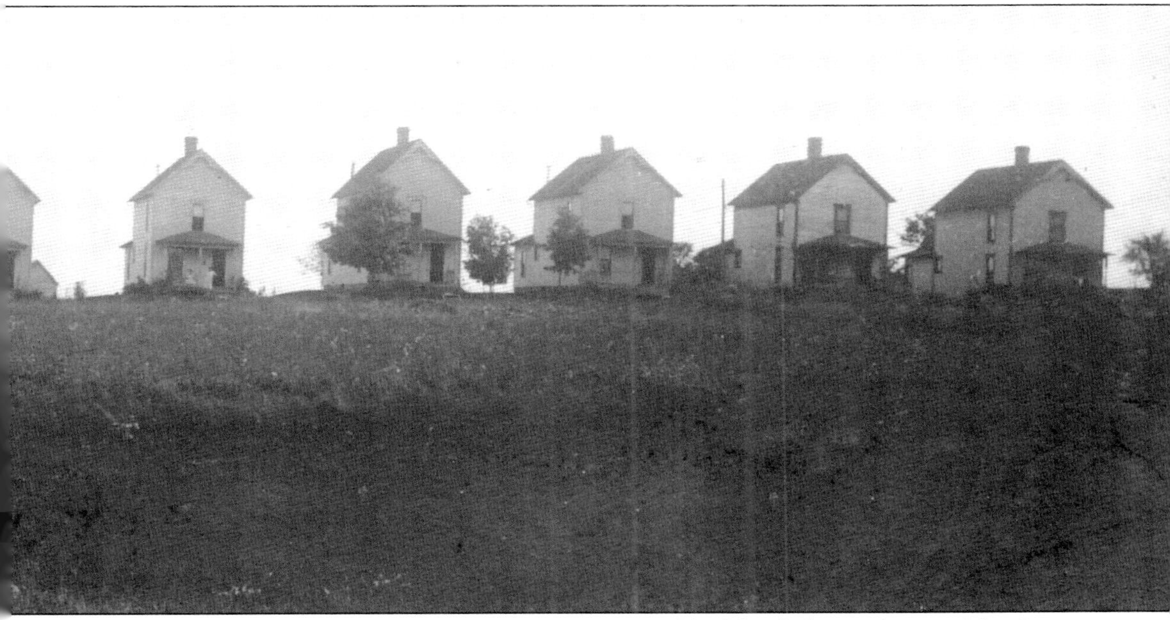

$750 each on Waddell Street, known then as "C" Street. Dubbed fondly by residents as "the dirty dozen," eleven of the homes are still standing.

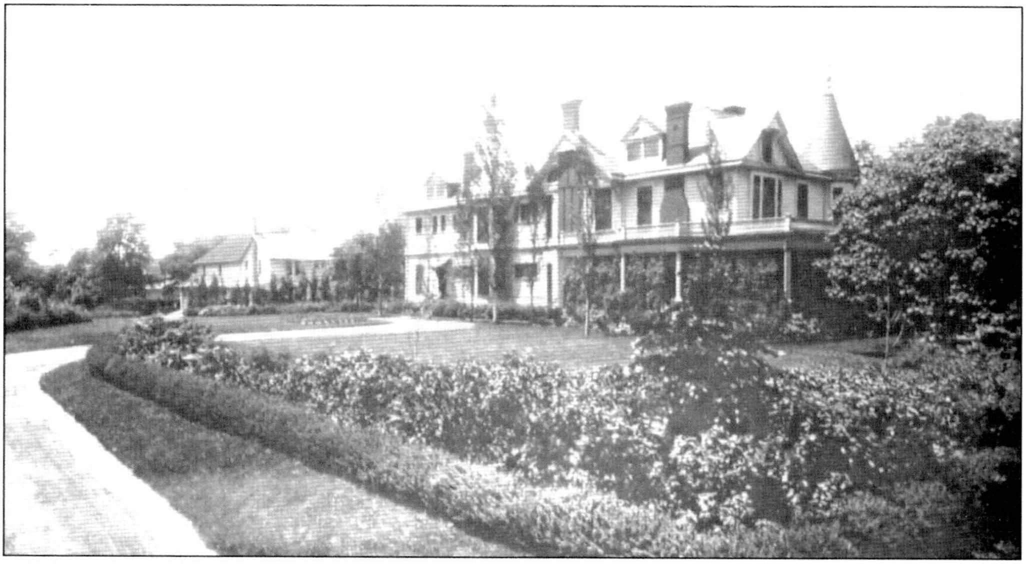

The home of Edward Lee and Lulu McClain stood at 330 S. Washington Street. The family moved in during 1887, after having it built to their specifications. It was demolished after Lulu's death in 1947, per her final request.

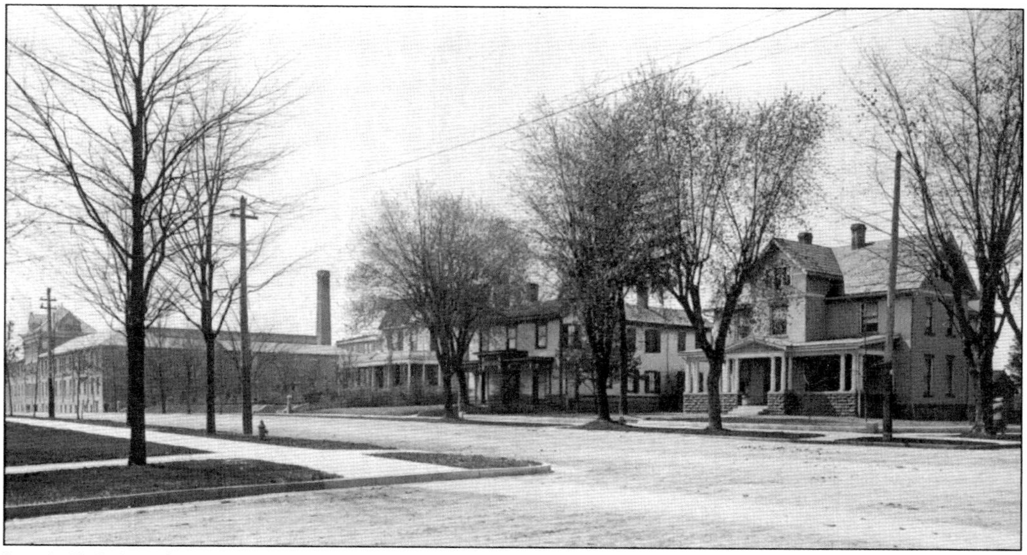

In 1915, S. Washington Street was lined with these beautiful homes. On the right is the Charles Mains Sr. home. Next door is the double home occupied by Dr. Bliss Glenn and George Morehouse, followed by the E.L. McClain home. TAPATCO is located just past the McClain home. The only structure remaining today is the Mains home, now the Anderson/Strueve Funeral Home.

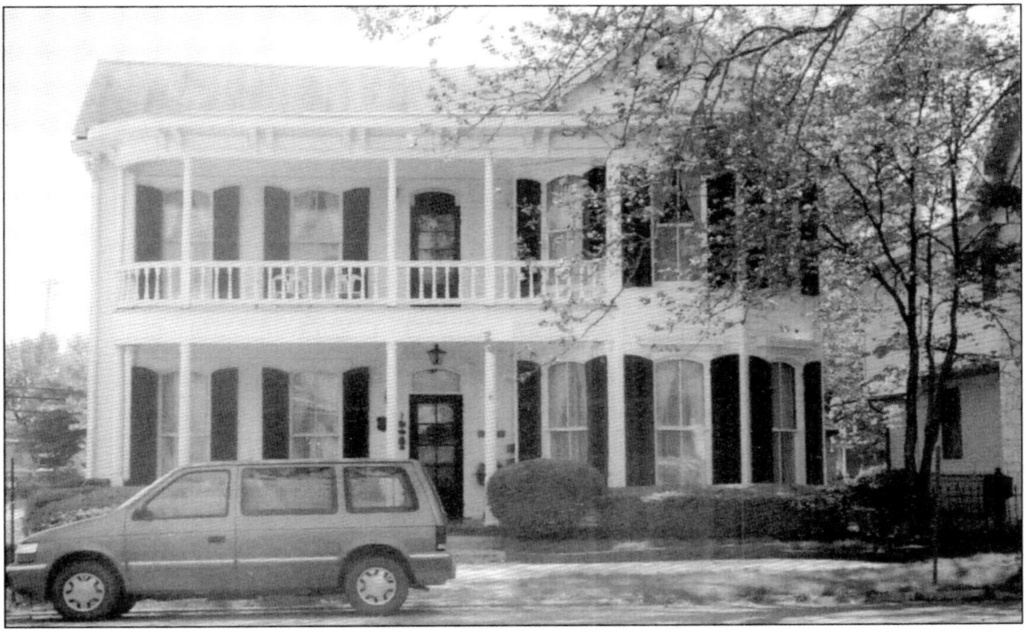

The home at 424 Jefferson Street was built in 1871 by Albert Mackerly (1850–1908). He studied law under Judge Alfred Dickey, was appointed postmaster in 1890, and was elected mayor in 1892. The house is referred to by some as the "Showboat House," as its long second-story porch resembles a Mississippi riverboat.

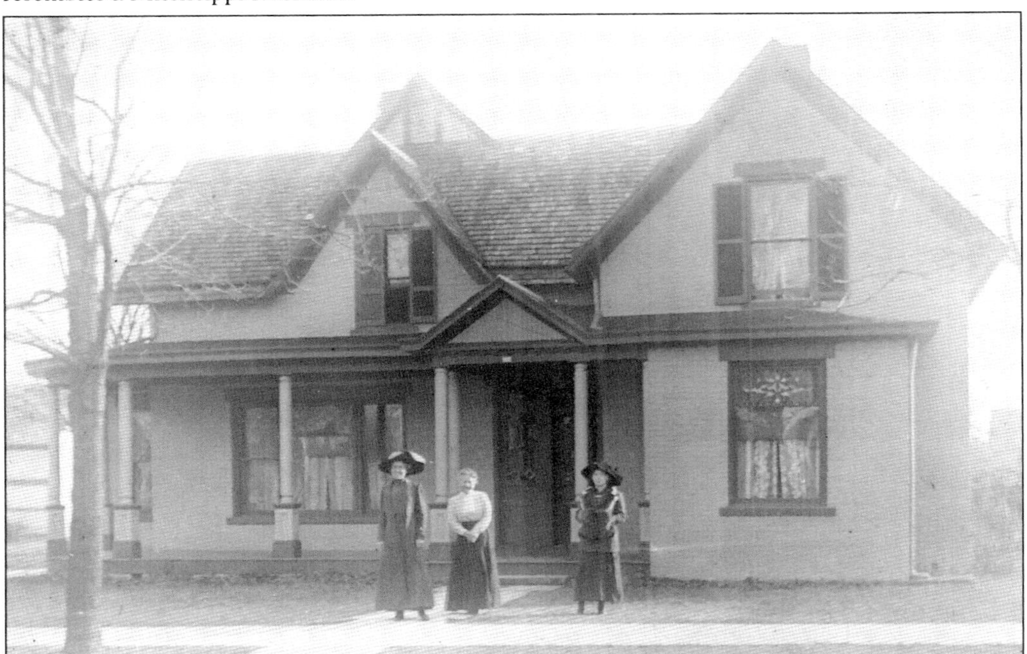

This home at 608 Jefferson Street was known as the James Fullerton House. The ladies pictured are believed to be Emma Fullerton, center, with her two daughters Elizabeth, left, and Emily. (Courtesy of Susan Thompson.)

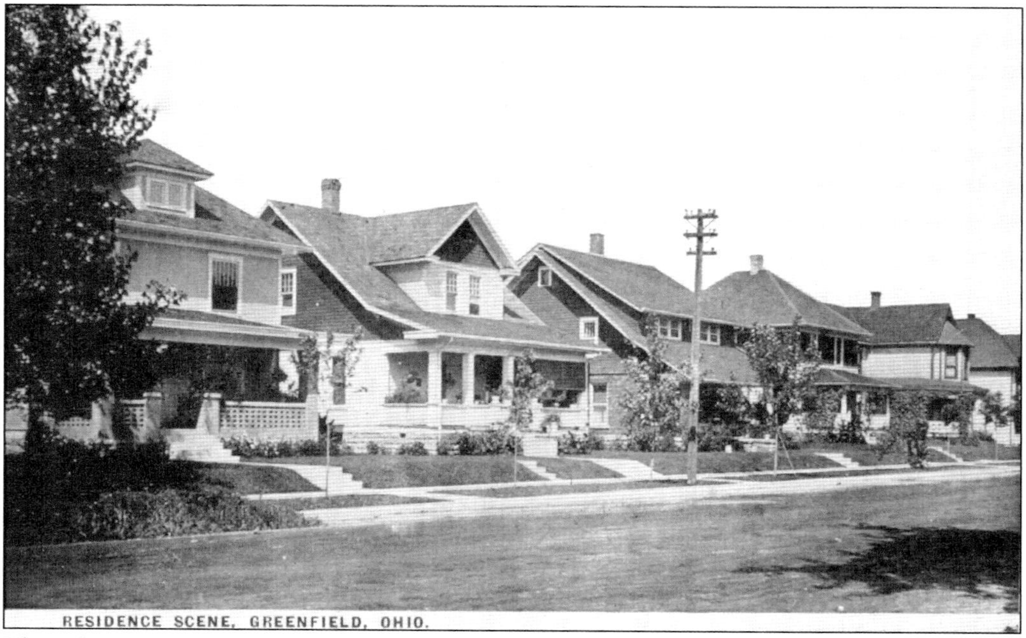

These homes are on the north side of Jefferson Street between Seventh and Eighth Streets. (Courtesy of Susan Thompson.)

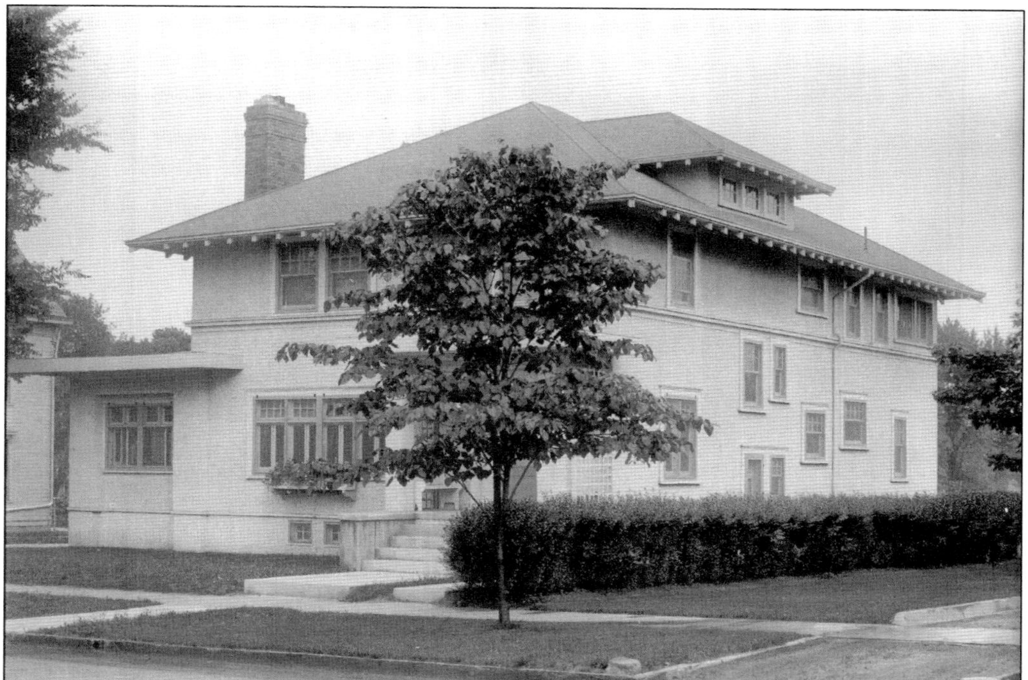

This is the South Street home of W. Forrest Woodmansee. After a career as an ice cream maker, he was elected mayor of Greenfield in 1939 with three consecutive terms, establishing a record tenure. He was the first mayor to devote his entire time to the duties of the office.

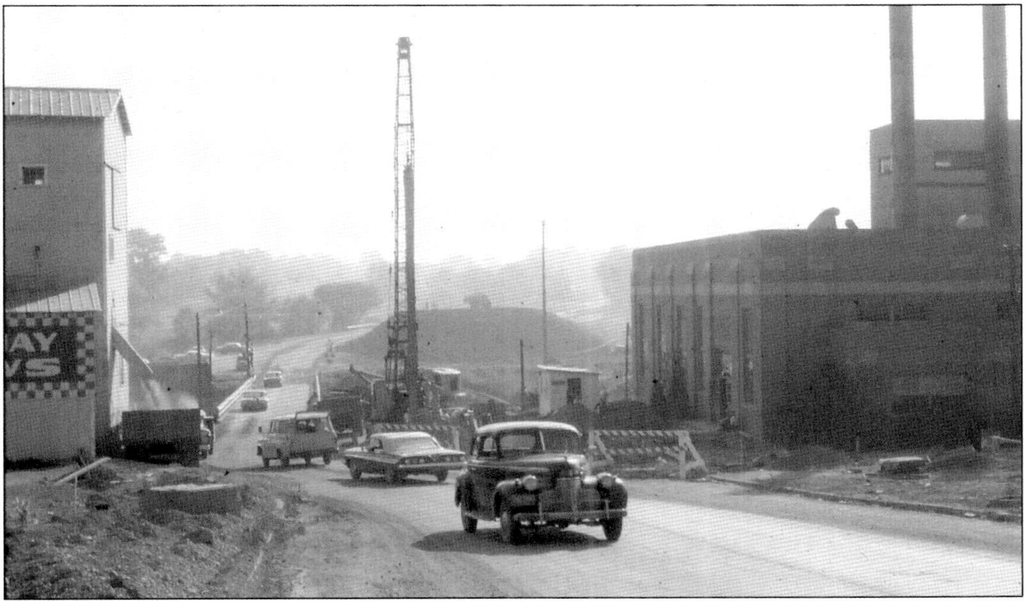

In 1962, the old bridge that carried State Route 28 over Paint Creek was replaced with a new modern bridge. The temporary bridge shown in this picture kept traffic moving throughout the construction process. On the right is the city power plant, while on the left is the grain mill of the Greenfield Grain and Hay. (Courtesy of Robert Smith.)

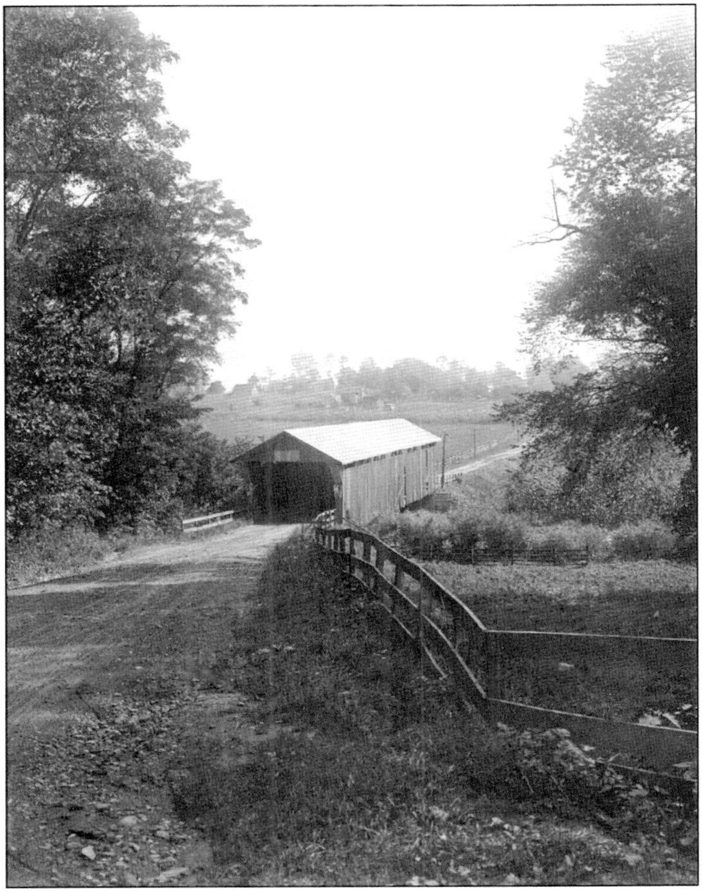

The covered bridge over Buckskin Creek in South Salem is called Caldwell Crossing Bridge and was built in 1873. Nameplates on both ends of the bridge were placed by Lee Nott. It has been said that the bridge is a nice place to rest on a hot summer day.

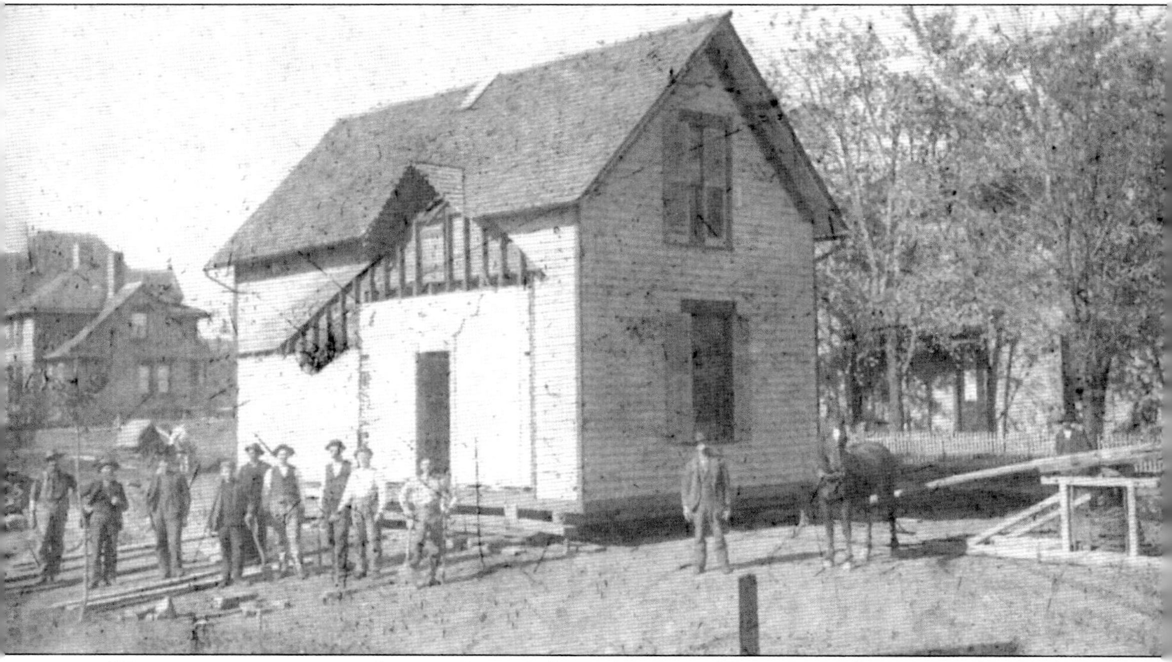

House moving was a much more frequently used option 100 years ago than it is today. J.H. Moon House Movers coordinated this house's relocation. The crew paused for this picture with the house sitting in the street in front of 127 South Street. The house to the left in the background is the D.O. Miller home on the corner of South and Second Streets. The new location of this house is unknown. (Courtesy of Bill and Terry Figgins.)

Six

School Bells

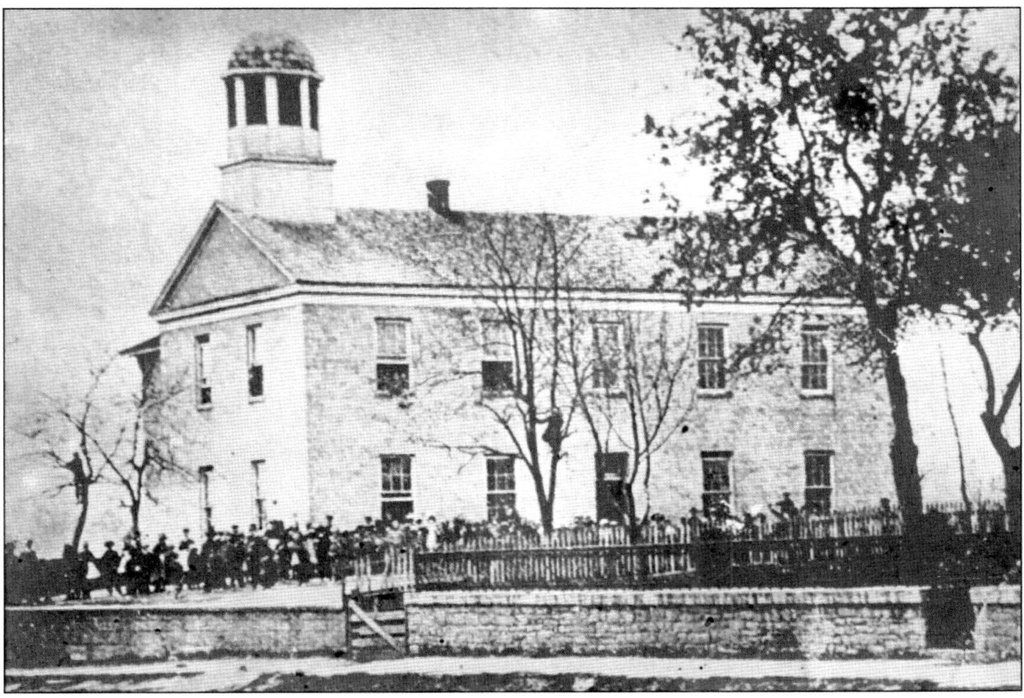

The creation of the Greenfield Seminary began with a September 1845 meeting of community leaders who hoped to provide a school that had "full collegiate powers." Ground breaking occurred on March 26, 1846, on two lots on the west side of S. Washington Street, almost opposite Pine Street. Pictured here is the seminary as it looked in 1851. The seminary operated only until 1852, but did serve as an educational facility for several years after that. The bell from this building is now located in the bell tower outside Greenfield Elementary School on Fifth Street. (Courtesy of Susan Thompson.)

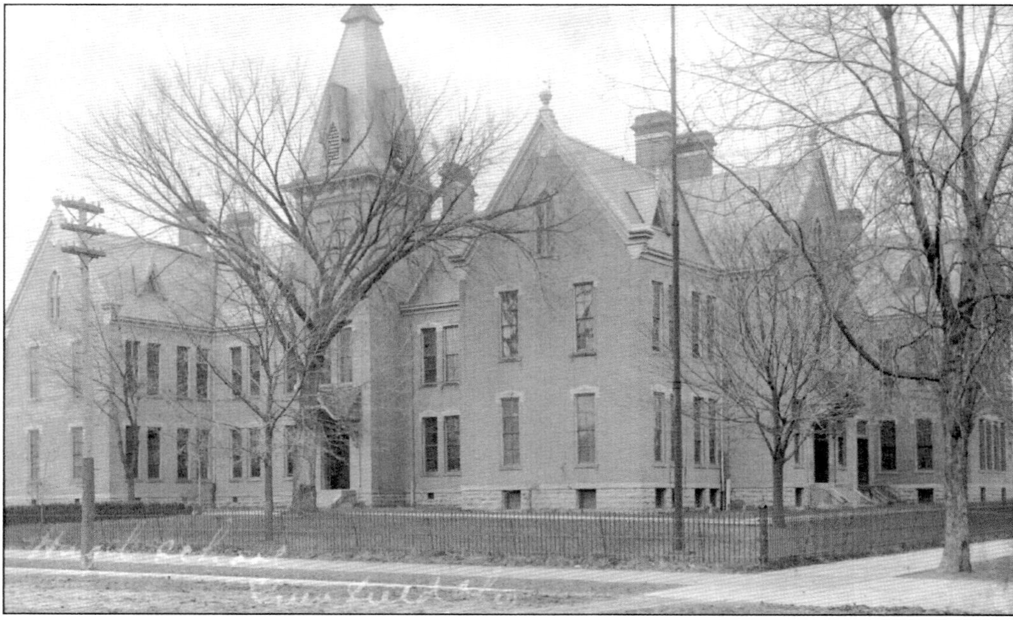

Central School was located at the present site of Greenfield Middle School. Affectionately referred to as "Old Central," it was constructed in 1884 to meet the expanding educational needs of a growing population. Central was surrounded by a spacious lawn, large trees, and a wrought iron fence to discourage trespassers after hours, as there were no extracurricular activities. (Courtesy of Susan Thompson.)

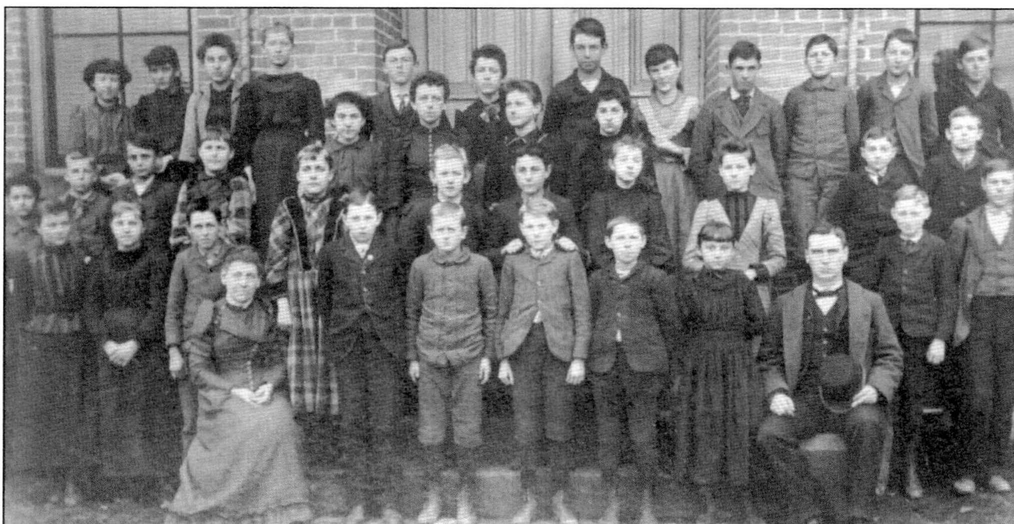

Addie Rhoten's seventh grade class of 1890 from Old Central poses here. They are, from left to right (first row) Mary Irons, Gertrude Love, unidentified, Miss Rhoten, Frank DePoy, Lou Anshutz, Charles Wilson, Otis Long, Bertha Mader, John S. Arnott, Carl Heimberger, and Frank Clouser; (second row) Caddie Ogle, Frank Harvey, Harry Kelso, unidentified, Mary Bell, unidentified, Dane Hyer, and unidentified; (third row) Nellie McCann, Edna Woodland, Minnie Leaverton, Etta Smith, Ott Allemang, Rosa Douglas, Lee Hayes, Mary Strider, unidentified, Algie Martin, unidentified, and George Wilson. (Courtesy of Patricia Smith.)

Greenfield High School's baseball and track teams from 1904 are featured in this composite image. From left to right, they are (top row) Head, Briggs, Barr, and Frazier; (second row) F. Hussey, Ellis, and J. Cleaveland; (third row) Doyle, M. Hussey, C. Cleaveland, and Ware; (fourth row) Brafford, Gossett, Caldwell, and Loggans.

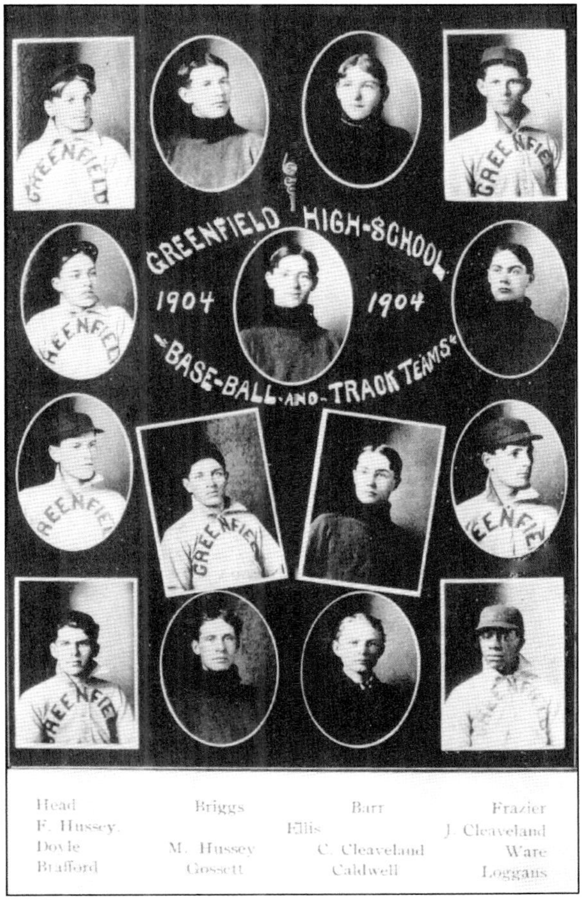

A junior high class from Old Central School is pictured here. The teacher is Miss Florence Kelso.

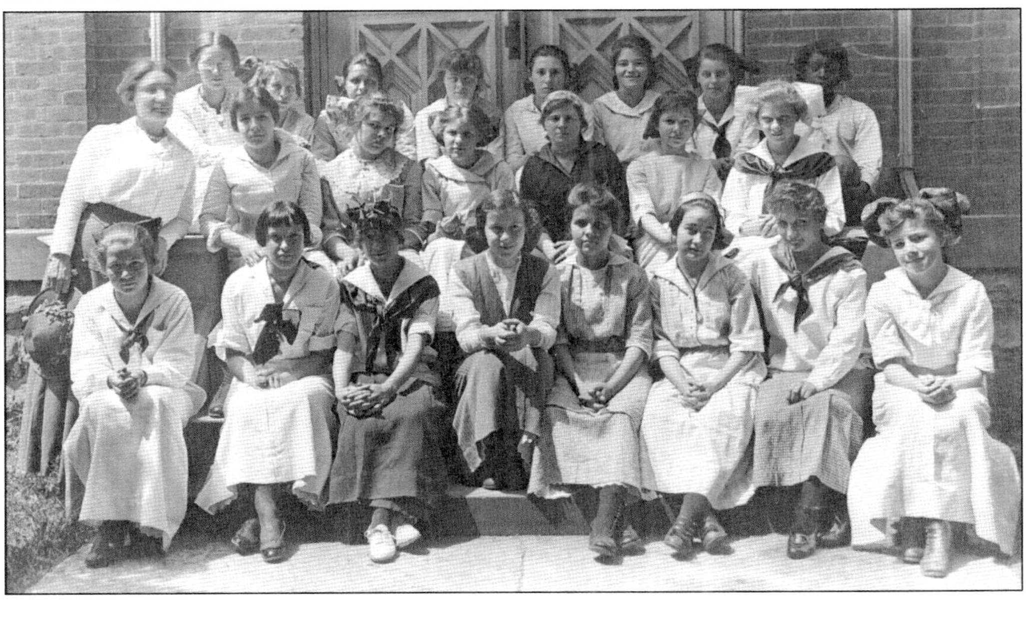

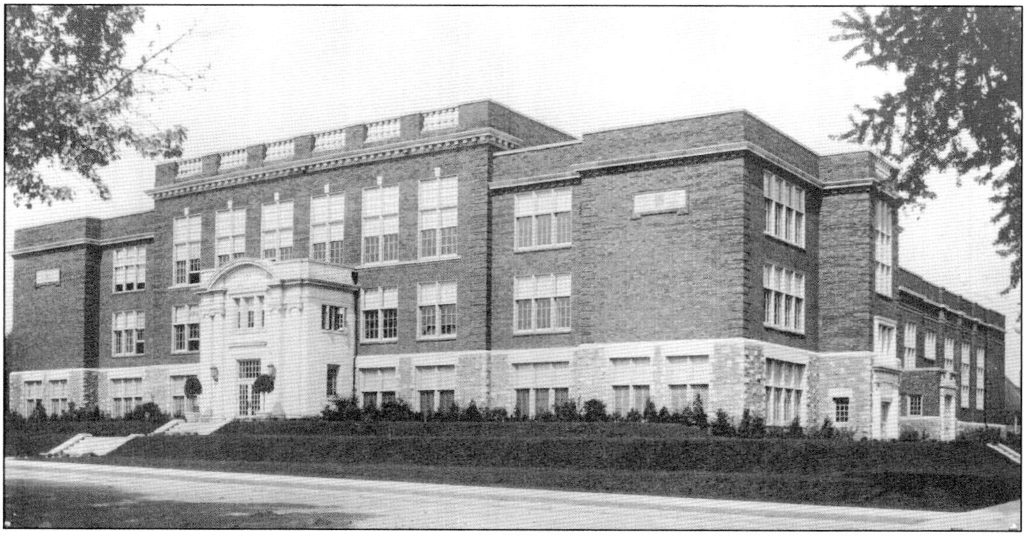

The generous gift of Edward Lee and Lulu McClain, McClain High School on Jefferson Street was dedicated on September 1, 1915. The school had roof gardens that, on September 23, 1915, were opened to the public for 15¢ admission.

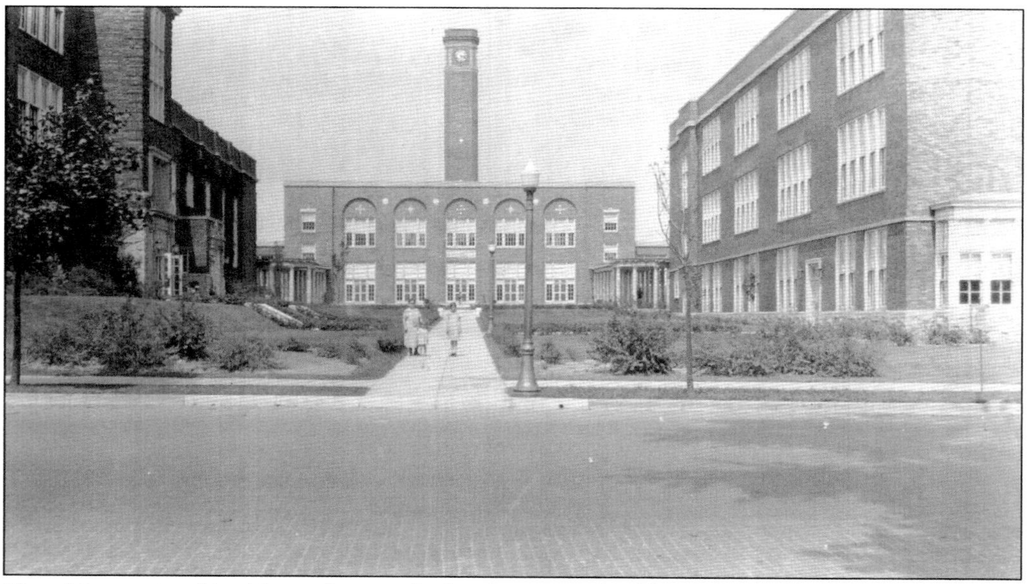

The old vocational building, along with the elementary building on the right, was completed in 1923–1924. The McClains offered to finance construction of the vocational building; in turn, citizens financed construction of the elementary to replace Old Central School, which was in need of extensive repair. The central courtyard and colonnades, along with residences for custodial and maintenance staff, completed the school campus as McClain intended it.

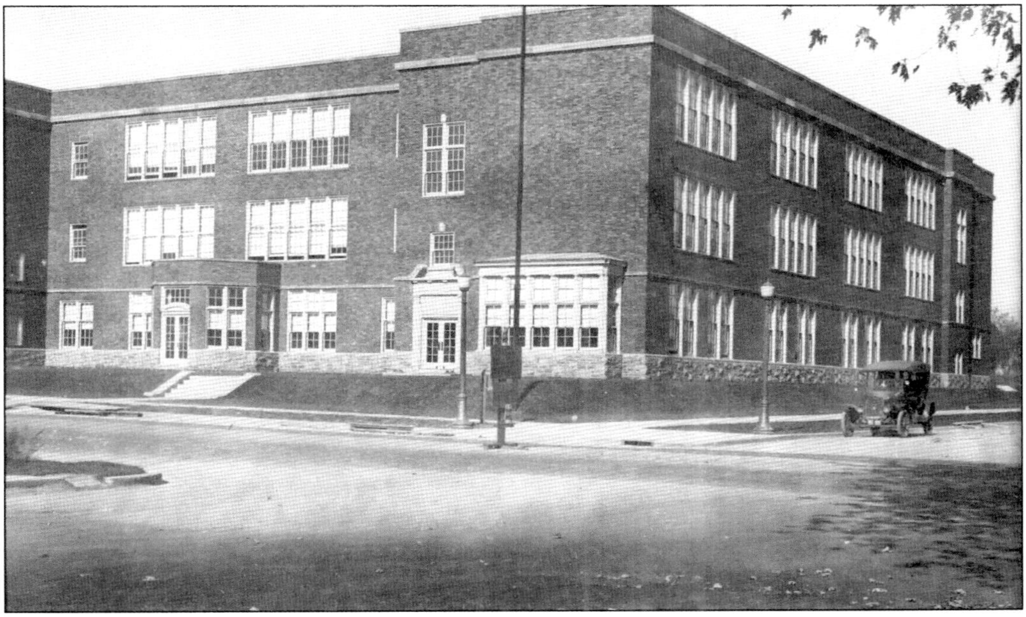

A view of the elementary school shows the 1924 building at the corner of Jefferson and Fifth Streets. In 1921, an overwhelming vote of 1,232 to 195 allowed for the construction of the new elementary school, now Greenfield Middle School.

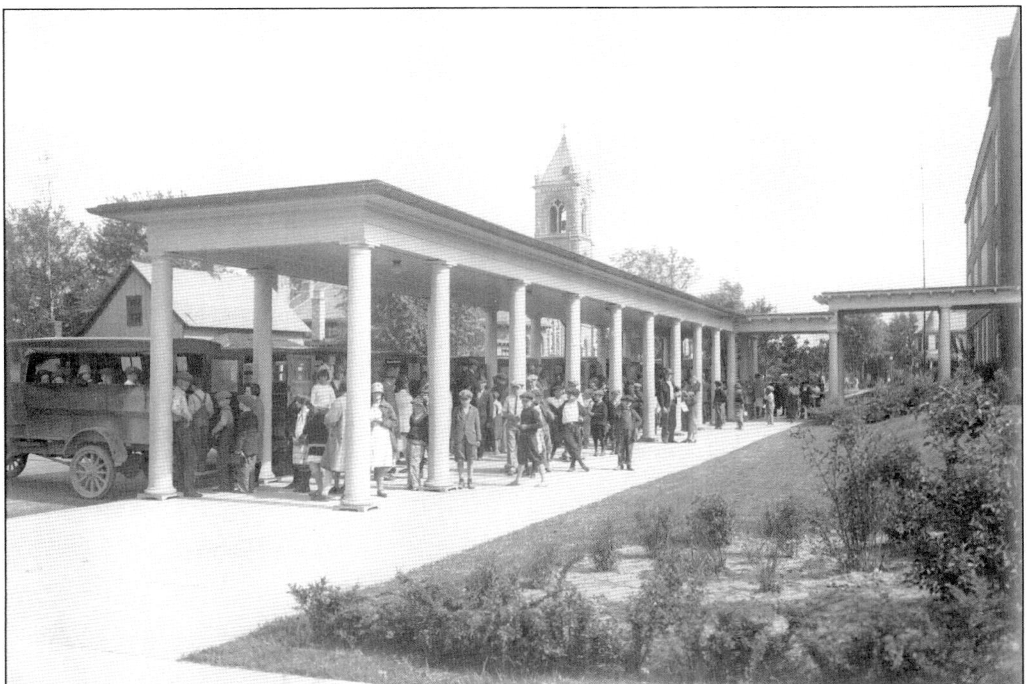

Since the use of school buses began, Greenfield students have been dropped off and picked up at the colonnades outside the elementary school (now Greenfield Middle School) on Fifth Street. Note that the students loaded and unloaded from the rear of the bus in those days.

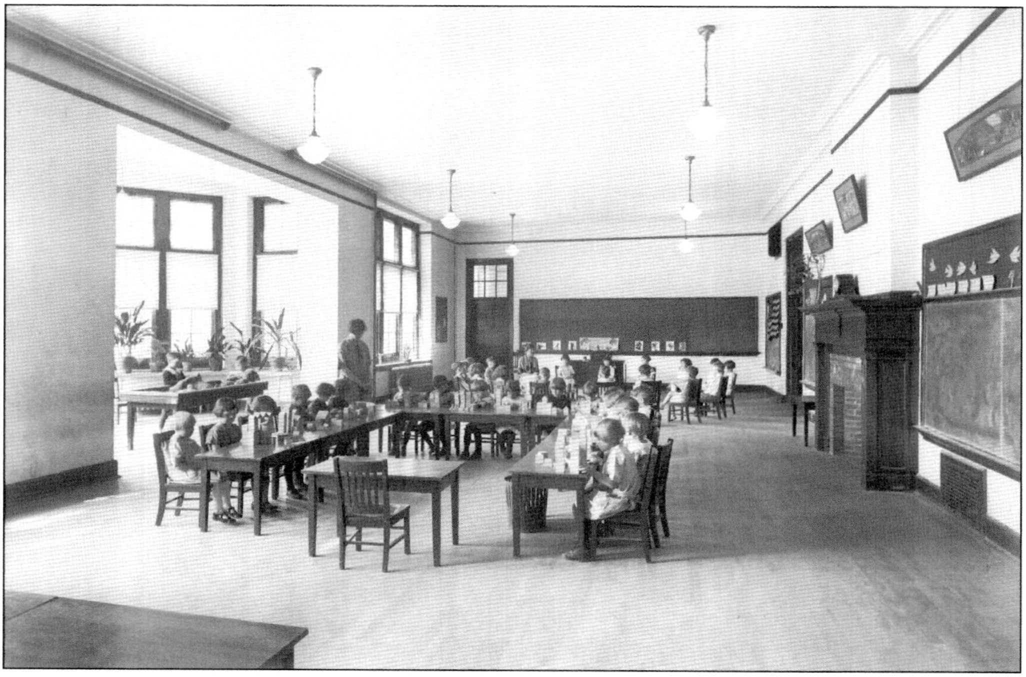

This spacious room is a kindergarten room with its own fireplace. Greenfield residents will recognize this room by its bow window on the left. The space was divided into smaller rooms and currently provides offices for the middle school principal.

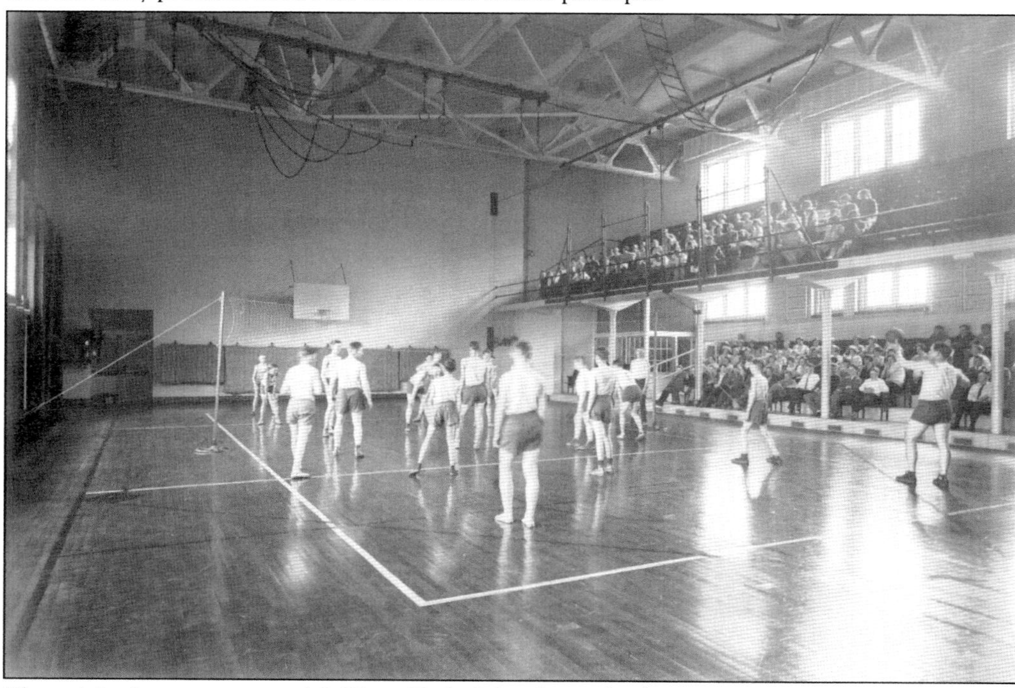

The original gymnasium at McClain High School is today known as the "old gym." This 1926 photograph shows a men's volleyball game in front of a crowd of onlookers.

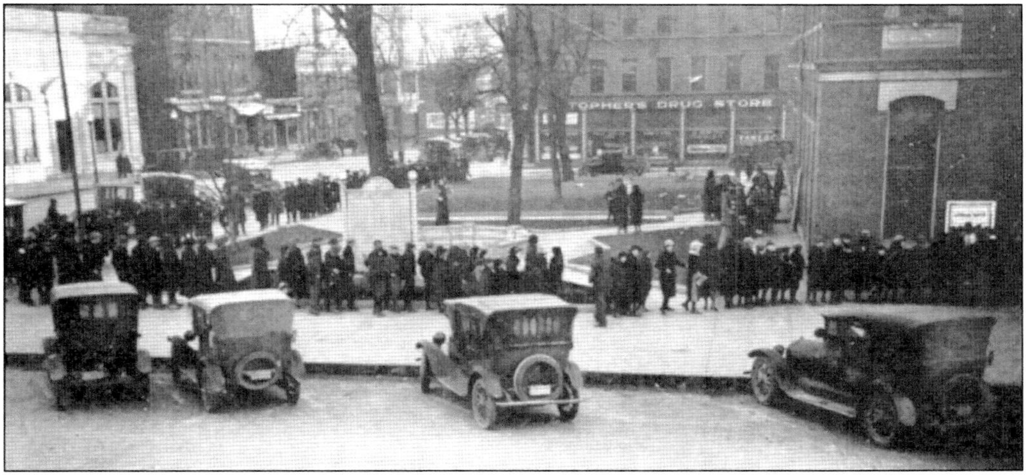

Greenfield's passion for high school basketball has a long history. In this picture, fans line up around the block for tickets to a game between the McClain Tigers and Dayton Stivers in 1922. This picture was taken from the 1922 *Dragon*, McClain High School's yearbook.

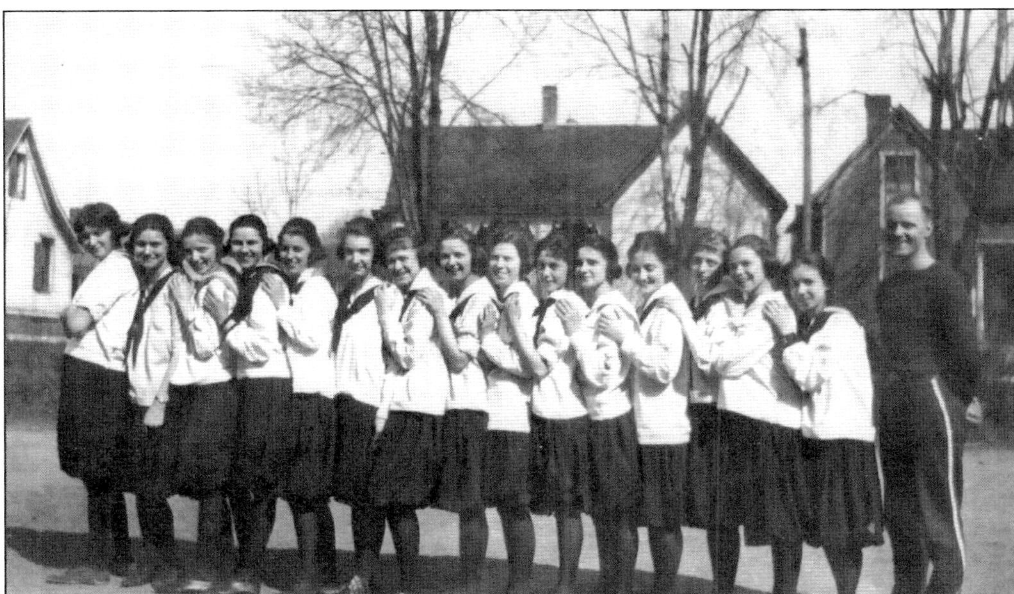

The 15 members of the 1920 McClain High School girls' basketball team are pictured here with their coach, the famed Duke Hayes. (Courtesy of Patricia Smith.)

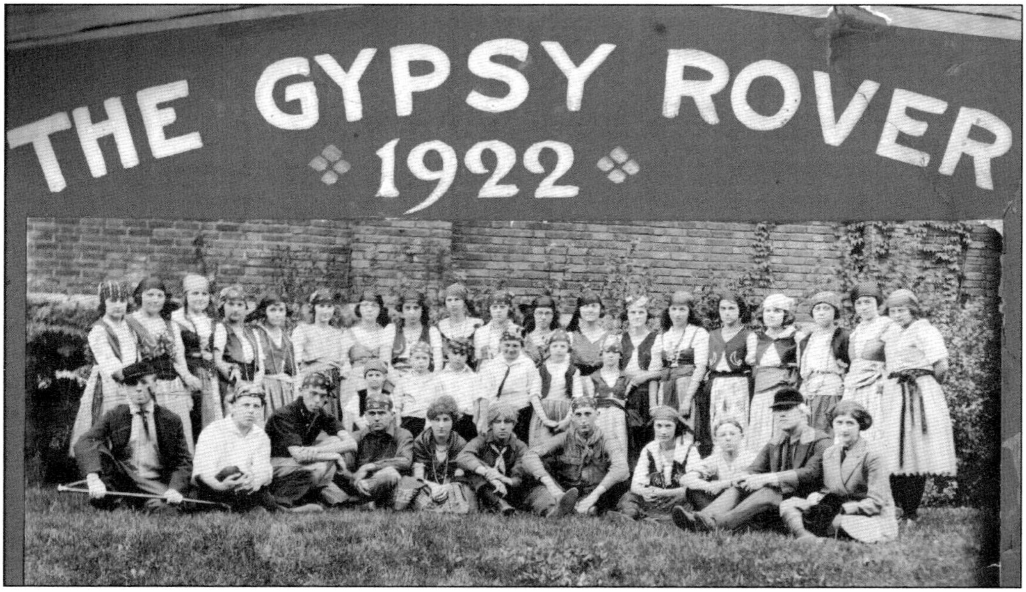

The romantic comedy musical in three acts called *The Gypsy Rover* was presented by the 1922 senior class and the glee club of McClain High School. Costumes were designed and made by the home economics department under the direction of Kathleen Doster.

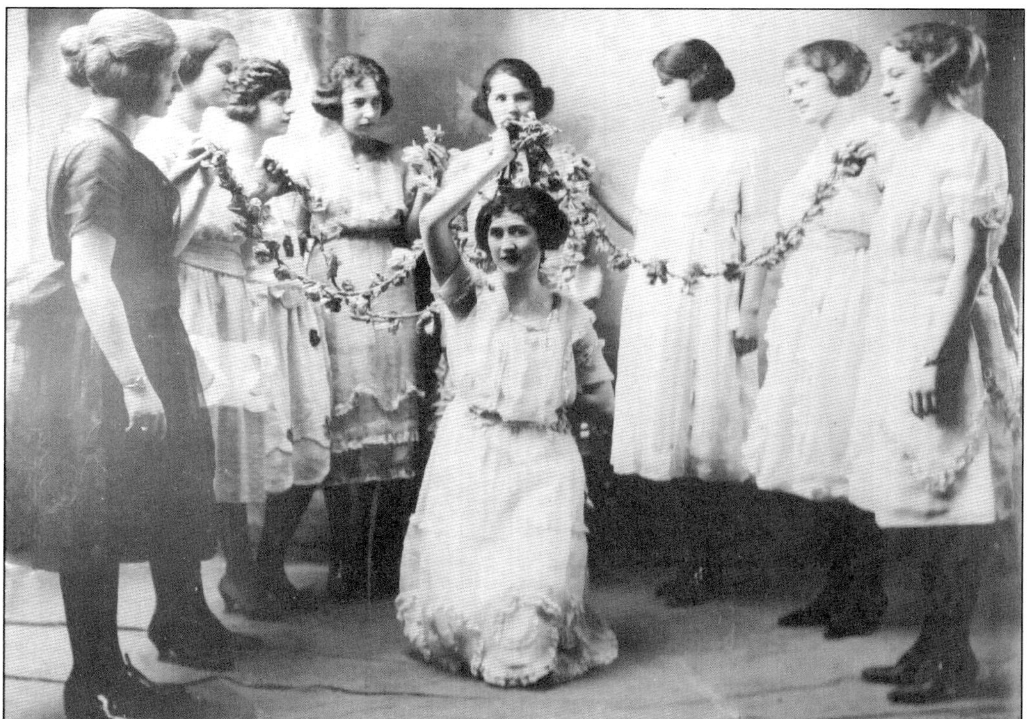

These young ladies are members of the cast and chorus of the 1922 production of *The Gypsy Rover* for McClain High School. The director was Ralph W. Price. These girls performed the "Flower Dance."

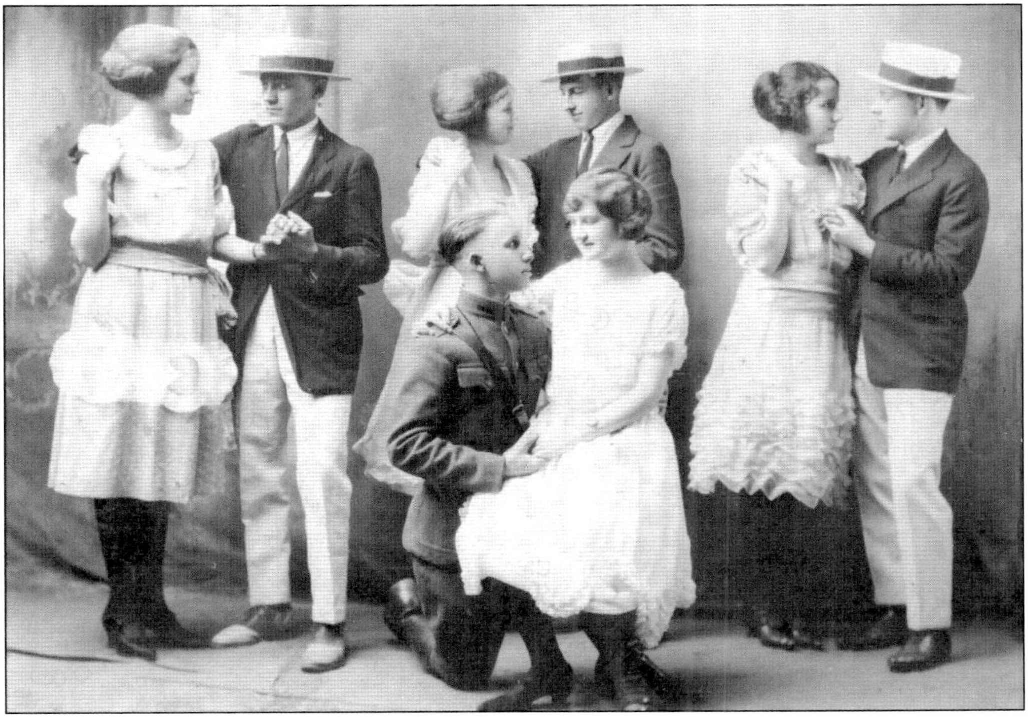

These couples danced the "Moon, Moon Dance" for the 1922 musical comedy *The Gypsy Rover*. Music for the show was by Price's orchestra with Dorothy Smith at the piano.

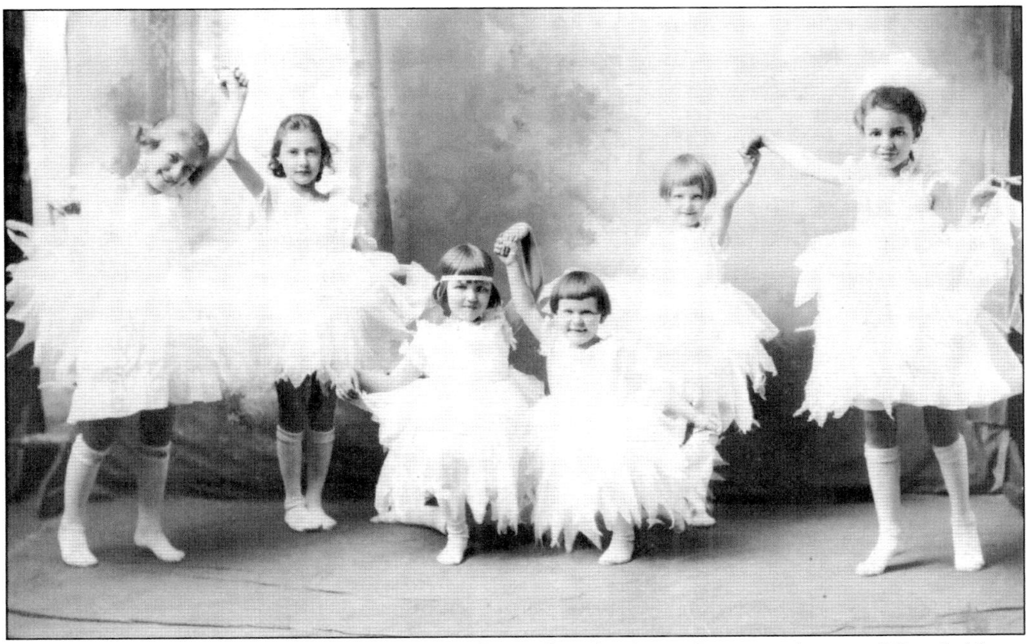

These younger children were cast as dancing fairies for *The Gypsy Rover* production. The children, in no particular order, were Mary Jane Mains, Helen Hiser, Grace Winfough, Pauline Gilliland, Sara Louise Limes, and Georgia Mertz.

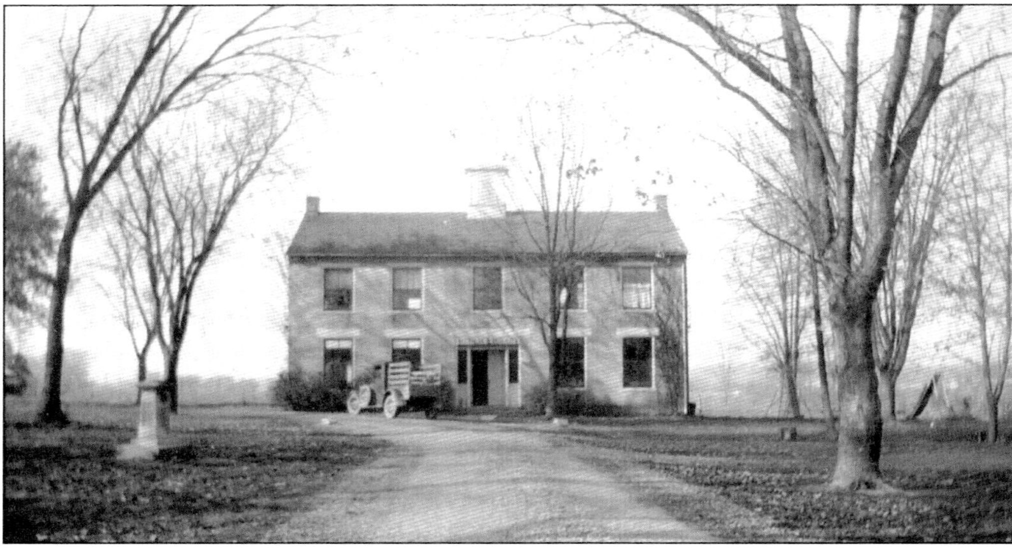

Salem Academy was opened in late 1842 by the South Salem Presbyterian Church. At one time, one-tenth of the graduates at Miami University were former Academy students. Most went on to become ministers, missionaries, and educators. South Salem grew up around the Academy as a place to house students. The Academy closed in 1907.

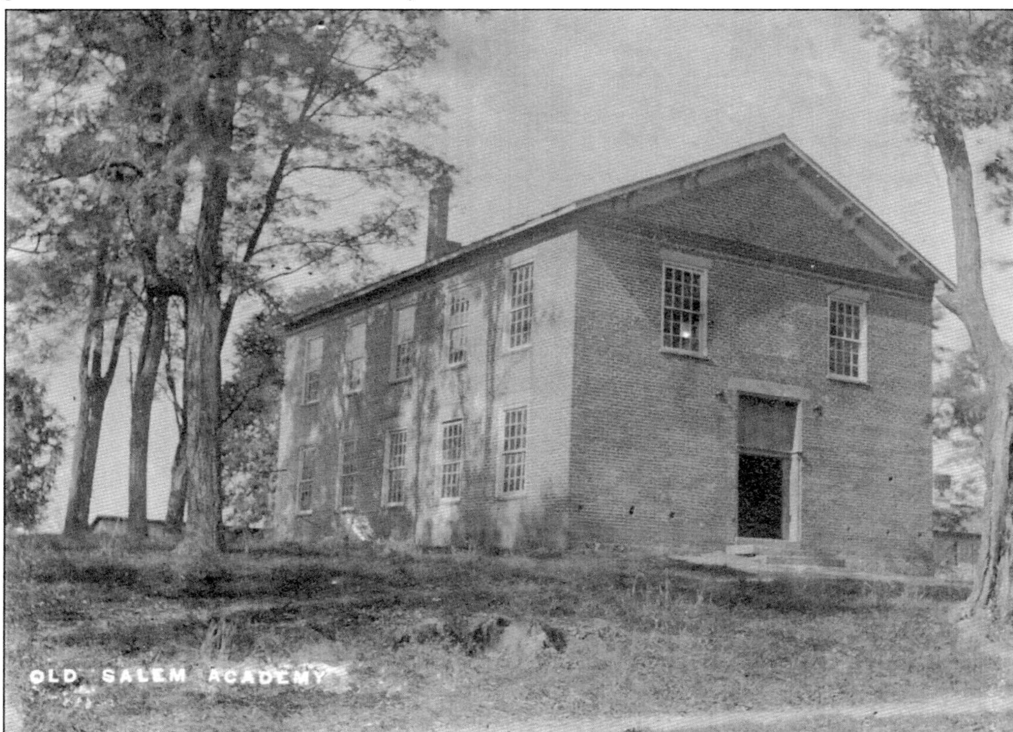

In 1856, a second building was constructed by Salem Academy to accommodate a growing student body. In later years, this building was used as a high school by the Buckskin Valley Schools. In 1929, it was torn down to construct the building that is currently Buckskin Elementary School

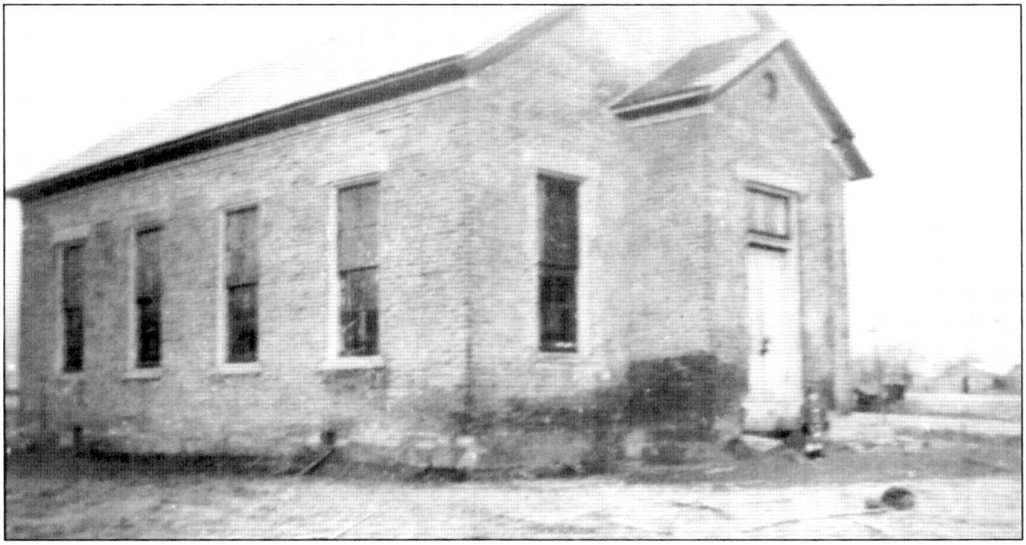

Lyndon is a small village on the B&O Southwestern Railroad line. It was the only town on the railway in all of Buckskin Township. At one time, Lyndon had about 200 inhabitants. Lyndon's one-room schoolhouse, pictured here in 1897, was on the southeast corner of State Route 28 and Wright Lane. (Courtesy of Lew Speakman.)

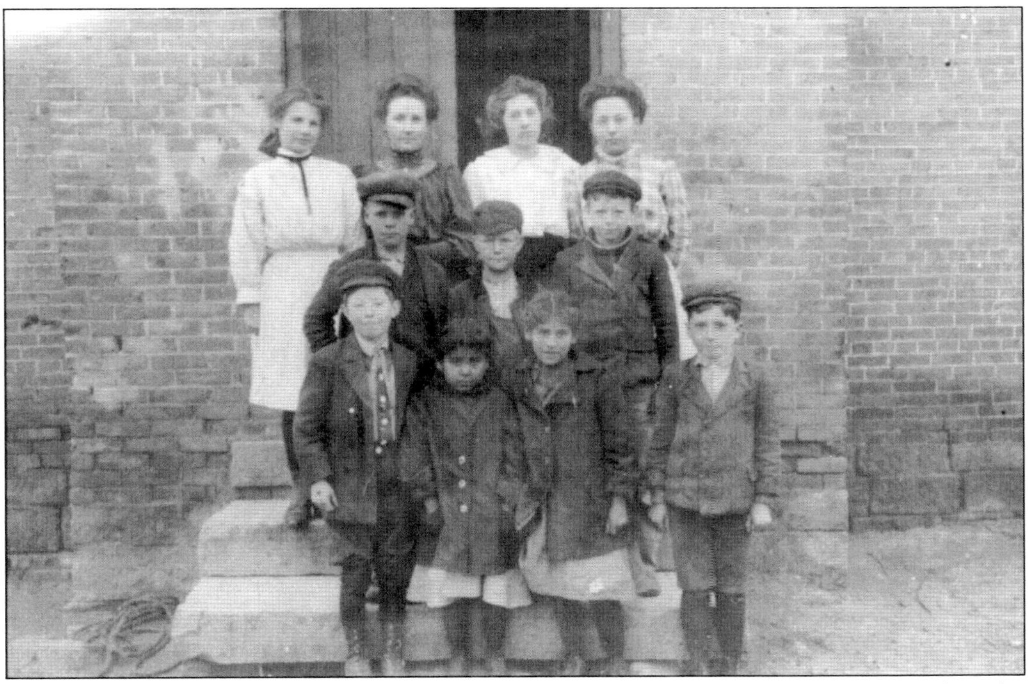

Lyndon, initially called Zora, was laid out in 1853 by John N. Huggins. Samuel Langdon, the first postmaster and first merchant in the village, renamed it Lyndon. Pictured here is a class of students from the Lyndon one-room schoolhouse. Mary DeHaas is in the third row. (Courtesy of Lew Speakman.)

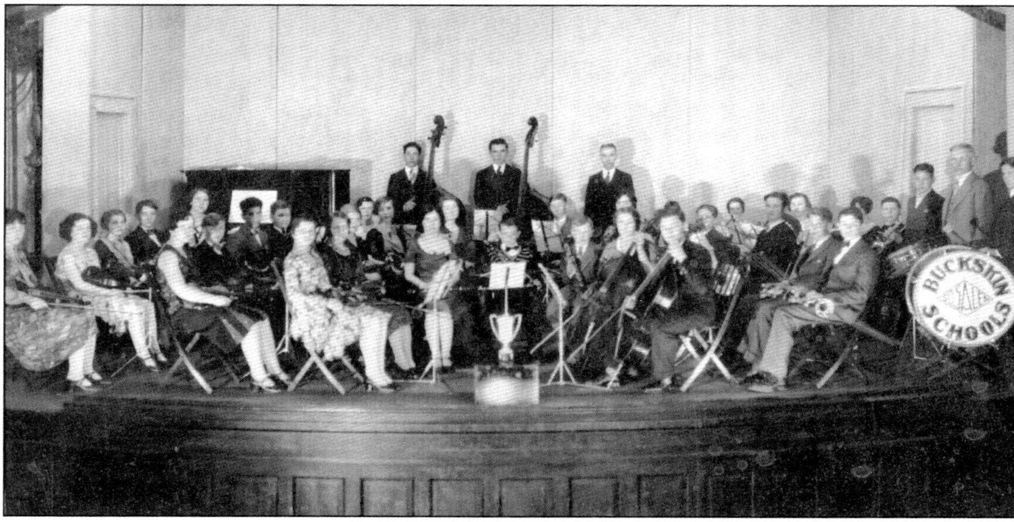

The Buckskin Orchestra performed on the Buckskin School stage in the early 1930s. The orchestra competed in contests, placing first in 1931 and 1933, and second in 1932. (Courtesy of Lew Speakman.)

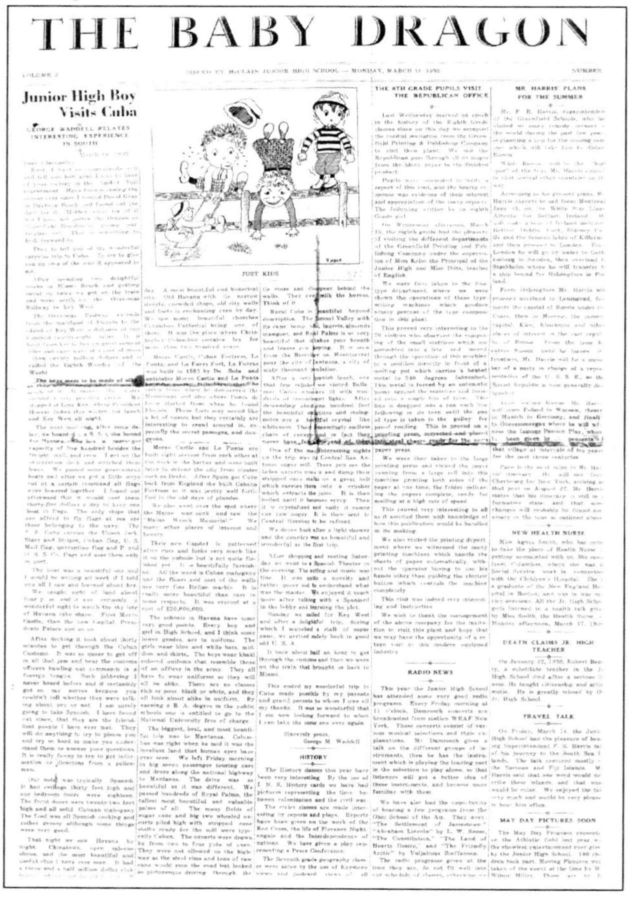

THE BABY DRAGON

ISSUED BY McCLAIN JUNIOR HIGH SCHOOL — MONDAY, MARCH 31, 1930

Junior High Boy Visits Cuba

GEORGE WADDELL RELATES INTERESTING EXPERIENCE IN SOUTH

JUST KIDS

THE 8TH GRADE PUPILS VISIT THE REPUBLICAN OFFICE

MR. HARRIS' PLANS FOR THE SUMMER

NEW HEALTH NURSE

DEATH CLAIMS JR. HIGH TEACHER

TRAVEL TALK

MAY DAY PICTURES SOON

RADIO NEWS

HISTORY

The McClain High School yearbook is known as the *Dragon*, and the McClain Junior High School put out a newspaper called the *Baby Dragon*. Headlining this Monday, March 31, 1930, issue is a story about a junior high boy's visit to Cuba.

Seven

Happenings Through the Years

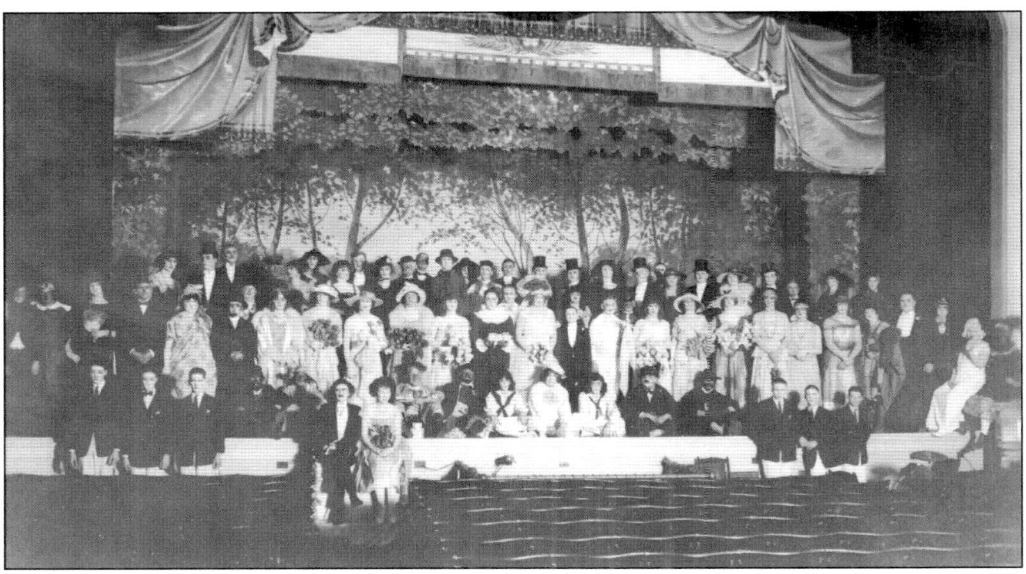

The cast of *The Womanless Wedding*, which was performed on March 22 and 23 in 1923, poses on the McClain High School stage. The production consisted of 78 male members of the community under the direction by Marie Simpson and was sponsored by the PTA. (Courtesy of Patricia Smith.)

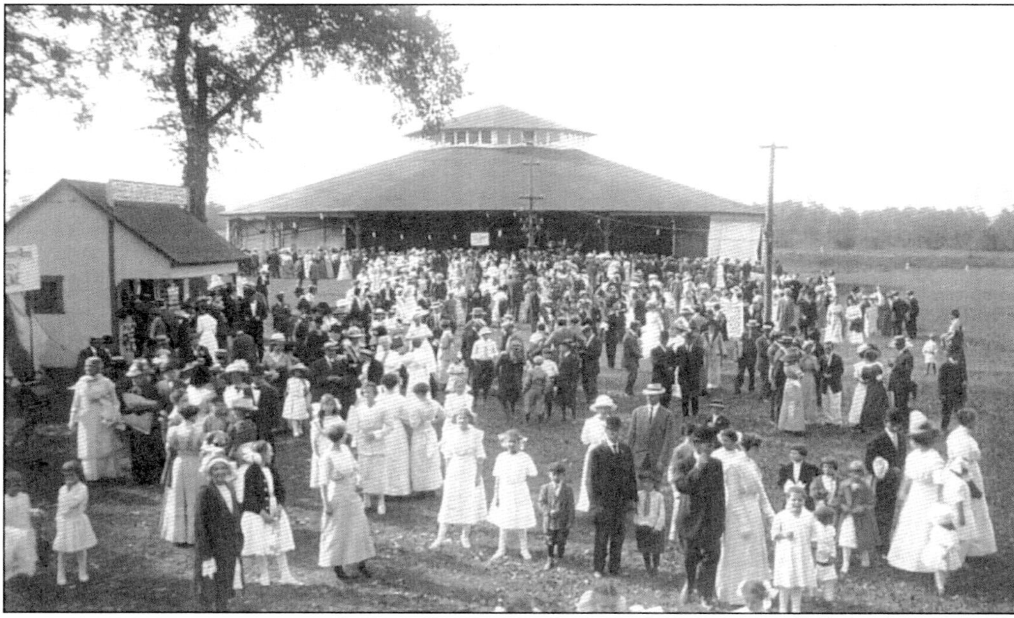

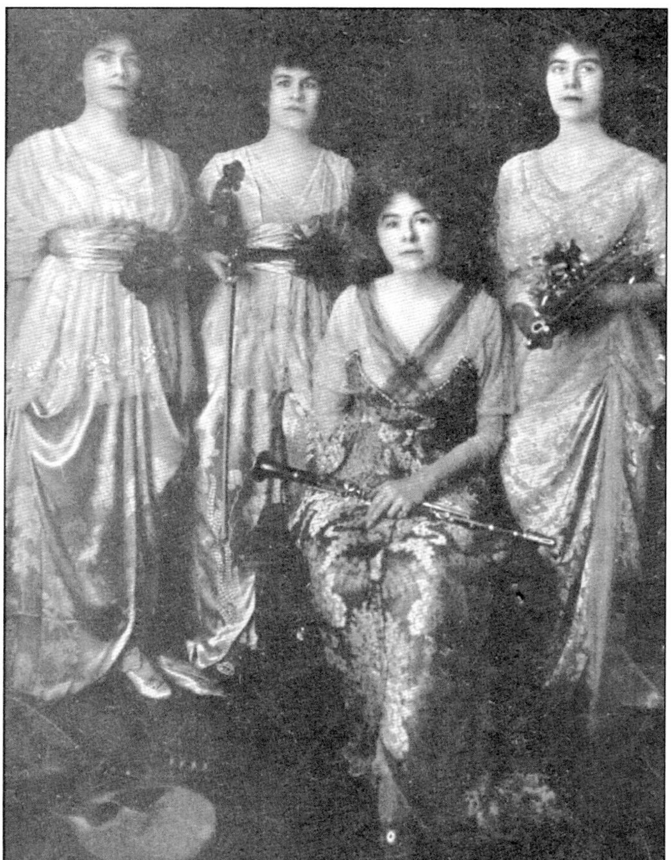

In 1906, Greenfield presented its first Chautauqua, bringing large crowds to the event held north of town on the Douglass land. The tent erected for Chautauqua seated audiences of 2,500. The large building pictured here is the steel auditorium built in 1915 to replace the tent. Chautauqua events occurred annually in Greenfield through the 1920s. The Christian Union campgrounds are currently located at this site.

One of the musical acts to perform at Chautauqua was the Hearon Sisters, shown here.

These young ladies were the Lyndon-Gordon Company, a musical act that performed for Chautauqua audiences.

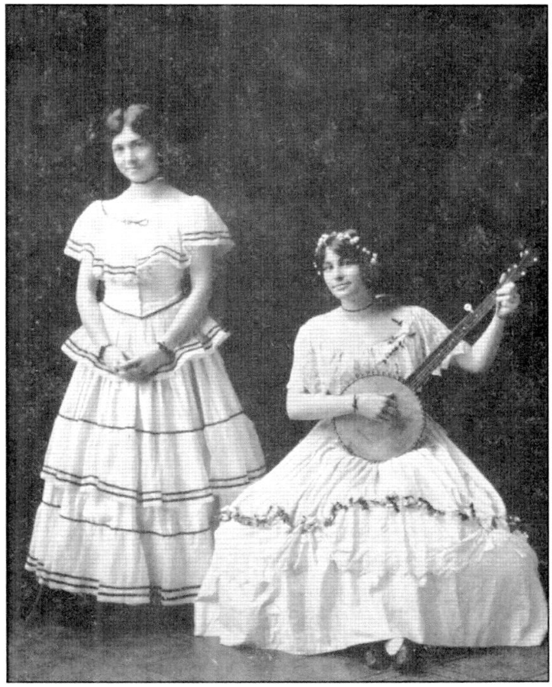

This baseball team competed in a tournament that occurred during the 10-day Chautauqua event. Teams from surrounding communities competed in the tournament. Dated Friday, August 3, 1906, this picture shows the victorious team after it defeated Sabina, 6-5, in 10 innings.

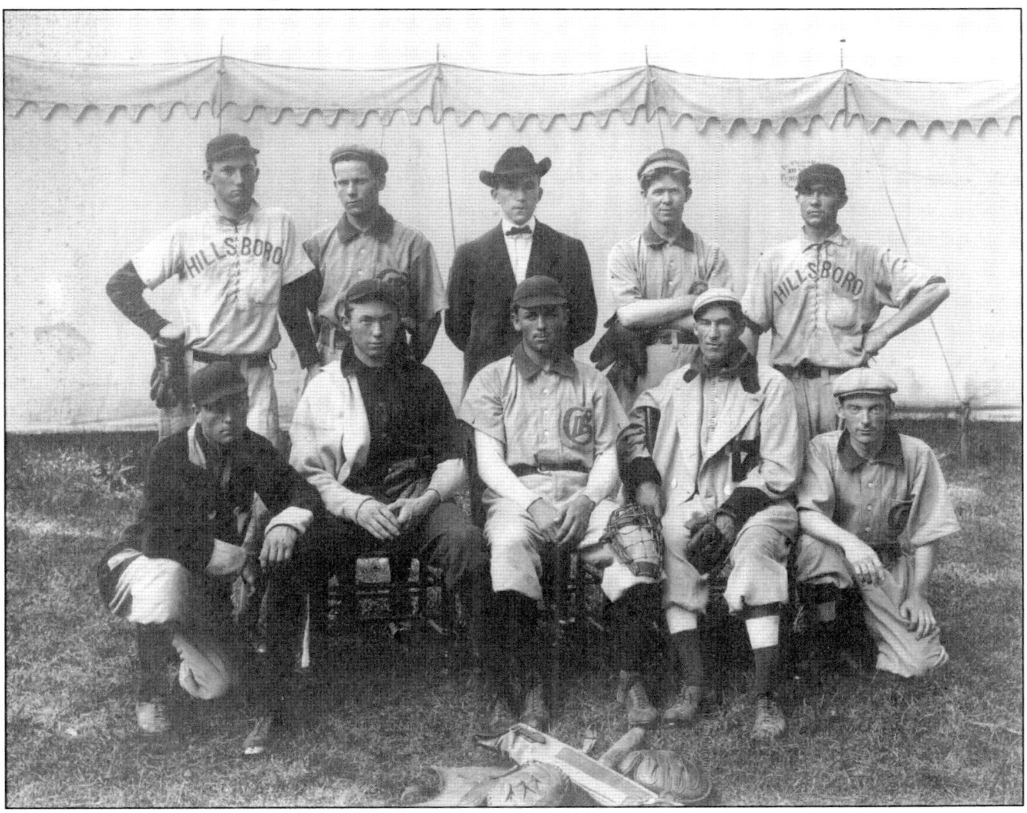

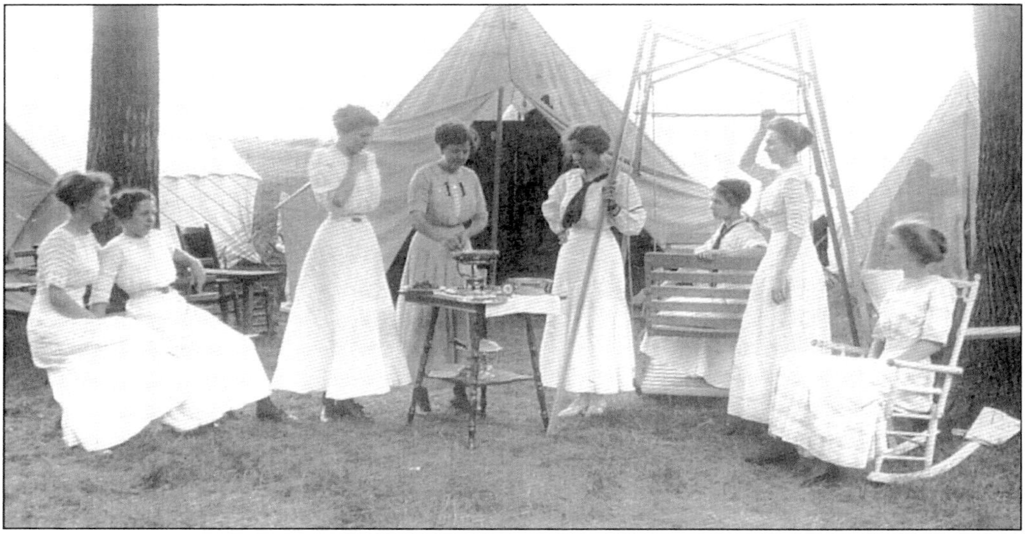

The Chautauqua movement started in New York and spread across America through the early 1900s. Chautauqua provided area residents opportunities to attend lectures throughout the day; in the evenings, guests could take in concerts and orations by statesmen and preachers. Children, too, were entertained by magicians and ventriloquists. These women are relaxing in front of a camper's tent with comforts from home like rocking chairs, dining tables, and garden swings.

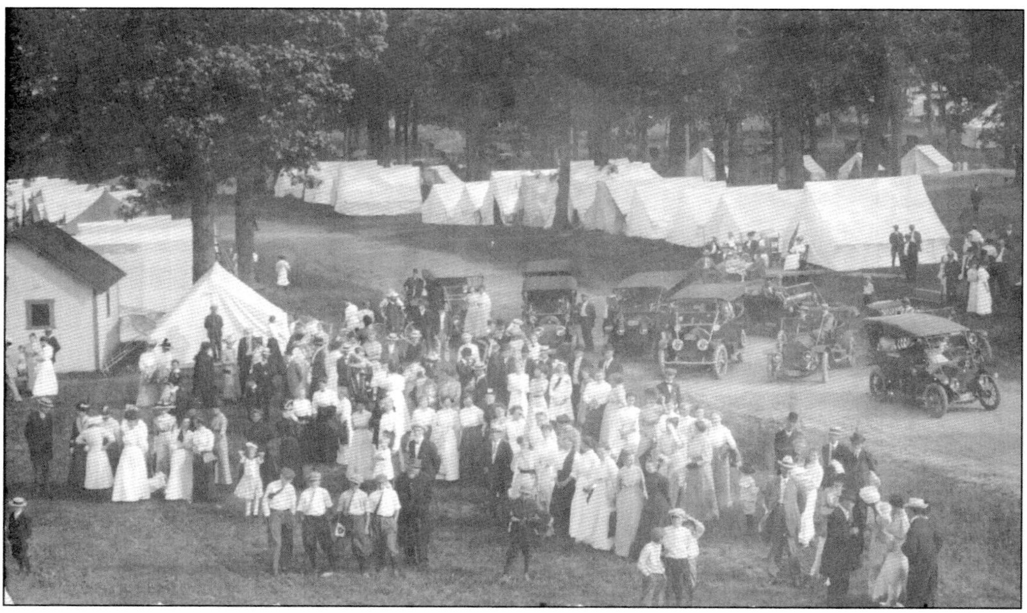

The wooded campgrounds provided an ideal setting for Chautauqua. Note the attire of the crowd: men and boys wore dress shirts and ties, while women wore fine summer dresses and bonnets. By the 1930s, interest in Chautauqua was waning, due largely to the increased popularity of the radio and the automobile.

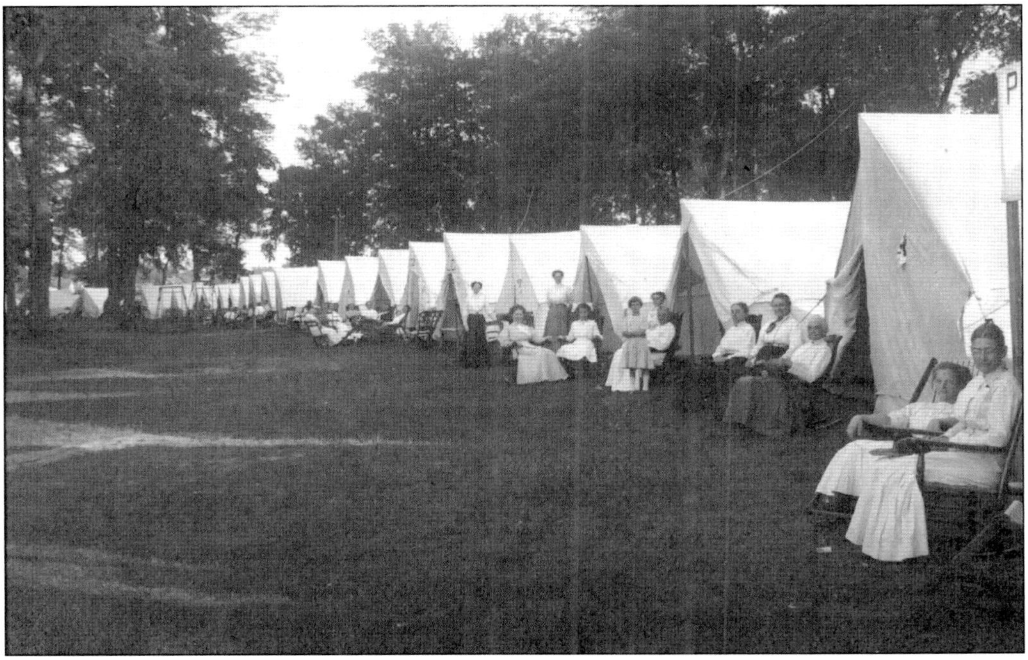

This photograph shows evidence of the extensive popularity of Chautauqua. The campground became known as "White City," because of the many white tents that families rented for $2.50 to $3.30.

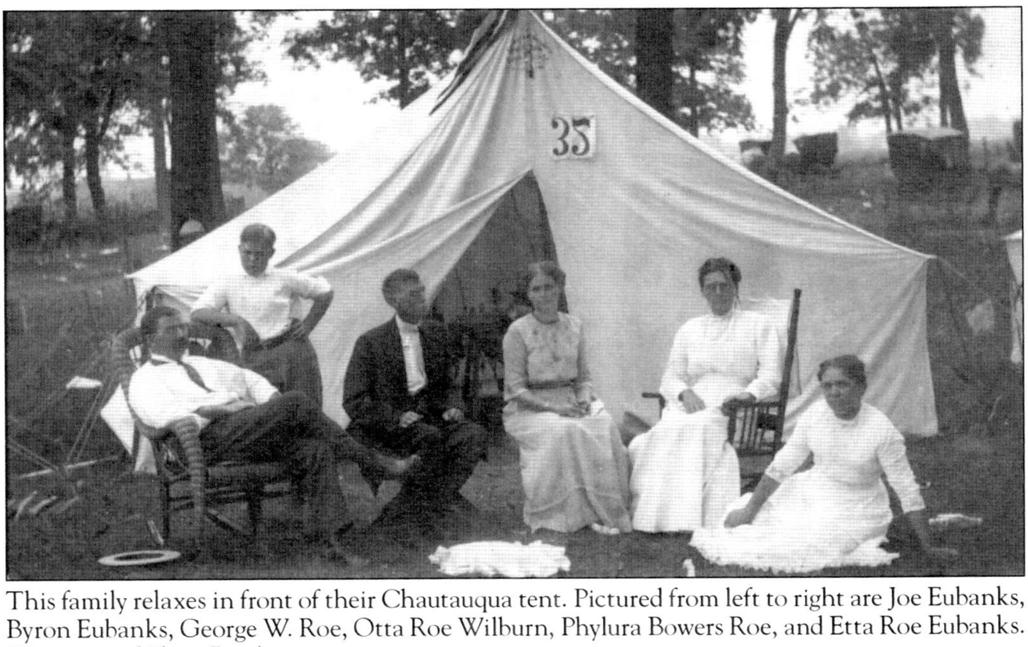

This family relaxes in front of their Chautauqua tent. Pictured from left to right are Joe Eubanks, Byron Eubanks, George W. Roe, Otta Roe Wilburn, Phylura Bowers Roe, and Etta Roe Eubanks. (Courtesy of Sheri Roe.)

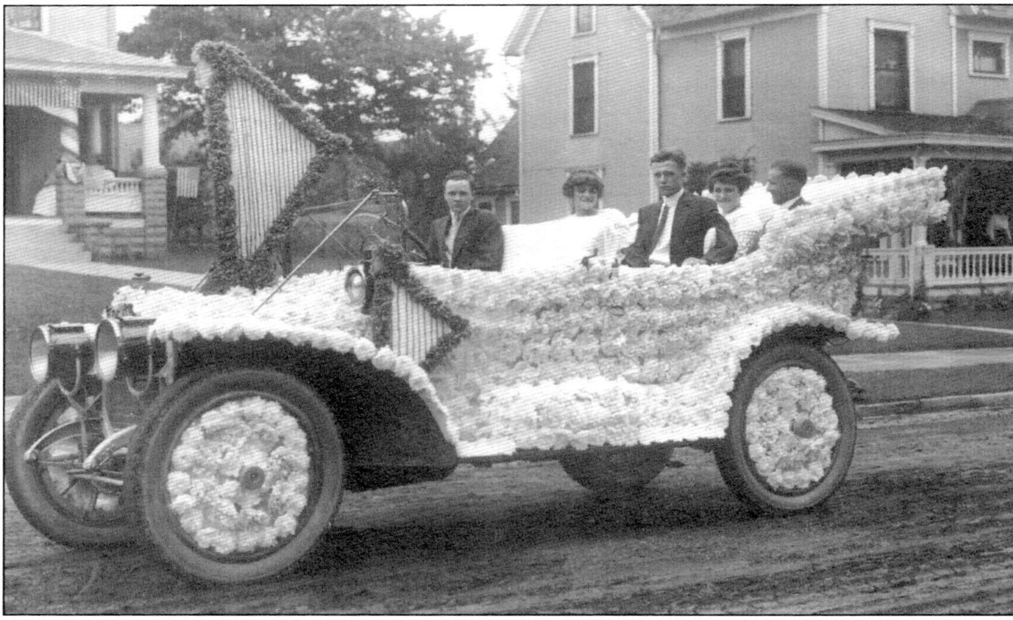

In 1912, Greenfield hosted artistically and beautifully decorated cars for its Fourth of July parade. The challenge published in the Chillicothe paper was to make the parade the largest, most successful automobile parade in southern Ohio. The prize for the top entry was a beautiful silver loving cup that was on display at DeVoss Jewelers in Greenfield. This parade float features one such decorated automobile.

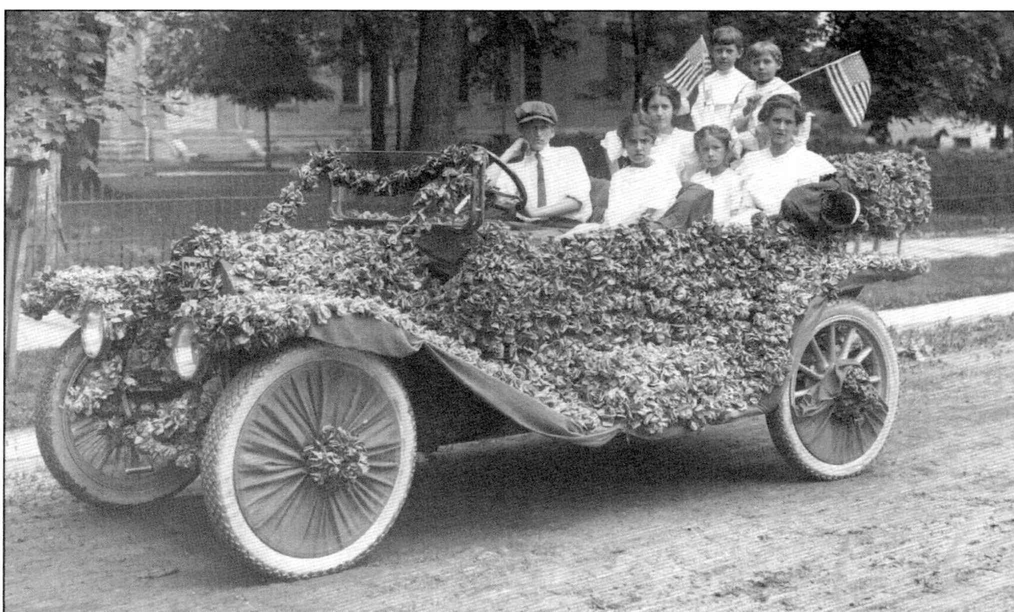

This early automobile is covered in ivy for the 1912 Independence Day parade. Even the wheels were festooned with fabric and florets.

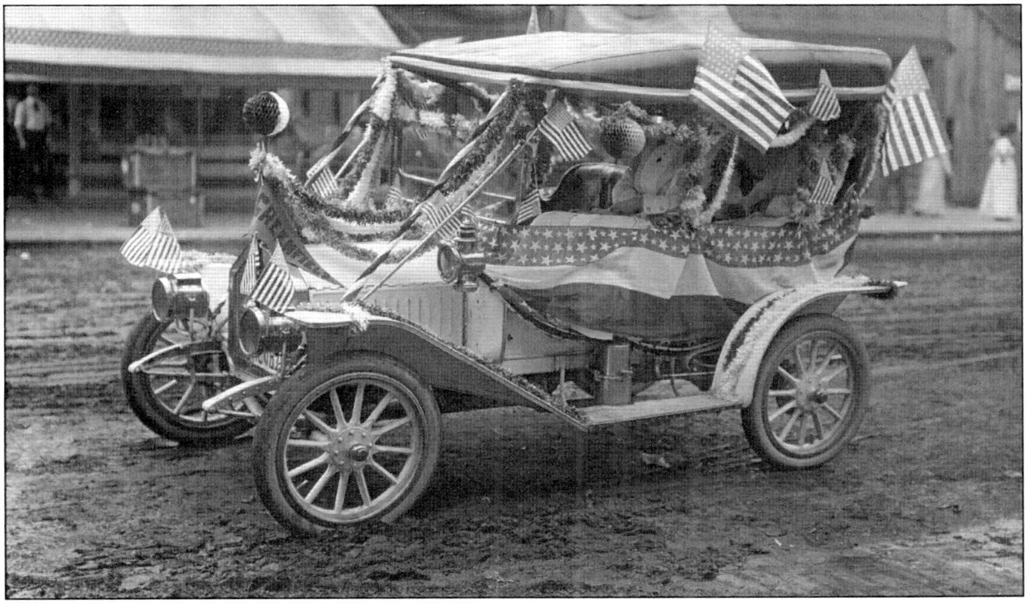

This patriotic 1910 Buick is draped with stars and stripes, not just in the numerous flags, but also in the bunting and streamers. The car was owned by George Ghormley. (Courtesy of Patricia Smith.)

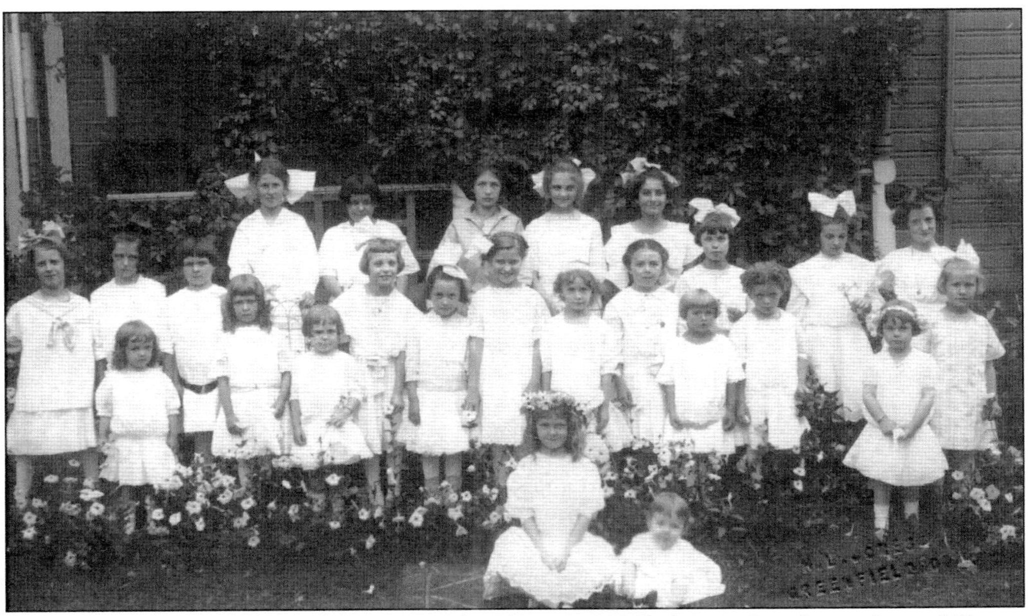

This group of girls with big white bows in their hair were dolled up and ready to ride on different floats in the big parade. (Courtesy of Patricia Smith.)

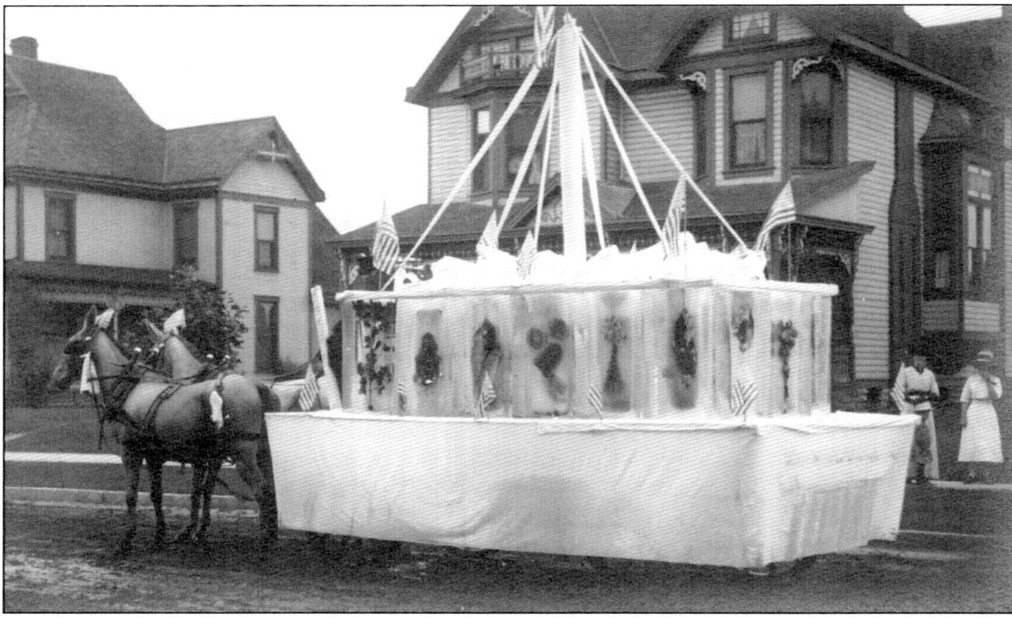

Horse-drawn floats were also included in the July 4, 1912 parade. This float was sponsored by the Greenfield Ice Company.

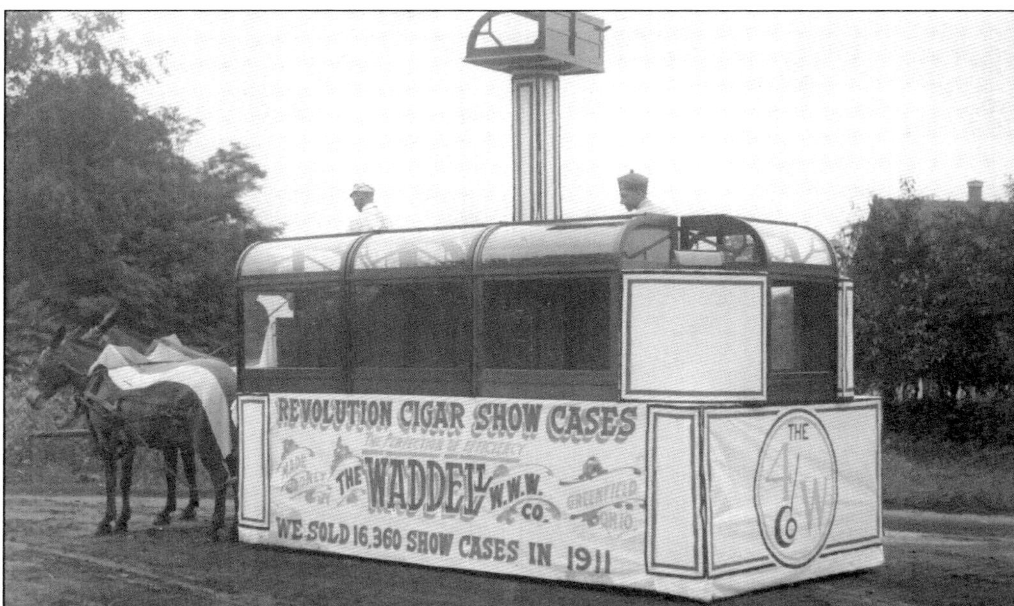

The Waddell Company float in the 1912 parade boasts "we sold 16,360 show cases in 1911." The "4/W" emblem on the back of the float represents the full name of the Waddell Company, Waddell Wooden Ware Works.

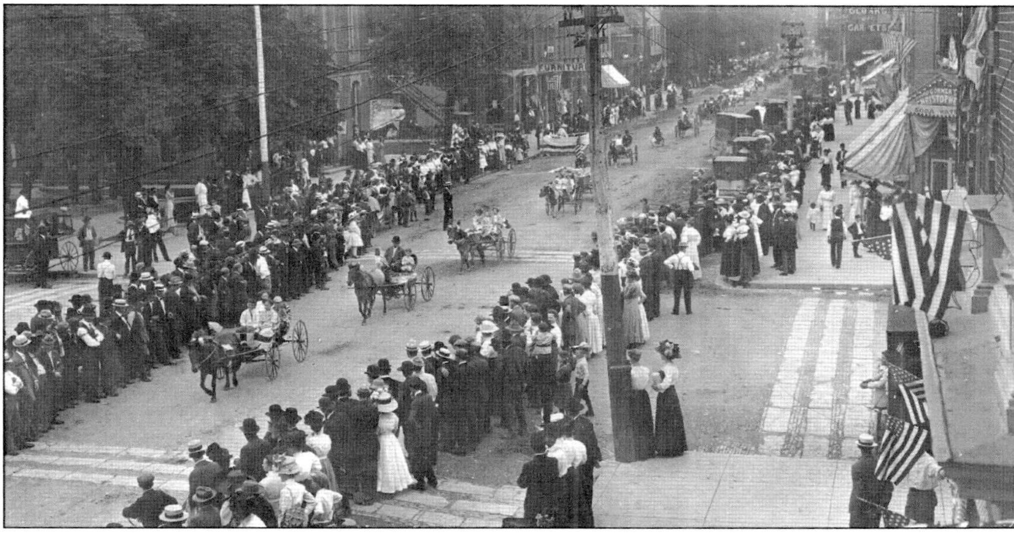

This c. 1920s pony parade marching through town features Dunlap Farms' high-grade Shetland ponies. Milton Irwin Dunlap founded his farm in 1905 and by 1915 it consisted of 1,100 acres, 100 of which were in the village limits in the vicinity of present-day Hillcrest Drive and Edgewood Avenue. At any given time, he had 500 to 600 ponies on hand. The farm had 12 residences and 16 barns, all consecutively numbered.

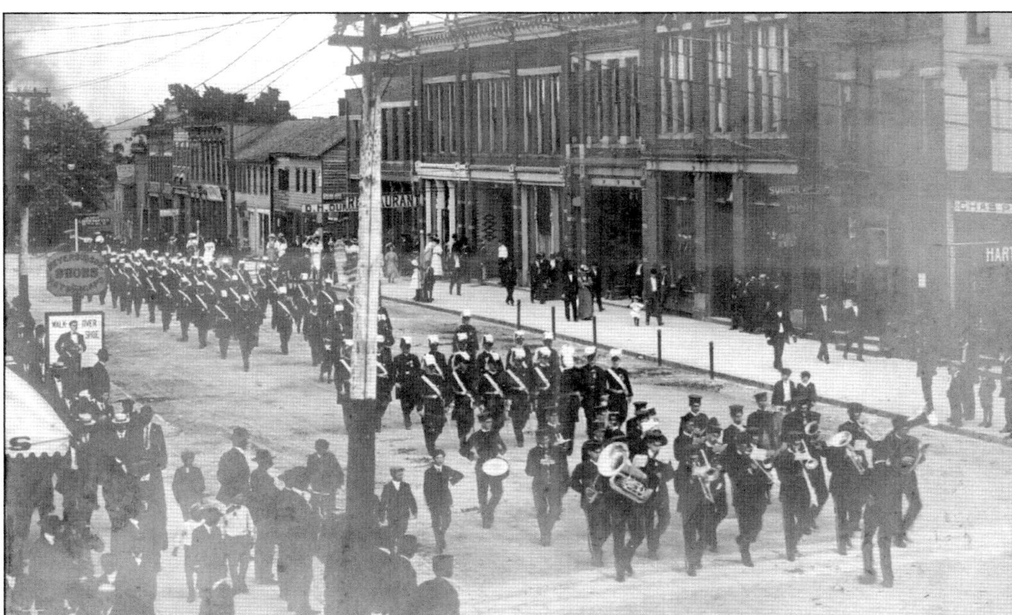

A marching band parades west on E. Jefferson Street.

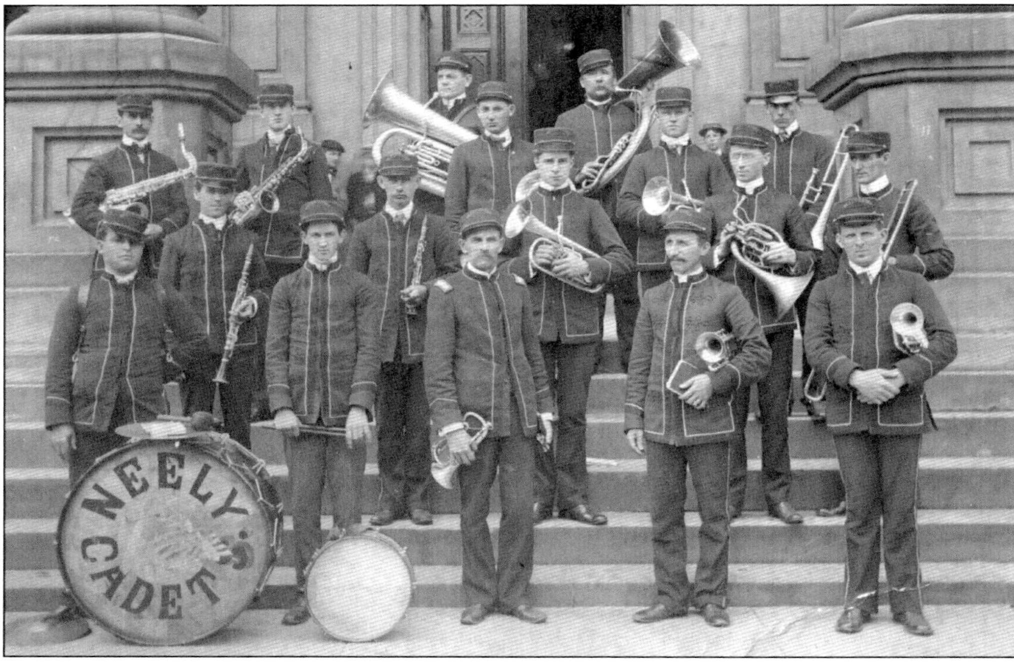

The Neely Cadet Band, formed by Joe Neely, was open to any young boy from the South Salem area; Neely even provided instruments for the young musicians. The band performed locally for graduations and ballgames, but gained a wider audience when it marched at the Chicago World's Fair. Legend has it that the band had no prior lodging arrangements in Chicago, so it marched until midnight before finding a hotel with openings.

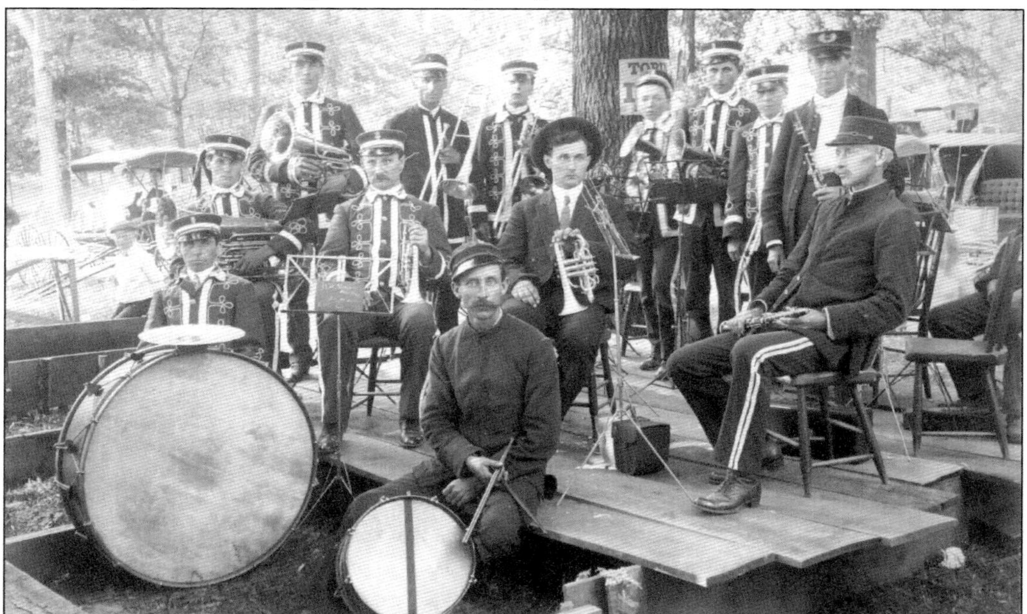

The Fruitdale Band poses in uniform as it prepares for a performance. Such bands often performed at functions such as the Lyndon Farmers' Picnic. (Courtesy of Lew Speakman.)

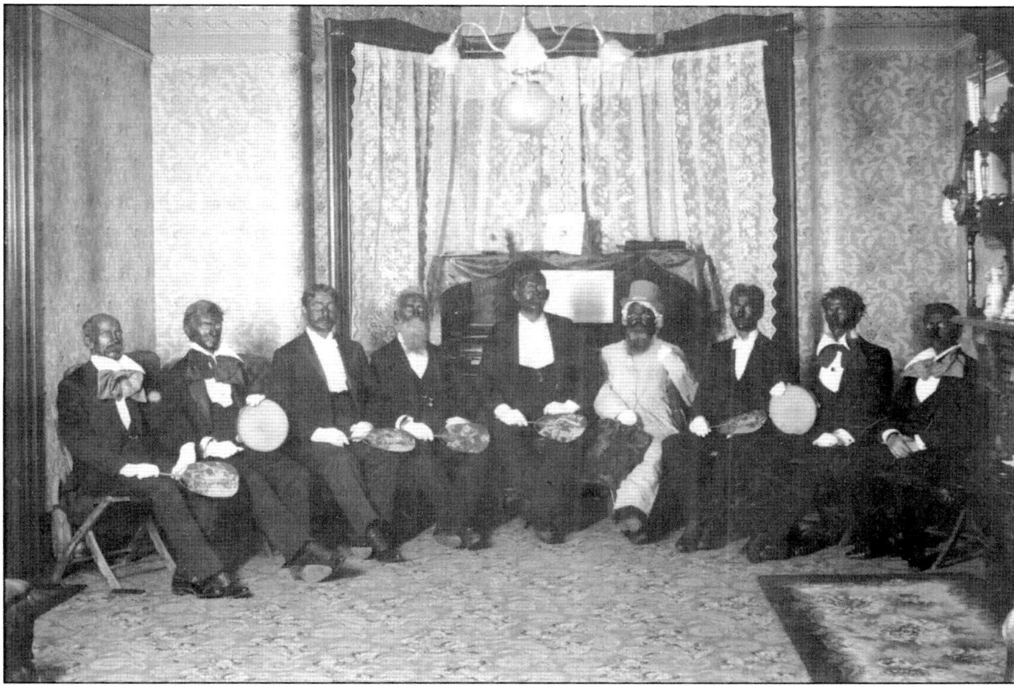

The Greenfield Glee Club posed for a group picture prior to a performance on April 26, 1895. Members included, from left to right, George Lowe, John Boggin, E.L. McClain, T.M. Elliott, Faye Baldwin, W.K. Dunlap, Stewart Jackson, Ralph Price, and M.W. Duncan.

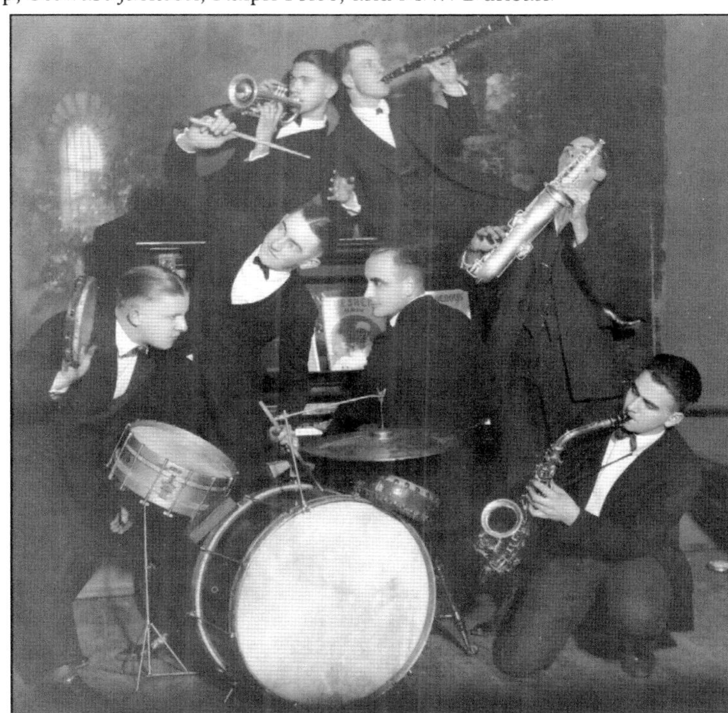

Likely a McClain High School jazz band, these musicians are ready to perform. On tambourine is Roger Donohoe; drums, Walter Smith; trumpet, Gerald Davis; clarinet, tenor saxophone, and piano, unidentified; and alto saxophone, Hugh Ghormley. (Courtesy Patricia Smith.)

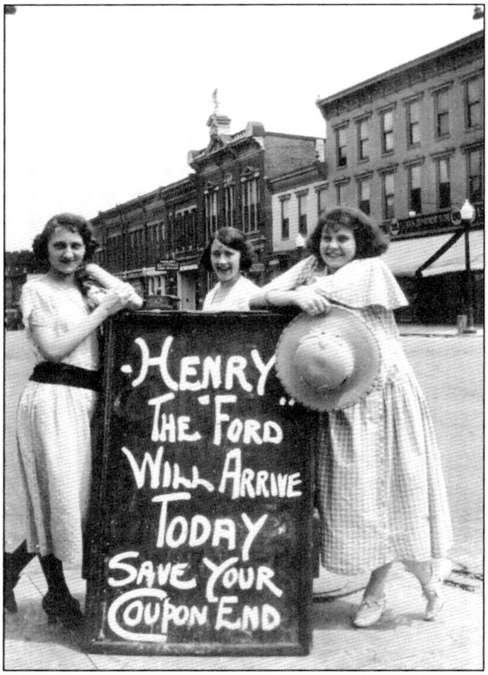

These three young ladies are prepared to welcome Henry the Ford in the 1920s. Pictured from left to right are unidentified, Helen Milner, and Frances McWilliams. (Courtesy Patricia Smith.)

In 1949, the Greenfield Sesquicentennial was held from September 2 to September 5. Dean T. Waddell chaired the sesquicentennial committee, and over 1,000 people helped in the planning and execution of the four-day event. The Grand Parade of the Years took place on Saturday, September 3 at 2:00 p.m. This float features an ox-drawn Conestoga wagon filled with children dressed in pioneer garb. The wagon is owned by the Greenfield Historical Society.

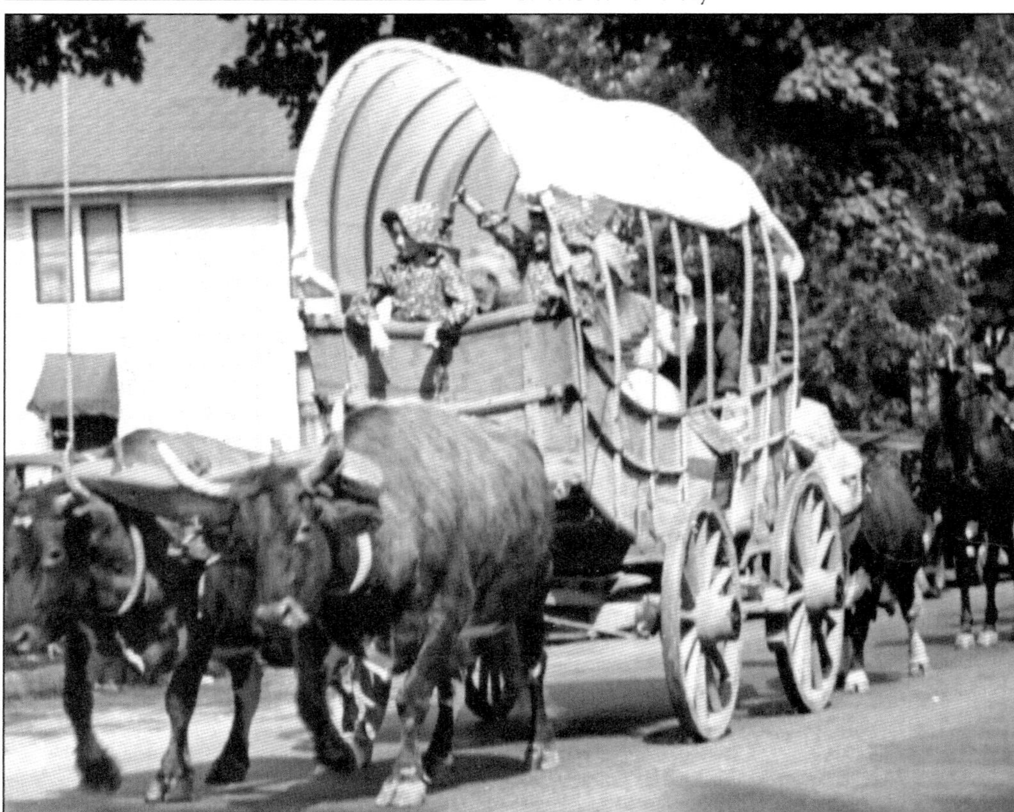

The Business and Professional Women float in the Greenfield Sesquicentennial Parade featured a huge birthday cake topped with 150 candles. This close-up view of the float shows little girls smiling out from the layers as they were met with cheers and applause. Girls in the first row are Vickie Mercer, Susan Winegar, Ann Marie Hayes, and LaVonne Jones. (Courtesy of Vickie Duff.)

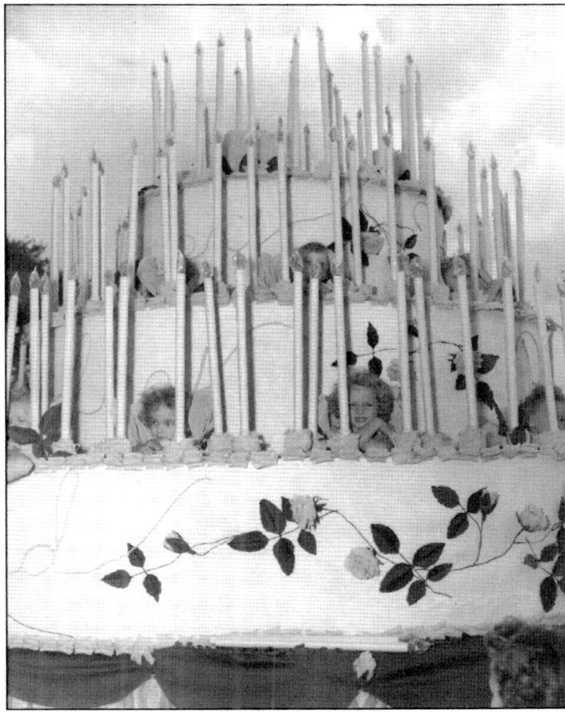

The McClain High School band marches in the Greenfield Sesquicentennial Parade.

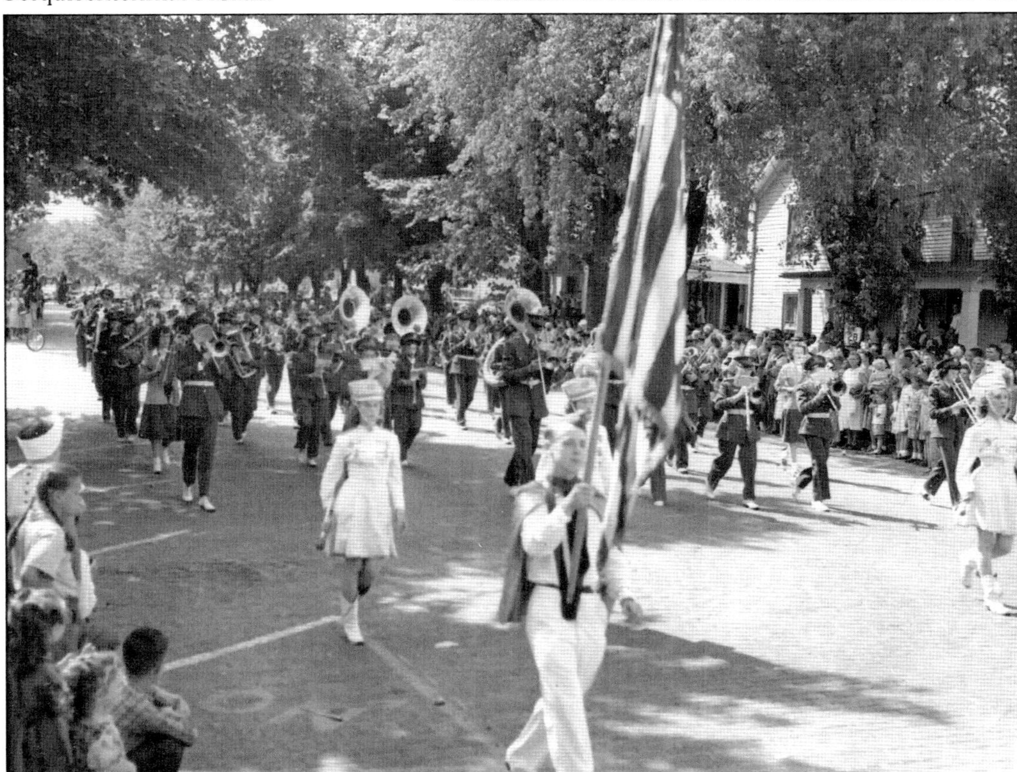

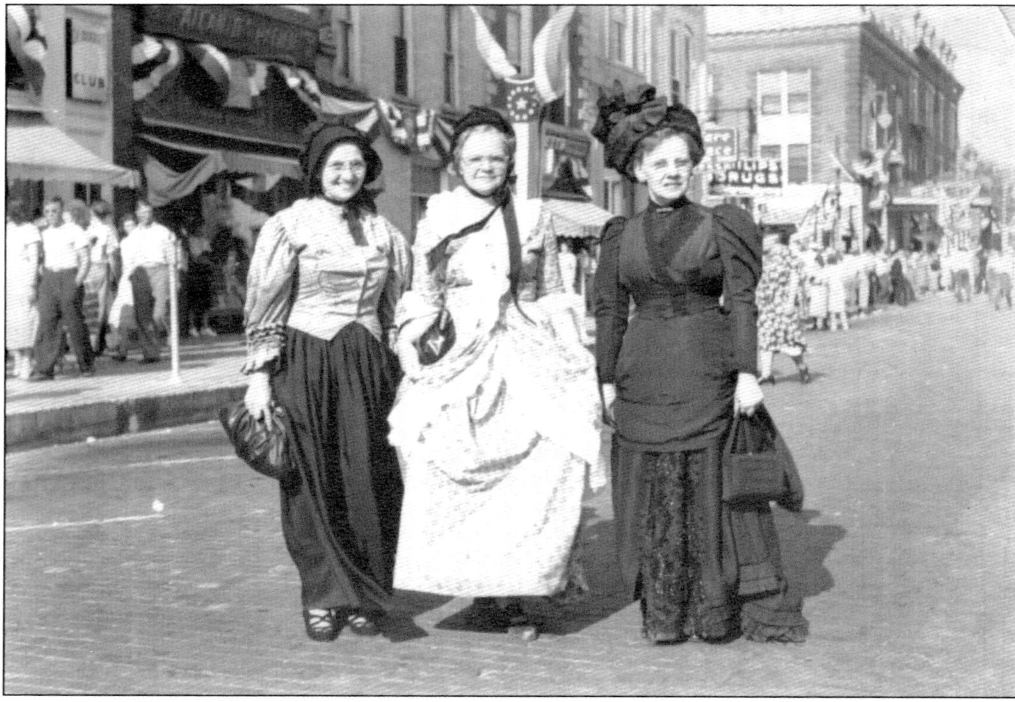

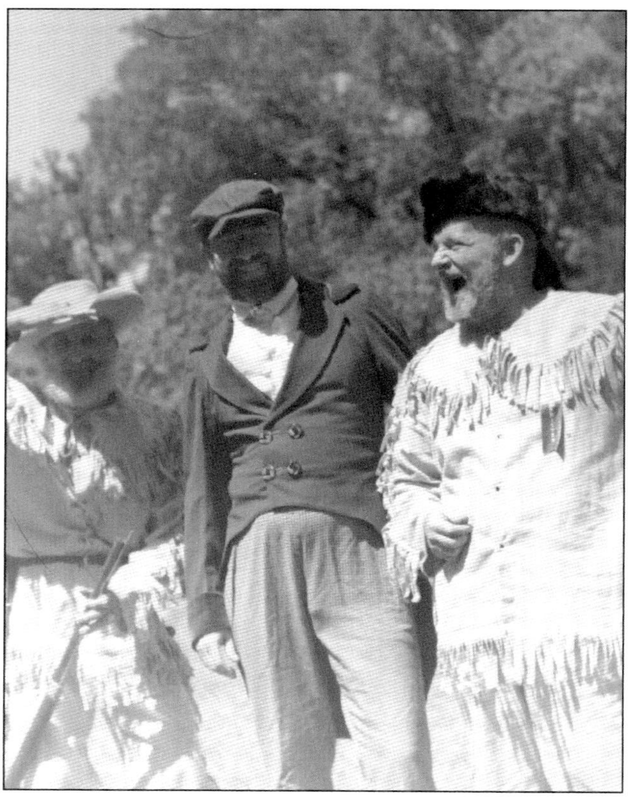

These ladies, dressed in their historical finest for the Greenfield Sesquicentennial Parade, are, from left to right, Marie Little, Gladys Hoisington, and Louise Sommers. Behind them is the north side of Jefferson Street, just west of the center of town.

Milt Sager, unidentified, and Maj. Roger Donohoe are dressed in period costumes to enjoy the festivities of the Greenfield Sesquicentennial Parade. Donohoe was the parade organizer. Records show that over 50,000 people watched the parade of 39 beautifully decorated floats and countless other bands, groups, and performers.

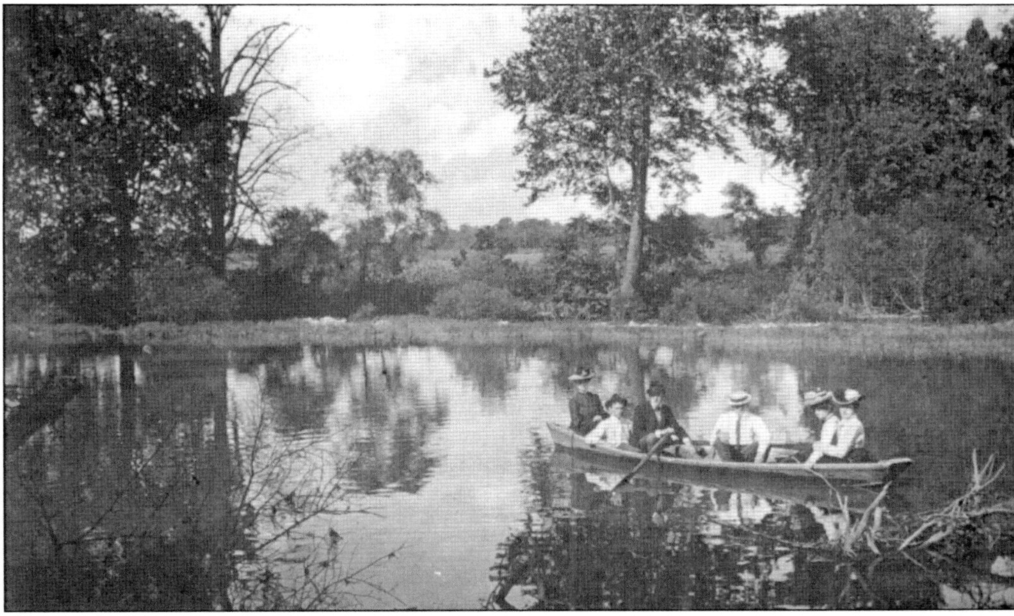

This six-member party enjoys a canoe ride on Paint Creek near Island Grove. The island was owned by Martha Mains, who entered into a five-year lease in 1891 with the management of Ohio Southern Railroad when the line realized possibilities for it. The railroad improved the island to become an area attraction, constructing a passenger platform and footbridge, a dance pavilion, and bandstand. Guests attended dances, picnics, and other functions here until 1894.

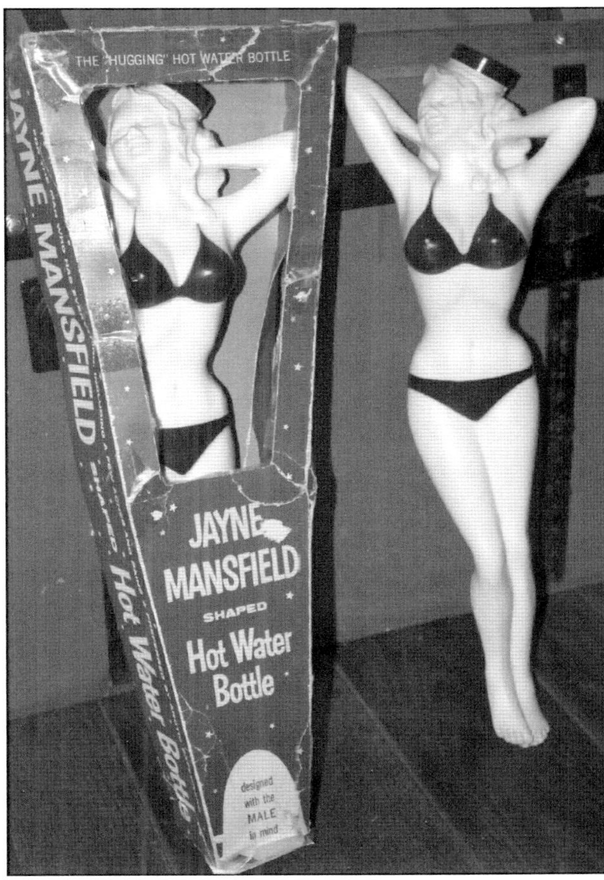

The Jayne Mansfield hot water bottle was made by TAPATCO in 1957. Mansfield granted permission to a Cincinnati group to use her likeness in an advertising gimmick. The McClain High School swimming pool was filled with them for a photo shoot. The hot water bottle was marketed "for the man who has everything, including a few aches and pains." (Courtesy of George Foltz.)